second edition

Computer Ethics

Deborah G. Johnson

Rensselaer Polytechnic Institute

PRENTICE HALL, *Upper Saddle River, New Jersey 07458*

Library of Congress Cataloging-in-Publication Data

Johnson, Deborah G.
  Computer ethics / Deborah G. Johnson.— 2nd ed.
    p. cm.
  Includes bibliographical references and index.
  ISBN 0–13–290339–3
  1. Electronic data processing—Moral and ethical aspects.
I. Title.
QA76.9.M65J64 1994
179—dc20   93-5847
                                       CIP

For my children
Jesse E. Johnson
Rose M. Johnson

Acquisitions editor: Ted Bolen
Editorial/production supervision: Merrill Peterson
Interior design: Joan Stone
Copy editor: Rene Lynch
Cover design: DeLuca Design
Cover photo: Michel Tcherevkoff/The Image Bank
Production coordinator: Kelly Behr
Editorial assistant: Nicole Gray

©1994, 1985 by Prentice-Hall, Inc.
A Simon & Schuster Company
Upper Saddle River, New Jersey 07458

Printed in the United States of America

10 9 8 7 6

ISBN 0-13-290339-3

PRENTICE-HALL INTERNATIONAL (UK) Limited, *London*
PRENTICE-HALL OF AUSTRALIA PTY. LIMITED, *Sydney*
PRENTICE-HALL CANADA INC., *Toronto*
PRENTICE-HALL HISPANOAMERICANA, S.A., *Mexico*
PRENTICE-HALL OF INDIA PRIVATE LIMITED, *New Delhi*
PRENTICE-HALL OF JAPAN, INC., *Tokyo*
SIMON & SCHUSTER ASIA PTE. LTD., *Singapore*
EDITORA PRENTICE-HALL DO BRASIL, LTDA., *Rio de Janeiro*

Contents

Preface

This edition of *Computer Ethics* could accurately be subtitled "Old and New." It contains, of course, a mixture of old material from the first edition and new material. More important, however, in this edition I introduce the idea that the ethical issues surrounding computers are new species of old and recurrent moral issues. Our society, and Western societies generally, have struggled with issues of privacy, property, responsibility, and power for centuries. The use of computers adds a new twist to some of these issues as computers structure, mediate, or expedite activities and relationships that existed without them. Sometimes the new twist arises from a change in the scale of thing as, for example, when computers allow a scale of record-keeping not possible before. Although privacy was an issue in our society long before computers, the use of computers creates new threats to individual privacy. Other times the new twist has to do with the very character of computer technology. For example, one can find numerous cases in the history of American intellectual property law in which there was a good deal of uncertainty and ambiguity about whether patent law should be extended to cover a new technology. In this respect, the intellectual property rights issues surrounding computer software are not new. Nevertheless, computer software challenges the intent and scope of both patent and copyright law in a way that they have never been challenged before. The challenge is new, but, in a sense, only a new version of a recurrent problem.

Those who have read and used the first edition of *Computer Ethics* will quickly see the changes that have been made in this edition. I have added an introductory chapter that asks and answers the question of why we need to study computer ethics and what it is all about. Among other things, I describe the important role that analogical thinking (making analogies between situations involving computers and familiar situations in which there is no computer) can play in working through computer ethical issues.

Chapter 2 on Philosophical Ethics has essentially the same structure as the chapter on ethical theory in the first edition with new material added here and there so as to extend discussion and, it is hoped, further clarify the role of ethical theory in discussions of computer ethics. I have changed Chapter 3, Professional Ethics, substantially. In rewriting this chapter I have made use of my recent work on engineering ethics so that the focus is more on the social responsibilities of computer professionals. I moved the chapter on property rights in computer software, Chapter 4, so that it appears earlier in the sequence of chapters. In addition to updating the material to reflect changes in the legal environment, I have taken on the issue of the moral permissibility of individual copying.

The thrust of the analysis in Chapter 5 on privacy is not so very different from that in the first edition. However, I have tried to update the discussion. Privacy legislation surrounding computers has become so complex that this chapter may well need to be supplemented. Chapter 6, titled Crime, Abuse, and Hacker Ethics, is an entirely new chapter. The discussion here focuses on a range of behaviors often referred to as "hacking," which includes such activities as gaining unauthorized access and planting viruses or worms. I have tried here to give hackers a fair hearing by taking the arguments used in defending their behavior and carefully examining them.

Much of the material from the first edition is still contained in Chapter 7 on responsibility and liability, but I have extended the discussion of responsibility and have added a discussion of liability for the contents of electronic bulletin boards. Chapter 8 resembles the chapter on computers and power in the first edition; however, I have focused this new chapter specifically on autonomy and access.

Each chapter now has study questions, and most chapters have essay questions and/or suggestions for class exercises. In addition, each chapter contains a list of suggested further readings.

Like the first, this edition is aimed at a variety of readers, including college students, computer professionals, and computer users. The teacher/reader might want to consider alternative paths through the book. For example, the material in Chapter 3 is placed near the beginning to draw in and connect with students who see themselves as becoming computer professionals in the future. However, for a class of students who see the issues as important because they will live in a world that will be significantly dependent upon computers, another path may work better. Chapter 3 might be skipped and returned to at the end as part of a discussion of ways to shape and control computer technology, a discussion that would follow nicely after Chapter 8.

Since 1984 when I completed the first edition of *Computer Ethics,* the number of courses being taught on this topic, the number of conferences and projects being undertaken, and the amount being written have grown enormously. However, this growth has been much too small in proportion to the importance of the topic. With this edition I issue "a call to arms." The world needs much more discussion and writing on the social and ethical issues surrounding computing. I hope readers of this edition will take up the challenge.

ACKNOWLEDGMENTS

I am most grateful to readers of the first edition of *Computer Ethics* who kindly told me how much they liked the book and generously offered ideas for this new edition.

In this edition I have incorporated material from several articles that I published elsewhere: "Computers and Ethics," originally appeared in *The Encyclopedia of Ethics* edited by Lawrence Becker; "The Social Responsibility of Computer Professionals," originally published in *The Journal of Computing and Society;* and "Proprietary Rights in Computer Software," originally presented at the National Conference on Computing and Values, Southern Connecticut State University, August 1991.

I am especially grateful to Rensselaer Polytechnic Institute's Undergraduate Research Program for providing support for two student assistants. During the spring semester of 1991, Paul Edelman helped me catch up on the property rights literature and issues. During the summer of 1991 and for the next two semesters, Dave Colantonio provided a variety of types of assistance. He got so involved in the project that he made it his own in many ways. He did bibliographic searches, read multiple drafts of each chapter (giving me feedback from the student reader's point of view), and wrote several scenarios, which I have used as chapter lead-ins.

I received many helpful comments and suggestions on early drafts of various chapters. I especially want to thank Jim Moor, Helen Nissenbaum, Keith Miller, and the reviewers for Prentice Hall: Lee C. Rice, Marquette University; Ernest A. Kallman, Bentley College; Russell E. Willis, Iowa Wesleyan College; James Moor, Dartmouth College; Helen Nissenbaum, Princeton University; Heinz C. Luegenbiehl, Rose-Hulman Institute of Technology; David Goodall, State University of New York, Albany.

I finished writing this edition while visiting in the School of Engineering at Princeton University under a grant from the National Science Foundation (HRD-9250118). In Princeton John Mulvey not only gave me helpful comments on several chapters but he pulled my attention to a new project so that I finally became anxious to finish this one.

The first edition of *Computer Ethics* was dedicated, in memory, to my parents, Edward and Rose Zimmerman. I dedicate this edition to my children, Jesse E. and Rose M. Johnson.

Deborah G. Johnson

CHAPTER 1

Introduction: What Is Computer Ethics?

SCENARIO 1.1: EXPLORING PRIVATE SYSTEMS

Dave, a sophomore in high school, is an avid computer fan. He has learned how to program in several languages and spends a good deal of his free time accessing local public bulletin board systems on his father's computer. Dave's father has a computer in their home so that he can work in the evenings and on the weekends when needed. Dave's father has encouraged Dave to learn about computers and has even set up a separate account on CompuServe for his son so that he can play games. Although Dave uses CompuServe occasionally, he has become interested in other private systems.

Inside one of the private systems is a message board where hackers exchange information on their various exploits in attacking other private systems. Dave carefully reads these messages and often writes some, explaining step by step how to access a local power company's system. Dave often jokes about how he knows his father's electric bill before it is even received in the mail. Dave explores other private systems, though he never changes the systems or any of the files available on-line. He simply enjoys the challenge of figuring out how to "crack" systems protection.

[Written by Dave Colantonio]

1

SCENARIO 1.2: POLICE SURVEILLANCE

Joe works as a computer systems operator for a local police force in the city of Omaha. Doris, a patrol cop, calls into the station from her patrol car. She has just observed a driver that looks suspicious. Although the driver was not breaking the law, he was pressing the speed limit and seemed to be continuously looking over his shoulder. Though it was hard to tell from a distance, he appeared to be unkempt and unshaven. Doris took down his license plate number and is asking Joe to check the driver out on the system. Joe uses the license plate number and calls up the file on Willis Hawk. Hawk, age twenty-five, was recently fired from his job at a local bakery. He is married, has two children under the age of five, and lives in a middle-class Hispanic neighborhood. Although he is in good standing with the local power and telephone companies and his credit card company, he is two payments behind on his mortgage. In the past five years Willis and his wife have attended several marriage counseling sessions. There is no record of Willis ever being arrested or convicted of a crime, but a year or so ago, the bakery that he worked for reported an internal theft and requested that Willis undergo a lie detector test. He was cleared.

Joe conveys all of this information to Doris and she decides to follow Willis for a while longer.

SCENARIO 1.3: BORROWING COMPUTER CODE

Jean, a systems programmer, is trying to write a new tutorial for use of her company's computer system, which will be used in other office branches nationwide. Now, after months of tedious programming, Jean has found herself stuck on several parts of the program. Her manager, not recognizing the complexity of the problem, wants the job completed within the next few days. Jean does not know how to solve the problems, but she realizes that there are several pieces of commercial software that handle similar problems quite nicely. Upon analysis of two of these programs, she sees two areas of code that could be directly incorporated into her own program. She uses these segments of code. The problems she was having are solved. She completes the project and turns it in a day ahead of time.
[Written by Dave Colantonio]

INTRODUCTION

Scenario 1.1 describes a type of behavior that is recognized in our society as problematic. Yet, while many believe it to be unethical, the popular press has often glorified activities of this kind, suggesting that the perpetrators are Robin Hood-types who reveal the foolishness of our blind faith in technology. Scenario 1.2 depicts the use of a database of information on citizens that could easily be put together now. However, many in our society fear this because of its potential for invasion of privacy and totalitarian government control. The third scenario is less dramatic but hints at the complexity of intellectual property rights in a computerized world.

All three of these scenarios raise questions about the use and abuse of computer technology. All three raise questions about right and wrong, good and bad. Are hackers heroes or bad guys? Should computers be used to do anything they make possible? What aspects of the technology should be owned? And, these questions lead to broader and deeper questions. Why do computers create ethical dilemmas? What is it about computers that both threatens us and promises us so much? Are the ethical issues surrounding computers unique?

New technologies often raise moral concerns. This seems to result from their creating new possibilities for human action, both individual action and collective or institutional behavior. Should I donate my organs for transplantation? Should lawyers be allowed to use DNA patterns as evidence in criminal cases? Will instantaneous global communication via fax machines, e-mail, and telephone be a good thing, or will it increase the pace and stress of modern life? The possibilities created by new technologies need to be evaluated. Will they make life better or worse? Are the benefits to be gained worth the negative effects or risk of negative effects? Can we do something to ensure that a new technology develops with a minimum of negative effects?

So it is with computers. The introduction of computers into our society has created possibilities for individual and institutional behavior that were not available before. We could not have reached the moon without computers, nor could we have the kind of global communication systems we now have. But, computers, like other technologies, create potentially undesirable as well as desirable possibilities. We now have a greater capacity to track and monitor individuals without their knowledge, to develop more heinous weapons systems, and to eliminate the need for human contact in many activities. These new possibilities need to be evaluated morally and in other ways.

A VACUUM OF RULES

In line with this idea that computers create new possibilities, James H. Moor (1985) has suggested that the study of computer ethics is needed because there is a vacuum of policies surrounding the new possibilities.[1] We face new choices about when and how to use computers, and we find a vacuum of policies on how to make these choices. The central task of computer ethics, Moor argues, is to determine what we should do and what the policies should be. This includes consideration of "both personal and social policies."

---

[1] James H. Moor, "What Is Computer Ethics?" *Metaphilosophy*, 16, no. 4 (October 1985), 266–75.

The sense in which there is a vacuum of policies surrounding computers can be illustrated by examples from the days when computers were relatively new. Consider the lack of rules regarding access to electronically stored data when computers were first created. Or consider the lack of policies about the ownership of software when the first software was being written.

Many laws and policies have been created in the last two to three decades, but vacuums still exist. They are most apparent when one looks at newer computer applications. There are, for example, few rules or conventions regarding various forms of on-line communications such as electronic mail and bulletin boards. Are such communications private? Who is liable for inaccurate, slanderous, or illegal information that appears on electronic bulletin boards? And what about computer graphics? Should computer graphical recreations of incidents, such as automobile accidents, be allowed to be used in courtrooms? Is it right for an individual to electronically reproduce and then alter an artistic image originally created by someone else? Vacuums still surround computers, and more are likely to arise as new applications develop.

CONCEPTUAL MUDDLES

We might jump to the conclusion that all we have to do to fill these vacuums and resolve computer ethical issues is to take our traditional moral principles and norms and apply them to the new situations created by computers. For example, when it comes to computer software, we might simply take our general rules regarding property and figure out what they imply about the ownership of software; or when it comes to on-line communication, we might simply take our conventions surrounding face-to-face communication (for example, certain words or questions are considered impolite, certain kinds of conversations are considered private) and extend them to on-line communications.

This, however, will not work in many cases because computers create conceptual muddles.[2] Computer software is a good example of this. A complex body of law regarding ownership of new inventions already existed long before computers, yet extending this body of law to computer software turned out to be troublesome because it has not been clear what software is. When one writes a program, is the program a product or a service? That is, should those who create programs be seen as providing a service or selling a product? The answer to this question makes all the difference in considering which laws or principles are relevant. Or should a program be seen as the expression of an idea? If so, would it be a form of intellectual property for which copyright law is appropriate? Or should a program be seen as a process for changing the internal structure of a computer? Or perhaps a program should be seen as a series of

---

[2] Moor, "What Is Computer Ethics?" p. 266.

"mental steps," capable, in principle, of being thought through by a human and not therefore appropriate for ownership.

We will take up questions about the nature of computer software in Chapter 4. For now, the point is that we cannot simply and mechanically apply traditional legal and moral principles to cases involving computers until we clear up the conceptual muddles. This is not to say that traditional moral norms and categories are irrelevant. On the contrary, we want to clear up the conceptual muddles so that we can see computers and situations involving computers in relation to our traditional moral norms and values.

COMPUTERS USED IN A SOCIAL CONTEXT

While Moor seems to be right, then, in arguing that we find a vacuum of policies and rules surrounding computers, it is important to point out that *computers are not used in a vacuum.* Computers are used by people for a whole variety of purposes and in a wide variety of contexts: in business, homes, criminal justice systems, educational institutions, medicine, science, government, and so on. In each one of these environments, there are human purposes and interests, institutional goals, social relationships, traditions, social rules, regulations, and so on.

It is important to recognize that these contexts shape the way computers are used. The conventions, rules, or policies created around computers are not likely to be created "out of the blue" but rather are likely to arise from the environment in which the computers are being used. The type of activity, institutional goals, as well as social, political, cultural, and economic factors will all influence perceptions of what is needed and what rules and policies are eventually adopted. For example, by some absolute measure of efficiency, it might be best for our society, as a whole, to create one master database of information on individual citizens, with private and public agencies having access to appropriate segments of the database. There are, however, a variety of reasons why such an arrangement has not yet come about and is not likely to come about in the near future. The factors include such things as social fears of powerful centralized government, which go to the heart of the historical experience of U.S. citizens. As well, the powerful private interests that have already invested in gathering and selling information will resist such an alternative.

Social context shapes the very character and direction of development of the technology. This is true at the broad level when we think about the development of computer technology over time, as well as at the micro level when we focus on how automation takes place in a small business, college campus, or government agency. Imagine, for example, the process of automating criminal justice records in a local police station. What the system looks like, who has access, and how records are processed will largely be determined by such factors as the unit's understanding of its mission and priorities, the existence of laws specifying the legal rights of citizens who are arrested and accused, the agency's budget, the relationships that the unit has already established with other criminal justice agencies, and so on.

One of the reasons that the study of computer ethics is so fascinating is that in order to understand an ethical issue surrounding computers, we have to understand the environment or environments in which computers are being used. In this respect the study of computer ethics turns out to be the study of human beings and society—our goals and values, our norms of behavior, the ways we organize ourselves and assign rights and responsibilities, and so on. In order to understand the impact of computers in education or government, for example, we have to learn a good deal about what goes on and is supposed to go on in these sectors. In order to figure out what the rules surrounding electronic communication should be, for another example, we have to explore the role of communication in whatever sector we are dealing with, for example, business or education, and we have to come to grips with the special importance of freedom of speech in American traditions and in a democracy.

The use of computers mirrors society. The study of computer ethics may be seen as a window through which we view a society—its activities and ideals; the social, political, and economic forces at work. Perhaps the most important thing about computers is their malleability: They can do almost anything, anything that can be thought of in terms of a series of logical steps or operations, with input and output. Because of this malleability, computers are used in a wide range of activities touching every aspect of human endeavor.

Computers can be used as much to keep things the same as to cause change. Indeed, when computers enter a new environment, we tend, initially at least, to map the way we had been doing things onto the new computer system. The process of automation is generally a process that involves looking at the way people have been doing a particular task or set of tasks, such as bookkeeping, word processing, manufacturing, or communicating, and then automating those activities.[3] Over time, especially as we become more familiar with computers, we may see their deeper potential; that is, we may begin to see entirely new things to do. Nevertheless, the fundamental activities are not likely to change. Manufacturers will want to produce products, record-keepers will want to keep and process records, businesses will want to serve customers, government agencies will want to achieve their missions, and so on.

So it is important to recognize that while computers and computer systems may be new, the environments they are brought into are rarely new. There

[3] James Rule and Paul Attewell (*Social Problems*, 36 (1989), 225–41) examined 184 private sector establishments to see how they were using computers. They coded each application in terms of whether the purpose it served was qualitatively new to the firm with computerization or whether the computerized application represented some form of conversion of activities previously carried out with prior technologies. They reported that "the overwhelming majority of these applications are the result of direct conversion from conventional to computer technologies; they were new ways of performing long-standing activities rather than fundamental revisions of organizational agendas" (p. 231).

may be a vacuum of policies with regard to many computer capabilities, but computers are never used in a vacuum. Rules and policies for activities involving computers can only be developed by understanding their environments; the nature of the human relationships involved; and the institutional purposes, ideals, and norms of behavior that have been operative. These and more are relevant to the ethical character of the situation.

LEGAL AND MORAL ISSUES

To say that computer ethical issues arise because there is a vacuum of policies leaves open the question of whether the vacuum should be filled with *laws* or something else. It is quite possible that some vacuums will be better left to personal choices, private institutional policies, or social conventions than to the imposition of law. For example, we may not want to prohibit the use of crude language in on-line communication, we may leave this to personal choice. As well, we may not want to make all on-line communications private, it may be best to allow some public forms and let individuals decide whether they want to participate or not. We may want companies to set their own policies for internal on-line communication or use of their proprietary information.

In many cases, we will need a variety of types of responses. For example, when it comes to the ownership of software, while law now defines what can and cannot be owned, there are still ambiguities. Corporations and government agencies supplement the law with internal policies applying to their employees. These policies serve to interpret the law in the company or agency context and specify how to handle ambiguities. As well, individuals must develop personal policies on the use of proprietary software, for example, whether to obey the law or not, how to behave when the law is unclear.

Law is neither the beginning place nor the ending place when it comes to ethics. Moral analysis precedes law when it is the basis for creation of a law— that is, our moral ideas often give rise to and shape the character of our laws. Think, for example, of minimum wage laws, or laws against racial and sexual discrimination. Or think of the way we have designed our criminal justice system to recognize the rights of the accused as well as the rights of the accuser. These aspects of our system of laws come from a shared sense of what is just and what is good. Criticisms of law and proposals for change in our laws are also often based on a shared moral ideal that is not being achieved. In this regard, law is often not the final word either. Think of the abortion debate or the debate about whether we should have compulsory or voluntary military service: issues that have been decided by legislation but in which individuals have persisted to have contrary moral opinions.

So, to say that computer ethics is needed to fill the vacuum of policies surrounding computers is not simply to say that we need laws. In some cases we do need laws; in other cases we may need personal policies or institutional policies or social conventions or several of these. In all cases, we need ethical analysis to help us understand the basis for adopting this type of policy or that.

WORKPLACE MONITORING

We can examine computer surveillance in the workplace to illustrate some of the ideas just discussed. As a result of computers, employers can now obtain a record of everything an employee does during the day while working on a computer. The employer can see how much time a worker spends on each task; how many errors are made before a programmer gets a program to work; how many and how long are the worker's breaks from work at the terminal; what the worker says in correspondence, electronic mail, or on-line forums; and so on. And this information can be tracked over any period of time. How many lines of code can a programmer write in a week? Over the past five years, how many employees hired by the personnel director turned out to be first-rate workers? And so on.

The important ethical question is, Is it right or good for employers to use this new technological capability? Some might argue that since it isn't illegal, it is all right to do. But this position blurs more than it clarifies. An ethical analysis would help us to understand what is at stake in using this technology. A good analysis would help us decide whether this use of computers should be made illegal or whether we personally would want to use the technology or work under such surveillance.

Workplace surveillance technology illustrates the ways in which there are and are not vacuums surrounding new computer applications. There are no laws prohibiting or constraining when or how employers can use this technology, and in this sense there is a vacuum surrounding it. Nevertheless, while there is a vacuum in this sense, there is no vacuum of ideas about the rights and interests of those who want to monitor (employers), nor about the rights and interests of those who will be monitored (employees). Indeed, all parties acting in the workplace have beliefs about what is just and good in the workplace. A large body of law already exists that deals with employer-employee rights—in this respect, there is anything but a vacuum of ideas about the relationship between employers and employees. Policies on the new technology will have to be consistent with principles embodied in existent workplace policies.

Just as we often have difficulty resolving computer ethical issues because of conceptual muddles surrounding the technology, it is important to note that there are muddles of a different kind in the contexts in which computers are used. That is, we are often muddled and conflicted as a society. We value justice, democracy, privacy, and so on, but when these values come into conflict with one another, we are not clear on what we should do. Workplace monitoring is a good example of this. We recognize that employers have rights and that, to some extent, they ought to be able to control their businesses and their employees. We also recognize that employees should have rights in the sense, at least, that they should not be wholly at the mercy of their employers, as slaves would be. There is a tension here and we need to balance the rights and interests of both parties. Indeed, if we look to other employer-employee issues to try to garner some general principles to apply in the computer case, we find this tension prevalent. We have minimum wage laws and some protection from occupational health hazards, on the one hand, but we allow employers to hire and fire "at will," on the other hand.

Computer ethical issues are thus often difficult to solve, not just because of the conceptual muddles but because ordinary morality, social values, and norms are not clear on the details called into question by computer technology. Computer ethical issues often press us to clarify our values, priorities, and ideals in ways we have never had to before.

NEW SPECIES, OLD ISSUES

In trying to understand why computers raise moral concerns and in what ways they do and don't change the environments in which they are used, we inevitably face the question of uniqueness. Are the ethical issues surrounding computers really new? Are they unique? Or are the issues simply the same old ethical issues that have plagued Western society for centuries?

Arguments can be made on both sides. On the one hand, we can argue that "there is nothing new under the sun." Computers may well threaten privacy, but privacy issues have been around for ages, and they have often centered on new technologies. Consider concerns about the publication of photographs in newspapers, wiretapping, hidden cameras: There have always been debates about privacy and what is done with information about individuals. The same may be said about ownership of computer software. There is no doubt that it challenges our property laws, but so have other new technologies. Most recently we've had to decide whether new forms of life created by geneticists should be owned. Historically, we have had to deal with ownership of such things as telephone lines, radio and television bands, electromagnetism, and so on. So it can be argued that from the point of view of ethics, the issues surrounding computers are *not* new.

On the other hand, arguments can and have been made to the effect that the issues are new and unique. Computers have brought about the creation of new entities—programs, software, microchips. These kinds of "things" never existed before. The activity of encoding ideas on silicon chips could not have been conceived of sixty years ago.

In addition to creating new entities, computers have also changed the scale of many operations and some would argue that scale alone marks a fundamental difference. The scale of calculations made by computers has led to the creation, for example, of other inventions that were not possible before. Travel to outer space and medical imaging devices are just two salient examples. The increased scale of information processing and statistical analysis has meant, in effect, that there is knowledge that could not have existed before. We could not know certain facts about large populations, at least not with the certainty we now have, without the scale of information processing possible with computers. Nor could we know what we now know about the solar system.

Another argument that follows from increased scale might be made for uniqueness. We might argue that computer technology is unique because of its inherent unreliability. Here the argument would be that because of the complexity and scale of calculations that constitute computer systems, they cannot be built with reliability. Since no single individual can understand and check every step in certain computer systems, we cannot be as sure of those systems as we might be of other technologies. Often we cannot test complex computer systems under every possible condition in which they will operate. This calls, some would argue, for an entirely new way of thinking about liability.

The argument about the uniqueness of computers might also be made by focusing on the power and pervasiveness of the technology. That is, we might argue that computer technology, unlike most other new technologies, is more likely to change the fundamental character of everything that we do. It will have a transformative effect comparable to that of steam power during the industrial revolution. One can add to this argument the unusual character of artificial intelligence. No invention before has promised to take over the thinking and decision-making functions of human beings.

Arguments on both sides of this debate seem to capture some element of the truth. Perhaps, it is better *not* to take a side, but to accept both sides. I propose that we think of the ethical issues surrounding computers as *new species of old moral issues.* The metaphor of species and genus encompasses the element of truth on each side of the debate in that a new species has some unique characteristics making it different from any other species, but at the same time, the species has generic or fundamental characteristics that are common to all members of the genus. Computer ethical issues have some unique features, but they do not exactly create a new category of issue. Threats to privacy, for example, have never existed in quite the form that they do with computers, but threats to personal privacy have been around for a long time. Just as software challenges our notions of property, so have other new inventions. Think of genetically engineered forms of life, chemical processes, or electromagnetism.

We see then that the ethical issues surrounding computers are not wholly new. It is not as if we have to create a new ethical theory or system. We have to come to grips with new species, which have some unique features, but we can rely on our traditional moral principles and theories. The issues in computer ethics can be categorized using traditional concepts: privacy, property, crime and abuse, power and responsibility, accountability and liability, and professional practice.

THE ROLE OF ANALOGY IN COMPUTER ETHICS

Given what has just been said, it seems clear that filling the vacuum of policies and rules surrounding computers will involve working through conceptual muddles and understanding the environments in which computers are being used. One very useful way to do this is reasoning by analogy. Reasoning by analogy involves looking for familiar situations comparable to the one involving computers and then either accepting the equivalence of certain actions or identifying the significant differences between the cases.

Consider, for example, the first scenario at the beginning of this chapter. As already mentioned, the popular press seems to enjoy publicizing cases of this kind in which individuals (often teenagers) break into confidential computer files, apparently for the fun and challenge of it. In the early days of computing the popular attitude was to look on this with humor and not take it seriously as crime. That is, some people seemed implicitly to believe that it wasn't such "a big deal." Yet, if we make an analogy with breaking into someone's office and into their file cabinet, it is difficult to see the moral difference. Certainly, it is true that the physical behavior required to perform each act (getting access to an electronic file and breaking into an office and into a file cabinet) is different, but there appear to be no morally significant differences between the acts. Both involve obtaining access to information that an individual has stored with the understanding that others will not have access. If we can't find any morally significant difference between the two cases, then we cannot (with consistency) claim that one type of behavior is all right and the other is wrong.

Of course, individuals sometimes do not (or did not, when the technology was new) recognize the equivalence of the cases. This raises a number of very interesting psychological or sociological questions. Why is it that individuals do not see what they are doing as wrong, or if they acknowledge that it is wrong, why is it that individuals who apparently would not physically break into an office will break into on-line files? Although they are most interesting, these are not ethical questions. They have more to do with psychological and sociological attitudes toward computers than with right and wrong.

Consider a slightly more complicated example of reasoning by analogy. Isn't sitting at a terminal and "playing around" by seeing just what systems or files you can get access to comparable to walking down a street and testing the doors of every house on the street to see if they are locked? Suppose when you find a door unlocked (a file accessible) you go in and look around. You may not change or take anything from the house (file). You simply look at what the owner has put in his drawers (what she has stored in various files). What, if anything, is different about these two cases? From the point of view of the person who is being intruded upon, both are likely to feel their privacy and their rights have been violated.

This analogy can be carried a bit further: Suppose I forgot to lock my door; am I partially responsible if someone enters my house? Or suppose the analogy is made to yards and gates. I left my gate unlocked and I have a swimming pool in my yard. This complicates things a bit since the law generally recognizes that individuals have a responsibility to take measures to protect others from the dangers of their swimming pool; that is, many local statutes require that one build a fence around the pool. There are computer comparables here. Perhaps, we should expect individuals to take measures to protect their files, especially if they contain sensitive data. We could pass legislation to this effect, or through court cases set precedents that make the responsibilities of computer users clear, and diminish the responsibility of trespassers where owners have not made efforts to protect their files. Be that as it may, the point here is only that analogical thinking can often be helpful in sorting out a computer ethical issue.

Still, caution is in order. Reasoning by analogy has some dangers, which can only be avoided by fully developing the analogy. Analogies are useful because they allow us to draw upon situations or technologies with which we are familiar and help us to see rules or principles that might be relevant in the computer situation. The danger is that we may be so taken with the similarities of the cases that we fail to recognize important differences. For example, in arguing about on-line break-ins and viruses, hackers sometimes put forth the argument that they are providing a service by pointing out the flaws and vulnerabilities in computer systems, so that something can be done to fix them. Countering this argument, Eugene Spafford uses a powerful analogy.[4] He suggests that to put forth this argument is comparable to arguing that it is all right to set a fire in a shopping mall in order to show the flaws in the fire protection system. I do not want to deny that planting a virus in the Internet has some parallels to starting a fire in a shopping mall, but I do want to point out that the analogy is so powerful that we might simply jump to the conclusion that because one is wrong, the other must be, before we have asked if there are any important differences between the cases and before we have asked why the first is wrong. Some might argue that lighting a fire in a shopping mall puts individual lives at risk, while most viruses do not. Both actions cause property damage, but the damage done by a virus can be repaired much more easily. And so the arguments go.

The important point to note is that while analogical thinking can be extremely useful, it also has dangers. Be sure to identify the differences between the computer and noncomputer cases. Be wary of what is brought into the discussion by the use of an analogy.

---

[4] Eugene H. Spafford, "Are Computer Hacker Break-Ins Ethical?" *Journal of Systems and Software*, 17, no. 1 (1992), 41–47.

THE GRAND ANALOGY

One analogy that may be helpful in setting the scene for the rest of this book is to think of computers, computer systems, and computer technology as a newly discovered island. Suppose in the case of the island that no one knew that it existed until recently, when it was discovered by an international team of explorers. It is uninhabited but very habitable. It is rich in natural resources, has a moderate year-round climate, and so on. The news of the discovery has generated a good deal of interest around the world and many individuals and corporations want to move there. Those who want to move there see the enormous potential. Some see the island as an opportunity for building a new society, an exemplar of democracy, a world community (nonnationalistic). Others see the potential for exploiting the natural resources on the island; yet others see the potential for developing the island as a grand international center for tourism. The list of potential uses for the island can go on.

As more and more interest is expressed in the island, many recognize that what is needed first and foremost is a set of rules and laws. They fear that if the rules are not made quickly the island's potential will be destroyed. The rules must specify what sort of government there will be, what rights individuals will have, whether the island can be cut up and owned, how the resources can be used, and so on. All involved agree that the rules should be such that we make the most of the island; that we don't waste its great potential; that it be set up to become a good place, a model of human cooperation; and so on. All involved recognize that the laws, policies, rules, attitudes, and conventions that are developed will make all the difference in what happens to the island.

Computer technology is like the island. It is a vast new territory for human endeavors. It has enormous potential to serve humans and improve our lot. The rules, policies, attitudes, and conventions we develop regarding this technology will make all the difference in whether its potential is exploited for good or ill. We can develop laws and policies to ensure that this technology serves humankind, or we can allow its potential to be squandered and wasted by thugs.

John P. Barlow suggests a similar metaphor for computing. He writes:

> Imagine discovering a continent so vast that it may have no end to its dimensions. Imagine a new world with more resources than all our future greed might exhaust, more opportunities than there will ever be entrepreneurs to exploit, and a peculiar kind of real estate that expands with development.[5]

As he goes on, he begins to hint at some of the problematic features of the new territory.

---

[5] John P. Barlow, "Coming into the Country," *Communications of the ACM,* Vol. 34, no. 3 (March, 1991), 19–21.

> Imagine a place where trespassers leave no footprints, where goods can be stolen an infinite number of times and yet remain in the possession of their original owners, where businesses you never heard of can own the history of your personal affairs, where only children feel completely at home, where the physics is that of thought rather than things, and where everyone is as virtual as the shadows in Plato's cave.[6]

Barlow goes on to explain that such a place exists.

> It consists of electron states, microwaves, magnetic fields, light pulses, thought-itself—a wave in the web of our electronic processing and communication systems.[7]

The discussion undertaken in this book is done in the spirit of thinking of computer technology as a "new territory." The presumption is that we ought to create rules, attitudes, conventions, and laws that will encourage the development and use of computer technology for the good of humanity. We will need to think carefully and critically about the role that computer professionals can and should play in determining the development and use of this technology. We will need to consider what forms of ownership, if any, are most likely to encourage and facilitate the development of safe, reliable, and useful software. We will have to ask how we will protect privacy. We will have to consider how much security we want, at what cost. Do we want an open system of on-line communication or do we want limited access? Both have benefits and drawbacks. How will we enforce the rules? How will we deal with those who violate the rules? And so on.

A FINAL NOTE

Thousands of books and articles have been written about the future of computers, but too often these discussions take place in a context in which it is simply assumed that all the potentials of computers will eventually be developed. In this book, the assumption is made that computer technology has many more possibilities than those that will be developed. The discussion surrounding computers and the rules and laws that are put in place will make all the difference in determining which of the potentials of computer technology are ever realized. The aim of this book is to encourage a dialogue that will harness the development of computer technology for the good of the creatures of this earth, not allowing it to serve the interests of a few and to degrade the character of life on this planet.

[6] Barlow, "Coming into the Country," p.19.
[7] Barlow, "Coming into the Country," p.19.

STUDY QUESTIONS

1. In what sense do computers create a vacuum?
2. Why can't we mechanically apply standard moral rules or principles to computer cases?
3. What is the relationship between law and morality when it comes to computer ethics issues?
4. Is there anything new in the moral questions raised by computers? Give examples of ethical questions raised by computers and explain in what sense they are new and in what sense they are old?

ESSAY QUESTIONS/CLASS EXERCISES

1. Consider the scenarios at the beginning of Chapter 1 and ask the following questions about each: (A) What is wrong, if anything, with the behavior described in the scenario? (B) Can you think of analogies (with situations not involving computers) that reveal the moral character of the behavior? (C) If you think any of these behaviors should be discouraged or prevented, what rules, laws, or conventions might achieve this?
2. Play out the "grand analogy." If you were a member of the team deciding the rules for the newly discovered island, what rules, laws, or conventions would you recommend? Now ask about what these choices imply about computer technology?
3. Suppose a computer center and hundreds of microcomputers are being installed for the first time on your college campus. You are quite familiar with computers and with computer activities and problems on other campuses. Design a set of rules for use of computers on your campus.

SUGGESTED FURTHER READING

BYNUM, TERRELL W. (ed.). *Computers and Ethics.* New York: Blackwell, 1985. (Published as the October 1985 issue of *Metaphilosophy.*)

DUNLOP, CHARLES, AND ROB KLING (eds.). *Computerization and Controversy: Value Conflicts and Social Choices.* San Diego, Calif.: Academic Press, 1991.

ERMANN, DAVID M, MARY B. WILLIAMS, AND CLAUDIO GUTIERREZ (eds.). *Computers, Ethics, and Society.* New York: Oxford University Press, 1990.

FORESTER, TOM, AND PERRY MORRISON. *Computer Ethics: Cautionary Tales and Ethical Dilemmas in Computing.* Cambridge, Mass.: MIT Press, 1990.

JOHNSON, DEBORAH G, AND HELEN NISSENBAUM (eds.). *Computers, Ethics, and Social Values.* Englewood Cliffs, N.J.: Prentice Hall, forthcoming.

PARKER, DONN B., SUSAN SWOPE, AND BOB BAKER. *Ethical Conflicts in Information and Computer Science, Technology, and Business.* Wellesley, Mass.: QED Information Sciences, 1990.

CHAPTER 2

Philosophical Ethics

INTRODUCTION

Before embarking on an analysis of the ethical issues surrounding computers, it will be helpful to discuss the nature of ethical analysis in general and to become familiar with some traditional ethical theories and concepts. This chapter aims to describe how a dialogue on an ethical issue should proceed to produce insight and better understanding. It also aims to explain some of the concepts and theories that philosophers have found particularly useful in discussing ethical issues.

We often overhear or participate in discussions of ethical issues. Think, for example, of the heated discussions you have heard about government restrictions on individual freedom, for example, censorship of film or music, seat belt laws; or think of discussions of abortion and the distribution of wealth in our society. Individuals who express opinions on such issues often defend their position on the basis of their emotional responses or their strongly held intuitions about what is right and wrong, just and unjust. These responses can be the starting place for ethical analysis, but they are only starting places. Discussions at this level may quickly end unresolved because the individuals involved are not able to articulate coherent reasons for believing as they do. As such it is impossible to talk about the issues rationally, let alone resolve them.

This book is an undertaking in philosophical analysis, and philosophical analysis proceeds on the premise that we must examine the *reasons* we have forour moral beliefs. In ethical analysis the reasons are first articulated and then critically evaluated. The reasons one gives (for holding an ethical belief or taking a position on an ethical issue) can be thought of as an argument, an argument for a claim. The argument has to be "put on the table," and once there, it can be evaluated in terms of its coherence and consistency: We can ascertain whether the argument does, indeed, support the claim being made or the position being taken.

This critical evaluation is often done in the context of trying to convince someone to reject a position, or to adopt another position, but it may also be done simply to explore a claim. When we examine the argument supporting a claim, we come to understand the claim more fully. Individuals sometimes have strong moral intuitions or convictions but have not thought about the philosophical basis upon which these rest. An examination of the underpinnings of those moral beliefs or intuitions sometimes leads to a change in belief, but it may also simply lead to stronger and better understood convictions.

In philosophical analysis, not only must we give reasons for our claims but we are expected to be consistent from one argument or topic to the next. For example, instead of having separate, isolated views on abortion and capital punishment, we would be led by philosophical analysis to recognize that both our views on abortion and our views on capital punishment rest on a claim about the value of human life and what abrogates it. Philosophical analysis would lead you to inquire whether the claim you made about the value of human life in the context of a discussion of capital punishment is consistent with the claim you made about the value of human life in the context of a discussion of abortion. If the claims appeared to be inconsistent from the one context to the next, then you would be expected to change one of your claims or provide some account that would reveal that there is not a real inconsistency.

Philosophical analysis is an ongoing process. It involves a variety of activities: formulation of an argument (giving a reason or set of reasons); critical examination of the argument; reformulation of the argument, perhaps rejecting aspects of the original argument but holding onto a core idea; critical examination of the new argument; examination of counter-arguments. Philosophers often refer to this process as a "dialectic" (which is related to the word "dialogue"). We pursue an argument to see where it goes and to find out what we would have to know or assert in order to defend the argument and establish it on a firm footing.

In addition to moving from intuition to reasons, and from one formulation of an argument to another, better formulation, the dialectic also moves back and forth from cases to principles or theory. To illustrate, take the issue of euthanasia: Say you start out by making the claim that euthanasia is wrong; then you articulate a principle as the reason for this claim. Say, the principle is that human life is the highest value and therefore should never be intentionally ended. You might then test this principle by seeing how it applies in a variety of euthanasia cases, for example, when the person is conscious but in extreme pain, when the person is unconscious and severely brain damaged, when the person is terminally ill, when the person is young or elderly, and so on. You might also test the principle by applying it to completely different types of cases, such as war and capital punishment. Given your intuitions in these cases, you may want to qualify the principle or you may hold to the principle and change your mind about the case. For example, after seeing how the principle applies in a variety of cases, you might qualify it so that you now assert that one should never intentionally take a human life *except* in self-defense or except when taking a life will save a life. Or you might reformulate the principle so that it specifies that the value of human life has to do with its quality so that when the quality of life is significantly and permanently diminished, it is all right to let a person die. The dialogue continues as the dialectic forces a clarification of the principle—the process moves toward consistency and coherence.

The dialectic (from intuition to argument, from argument to better argument, and from theory to case, and back) does not always lead to definitive conclusions or unanimous agreement, so it is important to emphasize that knowledge and understanding can be gained, progress can be made, even when we have not reached final conclusions. If nothing else, we acquire "negative knowledge." We learn which arguments are inadequate and why. But more often than not, we do acquire positive knowledge. We develop a deeper and more coherent set of beliefs and we understand how ideas are interrelated and interdependent.

As you will see in a moment, a familiarity with traditional ethical theories will help in identifying the reasons for many of our moral intuitions. Ethical theories provide some common ground for discussion as well; they establish a common vocabulary and frameworks within which, or against which, we can articulate moral ideas.

DESCRIPTIVE AND NORMATIVE CLAIMS

In any discussion of ethics it is important to recognize the distinction between descriptive and normative claims. *Descriptive* statements are statements about how people in fact behave. The following are descriptive claims: "When people are shown this picture, 60 percent think it is a butterfly"; "Only 30 percent of all Americans believe that it is wrong to make a copy of a piece of proprietary software for personal use"; "In all human societies, there are some areas of life that are considered private." We call these statements descriptive or *empirical* because they describe what people do or think. They describe a state of the world and as such they may be confirmed or disconfirmed by observation.

Social scientists gather empirical data and report their findings, both on moral and nonmoral matters. When it comes to morality, psychologists and sociologists might do such things as identify processes by which children in our society develop moral concepts, or they may measure various values and value changes in people. When anthropologists go to other cultures and describe moral rules that are adhered to in those cultures, they also are doing empirical studies of morality. Similarly, historians may trace the development of a particular moral notion in a historical period. To use a computer example, sociologists might survey a group of people and find that the majority views the use of someone's computer account quite differently from using someone's bank account.

When social scientists do these studies, they are studying morality, but they are studying it as an empirical phenomenon. They are describing what people think and do. In contrast, philosophical ethics is *prescriptive*. It is concerned with showing not what people actually do but rather what people *ought* to do. Ethical theories are normative—they aim to provide the basis for saying that it is wrong for someone to behave in a certain way. Descriptive facts about the world may come into play in the dialectic about ethics, but it is important to keep in mind that the issues of philosophical ethics cannot be resolved just by pointing to the facts about what people do or say or believe. For example, the fact (if it were true) that many individuals view using someone's computer account as not wrong does not make it so. The fact that individuals hold such a belief is not an argument for the claim that it is morally permissible to use someone else's computer account.

The aim of this book is not to describe how people behave when they use computers. For this we must consult empirical scientists, such as sociologists and psychologists. Rather, the aim of this book is to make some headway toward understanding how people ought to behave when they use computers.

ETHICAL RELATIVISM

We can begin our examination of ethical concepts and theories by examining a common moral intuition in our society. Many readers are likely to believe that "ethics is relative." This idea needs to be examined critically. It can be formulated into a theory, though not without difficulty, and that is where we shall begin.

We begin with the common intuition that ethics is relative. The idea here seems to be something like this: "What is right for you may not be right for me" or "I can decide what is right for me, but you have to decide for yourself." When we take this idea and formulate it into a more systematic account, it seems to encompass a *negative claim* (something that it denies), and a *positive claim* (something that it asserts). The negative claim appears to be: "There are no universal moral norms." According to this claim, there isn't a single standard for all human beings. One person may decide that it is right for her to tell a lie in certain circumstances, another person may decide that it is wrong for him to tell a lie in exactly the same circumstances, and both people could be right. Right and wrong are "relative." So, ethical relativists appear to deny that there are universal rights and wrongs.

The positive claim of ethical relativism is more difficult to formulate. Sometimes ethical relativists seem to assert that right and wrong are relative to the individual, and sometimes they seem to assert that right and wrong are relative to the society in which the person lives. I am going to focus on the latter version, and on this version the relativist claims that what is right for me, an American living in the twentieth century, is quite different from what was right for a person living, say, in Asia in the fifth century.

The negative and positive claims of ethical relativism can, then, be summarized as follows: "There are no universal moral rights and wrongs. Right and wrong are relative to one's society."

Ethical relativists often cite a number of descriptive facts to support their claims. (1) They point to the fact that cultures vary a good deal in what they consider to be right and wrong. For example: in some societies infanticide is or was acceptable, while in other societies it is considered wrong; in some societies, polygamy is permissible and in others it is not; and so on. (2) Relativists also point to the fact that moral norms change over time so that what is considered wrong at one time in a given society may be considered right at another time. Slavery is a good example of this for it was considered permissible (by many) at one time in our society but is not considered permissible now. (3) Relativists also point to what we know about how people develop their moral ideas. These are usually taught to a person as a child and are the result of his environment. If I had been raised in certain Middle Eastern cultures, I might believe that it is wrong for a woman to appear in public without her face covered. Yet because I was raised in the United States, I do not believe this. A person acquires moral beliefs from his or her family, from experiences in his or her society, at school, at work, and so on.

Note that at this point we have made progress simply by clearly and systematically formulating an idea that you may have entertained or heard expressed but never had a chance to examine carefully. Moreover, we have been able to articulate some reasons thought to support relativism. Now that the idea and supporting evidence have been "put on the table," we can examine them critically.

The facts that ethical relativists point to certainly cannot be denied. That is, we cannot deny that there is and always has been diversity of opinion on right and wrong, that moral beliefs change over time, and that environment plays an important role in shaping the moral ideas we have. The question we have to ask is this: Do these facts support the relativist's claims? Do these facts support the claim that there are no universal moral rights or wrongs or the claim that right and wrong are relative to our society?

The answer appears to be "no." The fact that there is diversity of opinion on right and wrong is not evidence for the claim that there is no universal moral code. A moral code may apply to people even though they fail to recognize it.

(I am not claiming that there *is* a universal right and wrong. I am only claiming that the evidence cited by relativists does not support their claim.) Second, the fact that our moral beliefs are shaped by our environment says nothing about the rightness or wrongness of what we believe. Racism and sexism are good examples of moral attitudes we may acquire from our environment but which turn out upon reflection to be unjustified. (Again, I am not claiming that there *are* universal rights and wrongs; I am only claiming that the fact that moral beliefs are shaped by our environment implies nothing about what is right or wrong.)

Finally, while it cannot be denied that people differ in their ideas about morality, from society to society and from time to time, this does not establish anything about the universality of morality. The diversity might be superficial rather than real. Relativists seem to be focusing on specific practices, and there is still the possibility that universal norms underlie these. Moral principles such as "never intentionally harm another person" or "always respect human beings as ends in themselves" are of such generality that they could be operative in all cultures. In each culture or time period, the principle might be interpreted differently. What is meant by "harm," "respect," and "human being" varies, so it is possible that there are universal principles but that they are hidden from sight due to the diversity of expression or interpretation of the principle.

Social scientists have certainly tried to find patterns within the apparent diversity. Some have asserted, for example, that all cultures have prohibitions on incest or, more recently, that while there is a great deal of diversity about what is considered private, all cultures consider some aspect of the lives of individuals private. Although such patterns have important implications for the study of ethics, we have to remember that establishing patterns across cultures is still descriptive, and it is another matter to determine what these claims imply about how people ought to behave.

A little farther on, when we examine utilitarianism, we will see an example of a very general normative principle that is compatible with a diversity of practices. Utilitarianism is a form of consequentialism and such theories assert that individuals should always do what will maximize good consequences. Individuals in quite different situations may be doing very different things but all in accordance with this same principle.

So the facts pointed to by relativists do not seem to support the relativist's claim that there are no universal moral rights and wrongs. The facts cited by relativists also do not support the relativist's claim that right and wrong are relative to our society. Pointing to what people believe to be right and wrong tells us nothing about what *is* right or wrong. The fact that people behave in accordance with the norms of their society is not evidence for the claim that they ought to.

Indeed, if we look more carefully at the positive claim of ethical relativism, it appears that ethical relativism may be self-contradictory, at least in some formulations. In saying that right and wrong are relative to our society, ethical relativists might be claiming that we are bound by the rules of our society. This would seem to mean that people ought to abide by the rules of their society; that what is right for me is defined by my society, and what is right for members of an African tribe is what is set by the standards of their tribe, and so on. Notice, however, that if this is what relativists mean, they have slipped into inconsistency. While denying that there are universal rights and wrongs, the relativist appears to have asserted a universal norm, namely that every individual *ought* to abide by the rules of his or her society.

We can see how this happens if we look at what appears to be a common motive for adopting relativism. Recognizing the diversity of morals from culture to culture, and from individual to individual, relativists seem to be impressed by the problems created when individuals ridicule and condemn those with beliefs different from their own. Relativists want to say that we should not judge others by the standards of our own culture but we should recognize and respect differences. We should respect others and understand how they have come to develop their beliefs from their experiences in their own culture.

This seems a worthy position to take, but notice that in recommending that we respect others who are different from us, relativists seem to be asserting a universal norm. That is, they seem to be claiming that *everyone ought to respect everyone else.* Hence, they seem to be contradicting their claim that there are no universal norms. The motive giving rise to relativism seems inconsistent with the positive claim of ethical relativism.

Case Illustration

To see these and other problems with ethical relativism, consider a hypothetical case. Suppose, by a distortion of history, that computers were developed to their present sophistication fifty-five years ago. World War II is in progress, though the United States has not yet entered the war. You are an American in charge of international sales for a large American computer company. You have just been contacted by the German government because they want to purchase several of your largest computers. Rumors of what is going on in Germany have been reaching the United States so it is not difficult for you to imagine what the German government will use the computers for. The question is, should you sell the computers to Hitler?

In reality the decision would most likely not be entirely in your hands, but let us assume that it is. If you are an ethical relativist, it seems that you have no reason to refrain from selling computers to Hitler. You may know full well that Hitler plans to use the computers to keep track of all citizens, to identify and monitor Jews, to build more efficient gas chambers, as well as to wage war against other European nations. Such activities are considered wrong in your society but perhaps not in Hitler's.

Actually, there are some practical problems with ethical relativism that now begin to appear. How do we figure out what the standards of a society are? You might raise questions about whether Hitler is abiding by the standards of his own society or whether he is going against these. If he is going against these, then perhaps he is doing wrong and you would be doing wrong to support him, but it is not easy to tell whether Hitler is adhering to or rejecting the standards of his society. Are standards set by leaders, masses, majorities?

This leads to another problem with relativism. It seems to rule out any form of rebellion. If people rebel against the standards of their society, it would seem they are doing wrong for they are rejecting these standards. Many of our greatest heroes—Socrates, Martin Luther King, Jr., Gandhi, even Jesus—would, then, have to be considered bad by ethical relativists for they went against the standards of their society.

In any case, as an ethical relativist it appears that you can make no judgments about Hitler's activities. You have no moral basis for refusing to sell the computers. You can only claim that most people in your society believe it is wrong to do what Hitler does, which hardly seems an adequate reason for adopting this moral belief.

Still, even if the relativist could conclude that Hitler's actions and agenda are immoral, the moral question facing you is whether to supply computers to Hitler. You need to know what the rule in your society is regarding assistance to those engaged in immoral activities. But why use your society's norm? The fact that the norm is accepted in your society seems a weak reason for adopting it as your own.

Ethical relativism therefore seems to suffer from three types of problems. First, the evidence that is used to support it does not exactly support it. Second, proponents cannot make normative claims without inconsistency. (By claiming that everyone is bound by the rules of their society, the ethical relativist makes a universal claim.) And, third, the theory has problems that make it hard to use. How do we decide what group an individual belongs to, so as to know what code applies to that individual? How do we justify any of our moral beliefs except by saying "because those are the rules in my society"?

Thus, although we have succeeded in formulating one of our intuitions about morality into a theory, after examining the theory, we find it looks untenable. Of course, the dialectic is far from over. You may want to reformulate ethical relativism so as to avoid some of the arguments given against it. Or you may want, for the time being, to take what might be called "an agnostic position," holding that you don't know yet whether there are universal rights and wrongs. The dialogue here will continue by turning to a new theory, a theory that captures part of what relativists are after but that asserts a universal norm.

UTILITARIANISM

Utilitarianism is a form of consequentialism. Consequentialist theories evaluate behavior in terms of its consequences. Utilitarianism puts the emphasis on happiness-producing consequences. The term "utilitarianism" derives from the word "utility," as this theory proposes that ethical rules are derived from their usefulness (their "utility") in bringing about happiness. Utilitarianism claims to provide one simple moral principle, which everyone should use to determine what he or she ought to do in a given situation. The basic principle is this: *Everyone ought to act so as to bring about the greatest amount of happiness for the greatest number of people.*

Now, what is the "proof" of this theory? What arguments can utilitarians give to support their theory? What follows is the account that some utilitarians have given to support the theory.

Intrinsic and Instrumental Value

Utilitarians derive the principle of utility by focusing on values and asking what is so important, so valuable to human beings that we can use it to ground a moral theory. They note that of all the things in the world that are valued, we can distinguish things that are desired because they lead to something else from things that are desired for their own sake. The former may be called *instrumental* goods and the latter *intrinsic* goods. Money is a classic example of something that is instrumentally good—it is not valuable for its own sake but rather has value as a means to other things. On the other hand, something that is intrinsically valuable is desired for itself, for what it is, not just because it is a means to something else.

Having drawn this distinction, utilitarians ask: What is there that is intrinsically good? What is so valuable that we can use it to ground a theory of right? Utilitarians conclude that *happiness* is the ultimate intrinsic good, because it is not desired for the sake of anything else. Indeed, some utilitarians claim that everything else is ultimately desired as a means to happiness. To see this, take any activity that people engage in and ask why they do it, each time you will find that the sequence of questions always ends with happiness. Take, for example, your career choice. Say you have chosen to study computer science to become a computer professional. Why do you want to be a computer professional? Perhaps you believe that you have a talent for computing, and you believe you will be able to get a well-paying job in computer science—one in which you can be creative and somewhat autonomous. Then we must ask, why are these things important to you? That is, why is it important to you to have a career doing something that you have a talent for? to be well paid? to have work in which you can be creative and autonomous? Suppose that you reply by saying that being well paid is important to you because you want security or because you like to buy "things" or because there are people who are financially dependent on you, and so on. In turn we can ask about each of these. Why is it important to be secure? or to have material possessions? or to support your dependents? The questions may continue or you may end them by saying you want whatever it is because you believe it will make you happy. The questioning stops because it doesn't seem to make sense to ask why someone wants to be happy.

We could go off into a discussion of whether you are right in believing that any of these things will make you happy. For example, we might discuss whether being a computer professional or acquiring material possessions will really make you happy. But the point that utilitarians want to make is that the series of questions about your desires will not stop until we get to happiness.

It makes no sense, utilitarians argue, to ask why people value happiness. Happiness is the ultimate good, all our actions are directly or indirectly aimed at it, it is what we all strive for. In a sense, utilitarians believe that this is simply part of our nature, human nature. Human beings are creatures who seek happiness.

And since happiness is the ultimate good, utilitarians believe that morality must be based on creating as much of this good as possible. Thus they believe that all actions must be evaluated in terms of their "utility" for bringing about happiness. When an individual is faced with a decision about what to do, the person should consider his or her alternatives, evaluate the consequences of each alternative, and choose that action that brings about the most happiness–producing consequences.

The utilitarian principle therefore provides a decision procedure. When you want to decide what to do, consider the happiness-unhappiness consequences that will result from your various alternatives. The alternative that produces the most overall net happiness (good minus bad) is the right action. To be sure, the right action may be one that brings about some unhappiness but that is justified if the action also brings about so much happiness that the unhappiness is outweighed, or as long as the action has the least net unhappiness of all the alternatives.

Be careful not to confuse utilitarianism with egoism. Egoism is a theory that specifies that you should act to bring about the most good consequences for yourself. What is good is what makes *me* happy or gets me what I want. Utilitarianism does not say that you should maximize your own good. Rather, total happiness in the world is what is at issue. Thus, when you evaluate your alternatives you have to ask about their effects on the happiness of everyone. It may often turn out to be right for you to do something that will diminish your own happiness because it will bring about a marked increase in overall happiness.

The emphasis on consequences found in utilitarianism is very much a part of decision making in our society, in particular as a framework for law and public policy. Cost-benefit or risk-benefit analysis is consequentialist. It involves weighing the potential benefits of a project, such as construction of a new nuclear power plant, against the potential harms (the risk of harm) in undertaking the project. That is, it involves calculating and weighing the negative and positive effects (the net good) of a project in deciding whether to go forward with it. In the case of a nuclear power plant, for example, we look at the amount of energy it will produce and how this will allow people to maintain a certain life-style. We, then, balance this good against the risk of harm or other negative consequences.

Utilitarians do not all agree on what utilitarianism is. That is, there are different kinds of utilitarians. One controversial issue of interpretation has to do with whether the focus should be on rules of behavior or individual acts. Utilitarians have recognized that it would be counter to overall happiness if each one of us had to calculate at every moment what the happiness–producing consequences of every one of our actions would be. Not only is this impractical, because it is time consuming and because sometimes we must act quickly, but often the consequences are impossible to foresee. Thus, there is a need for general rules to guide our actions in ordinary situations.

Hence, *rule-utilitarians* argue that we ought to adopt rules which, if followed by everyone, would, in general and in the long run, maximize happiness. Take, for example, truth-telling. If people in a society regularly told lies, it would be very disruptive—one would never know when to believe what one was told. In the long run, a rule obligating people to tell the truth has enormous beneficial consequences. Thus, "tell the truth" becomes a utilitarian moral rule. "Keep your promises" and "Don't reward behavior that causes pain to others" are rules that can be justified in a similar way. According to utilitarians, if the rule can be justified in terms of the consequences that are brought about from people following it, then individuals ought to follow the rule.

Act-utilitarians put the emphasis on individual actions rather than rules. Take, for example, a case where lying may bring about more happiness than telling the truth. Say you are told by a doctor that tentative test results indicate that your spouse may be terminally ill. You know your spouse well enough to know that this knowledge, at this time, will cause him enormous stress. He is already under a good deal of stress because of pressures at work and because someone else in the family is very ill, and in this case the pain (stress) may be unnecessary in that the results of further tests may prove more positive. Your spouse asks you what you and the doctor talked about. Should you lie or tell the truth? An act-utilitarian might say that the right thing to do in such a situation is to lie, for little good will come from telling the truth and a good deal of suffering (perhaps unnecessary suffering) will be avoided from lying. A rule-utilitarian would agree that good might result from lying in this one case, but in the long run, if we cannot count on people telling the truth, more bad than good will come. Thus, it is morally wrong to break the rule against lying.

Act-utilitarians treat rules simply as rules of thumb, general guidelines to be abandoned in situations where it is clear that more happiness will result from breaking them. Rule-utilitarians, on the other hand, take rules to be strict. We justify moral rules in terms of the happiness consequences that result from people following them. If a rule is justified, then an act that violates the rule is wrong.

In either case it should be clear that the simple utilitarian principle can be used to generate a set of moral norms or practices. In fact, many utilitarians propose that the utilitarian principle be used to determine the laws of a society. Laws against stealing, killing, breaking contracts, fraud, and so on can be justified on utilitarian grounds. Utilitarianism or some other variation of consequentialism is also often used as a principle for evaluating the laws that we have. If a law is not producing good consequences or is producing a mixture of good and bad effects and we know of another approach that will produce better effects, that information provides the grounds for changing the law. Punishment is a good example of a social practice that can be evaluated in terms of its utility. According to utilitarians, since punishment involves the imposition of pain, if it does not produce some good consequences, that is, if it does not deter criminals, it is not justified.

To return to the point about how utilitarianism captures part of the idea in relativism, it should be noted that the morally right thing to do for an act-utilitarian will depend a good deal on the situation. In one situation it may be right to lie; in another where the circumstances are different, it may be wrong. Even rule-utilitarians must admit that the rule that will produce the most happiness will vary from situation to situation. For example, where water is scarce, a rule prohibiting individuals from filling their swimming pools and watering their lawns is justified and it would be wrong to break such a rule. On the other hand, where water is abundant, such a rule would not be justified and filling your pool or watering your lawn would not be wrong. To be sure, utilitarians assert a universal principle, that "everyone ought to act so as to bring about the greatest amount of happiness for the greatest number," but they recognize that this may mean quite different acts or quite different rules of behavior in different places at different times.

Now that the fundamentals of utilitarianism have been explained, it is worth remembering that we are engaged in a dialectic. We have developed the idea of utilitarianism; we have made the case for the theory. Now it is time for more critical scrutiny.

Critique of Utilitarianism

One of the traditional criticisms of utilitarianism is that when it is applied to certain cases, it seems to go against some of our most strongly held moral intuitions. In particular it seems to justify imposing enormous burdens on some individuals for the sake of others. According to utilitarianism, every person is to be counted equally—no one person's unhappiness or happiness is more important than another's. However, since utilitarians are concerned with the total amount of happiness, we can imagine situations where great overall happiness might result from sacrificing the happiness of a few. Suppose, for example, that having a small number of slaves would create great happiness for large numbers of people. Those who were made slaves would be unhappy but this would be counterbalanced by marked increases in the happiness of many others. Another more contemporary example would have us imagine a situation in which by killing one person and using all this person's organs for transplantation, we would be able to save ten lives. This would seem to maximize good consequences. Critics of utilitarianism say that such practices as slavery and killing individuals in order to save others cannot possibly be right, and if utilitarianism justifies such practices, then the theory must be wrong.

In response to this attack, some utilitarians argue that such practices are not (and never could be) justified in utilitarianism because of their long-term consequences. For example, a practice of slavery or of killing people for their organs could never be justified because such practices would lead to everyone living in fear that they might be the next one to be selected for sacrifice. The good produced could never counterbalance the bad effects of the fear.

Other utilitarians boldly accept and defend these practices where they are consistent with the utility principle. That is, they hold that if there are ever circumstances in which slavery would produce more good than ill, then it would be morally acceptable. If there are ever circumstances in which the bad effects of killing people for their organs are outweighed by the good results, then so be it. In other words, these utilitarians admit that there may be circumstances in which some people should be sacrificed for the sake of overall happiness. Let us explore this criticism a little further and contrast it with a Kantian or deontological approach.

Case Illustration

A few years ago, when medical researchers had just succeeded in developing the kidney dialysis machine, a few hospitals acquired a limited number of these expensive machines. Hospitals soon found that the number of patients needing treatment on the machines far exceeded the number of machines they had available or could afford. Decisions had to be made as to who would get access to the machines, and these were often life-death decisions. In response, some hospitals set up review boards composed of representative community members as well as medical staff to decide which patients would get access to the machines. Medical information was considered, but the decisions were made primarily on the basis of personal facts about the patients: age, job, number of dependents, social usefulness of job, whether the person had a criminal record, and so on. These committees appeared to be using utilitarian criteria. The resource—kidney dialysis machines—was scarce and they wanted to maximize the benefit (the consequences) to society. Thus, those who were most likely to benefit and to contribute to society in the future would get access, namely those who were the least ill or did not have other terminal illness, those who had dependent children, those who were doctors, those who were the youngest (had the longest to live), those who were not criminals, and so on.

As the activities of the hospital review boards became known to the public, they were criticized. Critics argued that one's value as a person cannot be measured by one's value to the community. Everyone, it was argued, has value in and of themselves. This response is consistent with Kantian theory, for according to Immanuel Kant you should never treat another person merely as a means; you should always respect individuals as ends in themselves. To treat another as a means to some end is the utmost in disrespect, and that is exactly what a policy of allocating scarce resources according to social value does. It says, in effect, that people have value only as means to the betterment of society. In contrast, Kantians argued that the only way to truly recognize the equal value of persons is to distribute scarce medical resources by a lottery. In a lottery everyone has an equal chance, everyone counts the same. Any other kind of distribution is unfair.

It is interesting to note that the kidney dialysis issue is just a microcosm of all medical resources. We have much less than is needed—of doctors, of money to be spent on equipment or research, and so on—and decisions have to be made about distribution. For our purposes here, the important point is that utilitarianism seems ill equipped to deal with issues of *distributive justice.* The core idea in utilitarianism does not address how benefits and burdens are distributed in a society. The criticism of the hospital review boards for distributing access to kidney machines according to social value goes right to the heart of this criticism. Critics argue that people are valuable in themselves, not for their contribution to society. They argue that utilitarian programs are often unfair because in maximizing overall good, they impose an unfair burden on certain individuals and as such treat those individuals merely as means.

We now need to look more closely at Kantian theory, but once again it is important to note that the dialectic might go off in a different direction. The debate about utilitarianism is rich and there are many moves to be made in reformulating the theory and defending it against its critics. It is also important to note that whatever its weaknesses, utilitarianism goes a long way in providing a systematic account of many of our moral notions.

DEONTOLOGICAL THEORIES

In utilitarianism, what makes an action right or wrong is outside the action; it is the consequences of the action. By contrast, deontological theories put the emphasis on the internal character of the act itself.[1] What makes an action right or wrong for deontologists is the principle inherent in the action. If an action is done from a sense of duty, if the principle of the action can be universalized, then the action is right. For example, if I tell the truth, not just because it is convenient for me to do so but because I recognize that I must respect the other person, then I act from duty and my action is right. If I tell the truth because I fear getting caught or because I believe I will be rewarded for doing so, then my act is not morally worthy.

[1] The term "deontology" derives from the Greek words *deon* (duty) and *logos* (science). Etymologically, then, deontology means the science of duty. According to the *Encyclopedia of Philosophy,* its current usage is more specific, referring to an ethical theory which holds that "at least some acts are morally obligatory regardless of their consequences for human weal or woe" (Paul Edwards, ed., *The Encyclopedia of Philosophy* (New York: Macmillan, 1967).

The difference between deontological theories and consequentialist theories was illustrated in the discussion of allocation of scarce medical resources. Deontologists say that individuals are valuable in themselves, not because of their social value. Utilitarianism is criticized because it appears to tolerate sacrificing some people for the sake of others. With the emphasis on maximizing overall happiness, there are no absolute prohibitions on how we treat others. By contrast, deontological theories assert that there are some actions that are always wrong, no matter what the consequences. The best example of this is killing. Even though we can imagine situations in which intentionally killing one person may save the lives of many others, deontologists insist that intentional killing is always wrong. Killing is wrong (even in extreme situations) because it means using the person as a means and does not treat the human being as valuable in and of himself. (Deontologists do often recognize self-defense and other special circumstances as excusing killing, but these are cases when the killing is not exactly intentional.)

At the heart of deontological theory is an idea about what it means to be a person, and this is connected to the idea of moral agency. Charles Fried puts the point as follows:

> the substantive contents of the norms of right and wrong express the value of persons, of respect for personality. What we may not do to each other, the things which are wrong, are precisely those forms of personal interaction which deny to our victim the status of a freely choosing, rationally valuing, specially efficacious person, the special status of moral personality.[2]

According to deontologists, the utilitarians go wrong when they fix on happiness as the highest good. Deontologists point out that this cannot be the highest good for humans because if this was what we were meant to achieve, we would have been better designed without minds. That is, if our function as human beings was simply to be happy, blind instinct would have suited us better. The fact that we are rational beings, capable of reasoning about what we want to do and then deciding and acting, suggests that our function must be something other than mere happiness. Humans differ from all other beings in the world insofar as we have the capacity for rationality. The behavior of other things is determined simply by laws of nature. Plants turn toward the sun because of photosynthesis—they don't think and decide which way they will turn. Physical objects fall by the law of gravity. Water boils when it reaches a certain temperature. In contrast, human beings are not entirely determined by laws of nature: We have the capacity to legislate for ourselves; we decide how we will behave.

---

[2] Charles Fried, *Right and Wrong* (Cambridge, Mass.: Harvard University Press, 1978), pp. 28–29.

So Kant identifies a fundamental feature of human beings—our capacity for rational decision making. Each of us has this capacity; each of us can make choices, choices about what we will do and what kind of persons we will become. This means that no one else can make these choices for us, and that each of us must recognize this capacity in the other.

Notice that it makes good sense that our rationality is connected with morality, for we could not be moral beings at all unless we had this rational capacity. We do not think of plants or fish or dogs and cats as moral beings precisely because they do not have the capacity to reason about their actions. We are moral beings because we are rational beings, that is, because we have the capacity to give ourselves rules and follow them. We are capable of determining our own behavior, in a way that other beings are not.

Where utilitarians note that all humans seek happiness, deontologists emphasize that humans are creatures with goals who engage in activities directed toward achieving these and they use their rationality to formulate their goals and figure out what kind of life to live. In a sense, deontologists pull back from fixing on any particular value as structuring morality and instead ground morality in the capacity of each individual to organize his or her own life, make choices, and engage in activities to realize his or her self-chosen life plans. What morality requires is that we respect all of these beings as valuable in themselves and refrain from seeing them or valuing them only insofar as they fit into our own life plans.

Although deontological theories can be formulated in a number of ways, one formulation is particularly important to mention. This is a rule Kant referred to as the *categorical imperative*. There are actually three versions of it, and the second version, as discussed earlier, goes as follows: Never treat another human being merely as a means but always as an end. This general rule is derived from the idea that persons are moral beings because they are rational, efficacious beings. Because we each have the capacity to think and decide and act for ourselves, we should each be treated with respect, that is with recognition of this capacity.

It is important to note the "merely" in the categorical imperative. Deontologists do not insist that we never use other persons, only that we never "merely" use them. For example, if I own a company and hire employees to work in my company, I might be thought of as using those employees as a means to my end (that is, the success of my business). This, however, is not wrong if the employees agree to work for me and if I pay them a fair wage. I thereby respect their ability to choose for themselves and I respect the value of their labor. What would be wrong would be to take them as slaves and make them work for me, or to pay them so little that they must borrow from me and must remain always in my debt. This would be exploitation. This would show disregard for the value of each person as a "freely choosing, rationally valuing, specially efficacious person."

Case Illustration

Though utilitarianism and Kantian theory were contrasted in the case illustration about allocation of scarce medical resources, another case will clarify things even more. Consider a case involving computers. Suppose a professor of sociology, at a major research university, undertakes research on attitudes toward sex and sexual behavior among high school students. Among other things, she interviews hundreds of high school students concerning their attitudes and behavior. She knows that the students will never give her information unless she guarantees them confidentiality, so before doing the interviews, she promises each student that no one (other than her) will have access to the raw interview data and that all publishable results will be reported in statistical form. Thus, it will be impossible to identify information from individual students.

Suppose, however, that it is now time to analyze the interview data, and she realizes that it will be much easier to put the data into a computer and use the computer to do the analysis. She will have to code the data so that names do not appear in the database and she will have to make an effort to secure the data. She has hired graduate students to assist her and she wonders whether she should let the graduate students code and process the raw data.

At first glance it would seem that from a consequentialist point of view, the professor should weigh the good that will come from the research, and from doing it quickly (on a computer), against the possible harm to herself and her subjects if information is leaked. The research may provide important information to people working with youth and may help her career to prosper. Still, the advantage of doing it quickly may be slight. She must worry about the effect of a leak of information on one of the students. Also, since she has explicitly promised confidentiality to the student-subjects, she has to worry about the effects on her credibility as a social researcher and on social science research in general if she breaks her promise. That is, her subjects and many others may be reluctant in the future to trust her and other social scientists if she breaks the promise and they find out.

Thus, it would seem from a consequentialist point of view that the professor should not violate her promise of confidentiality. Fortunately, there are ways to code data before putting it into the computer or turning it over to her graduate students. She must, however, do the coding herself and keep the key to individual names strictly to herself.

This is how a consequentialist might analyze the situation. A deontologist would probably not come to a very different conclusion, but the reasoning would be quite different. The sociologist is doing a study that will advance human knowledge and, no doubt, further her career. There is nothing wrong with this as long as it does not violate the categorical imperative. The question here is, is she treating her subjects merely as means to knowledge and her own advancement, or is she truly recognizing those subjects as ends in themselves? The categorical imperative requires that the sociologist seek the permission of each subject before she gathers data on their sex lives. In seeking the permission of each subject, she respects each as an individual who has her or his own desires, needs, and plans, and the ability to make her or his own choices about what to do or not to do. If, however, the sociologist were to ignore her promise of confidentiality, she would not be treating each subject as an end. After all, each student made a choice based on her pledge of confidentiality, and she must acknowledge and respect that choice. Thus, out of respect for the subjects, the sociologist must code the data herself and maintain confidentiality.

The two theories do not, then, come to very different conclusions in this case. However, the analysis is very different; that is, the reasons given for coming to a conclusion are very different. In other cases, these theories lead to dramatically different conclusions.

Our dialogue on utilitarianism and Kantian theory could continue. I have only sketched each theory, and there are many aspects of each that might be explored further. The dialogue could go off in any number of directions. However, in the interest of getting to the issues surrounding computers, we must move on. A few more new ideas need to be put "on the table."

RIGHTS

So far, very little has been said about "rights," though we often use the concept of rights when discussing moral issues. Rights are generally associated with deontological theories. The categorical imperative requires that each person be treated as an end in himself or herself, and this might be understood to mean that individuals have "a right to" the kind of treatment that is implied in "being treated as an end." The idea that each individual must be respected as valuable in himself or herself implies that we each have rights not to be interfered with in certain ways, for example, not to be killed or enslaved, to be given freedom to make decisions about our own lives, and so on.

An important distinction that philosophers often make here is between negative rights and positive rights. Negative rights are rights that call for restraint by others. For example, my right not to be killed requires that others refrain from killing me; it does not require that others do anything to or for me. Positive rights imply that others have a duty to do something to or for the right holder. For example, if we say that I have a positive right to life, this implies not just that others must refrain from killing me, but that they must do such things as feed me if I am starving, give me medical treatment if I am sick, swim out and save me if I am drowning, and so on.

Positive rights are more controversial than negative rights because they have implications that are counterintuitive. For example, if every person has a positive right to life, this seems to imply that each and every one of us has a duty to do whatever is necessary to keep all people alive. This seems to suggest that, among other things, it is our duty to give away any excess wealth that we have, to feed and care for those who are starving and in ill health. It also seems to imply that we have a duty to supply extraordinary life-saving treatment for all those who are dying. In response to these implications, some philosophers have argued that individuals have only negative rights.

In any case, while "rights-talk" is typically associated with deontological theories, it is important to note that utilitarians may also use the language of rights, for one can argue for recognition of individual rights on utilitarian grounds. For example, suppose we ask why individuals should be allowed to have private property in general and, in particular, why they should be allowed to own computer software. Utilitarians would argue for private ownership of software on grounds that much more and better software will be created if individuals are allowed to own (and then license or sell) it. Thus, they argue that individuals should have a legal right to ownership in software. This is very different from arguing that one has a natural right to own what one has created. The natural rights argument claims that since no one is entitled to own another person, and since my labor is an extension of my person, then no one can own what I create. Since computer software is the product of individual labor, those who create it have a right to own and control it.

This debate will be taken up fully in Chapter 4 on property. The important thing to remember now is that rights-claims are usually embedded in a theory and should not be accepted as primitive truths. Rights-claims should be analyzed, their underlying rationale should be uncovered, and they should be critically examined.

The other important thing to remember about rights is the distinction between legal and moral (or natural or human) rights. Legal rights are rights that are created by law. Moral, natural, or human rights are claims independent of law. Such claims are usually embedded in a moral theory, or a theory of human nature.

MACRO AND MICRO SOLUTIONS

One final distinction will be helpful. In examining problems or issues, it is important to distinguish levels of analysis, in particular that between macro- and micro-level issues or approaches. We can approach a problem from the point of view of social practices and public policy or from the point of view of individual choice. Macro-level problems are problems that arise for groups of people, a community, a state, a country. They usually call for a solution in the form of a law or policy that specifies how people in that group or society ought to behave, what the rules of that group ought to be. When we ask the following questions, we are asking macro-level questions: Should our society grant software creators a legal right to own programs? Should computer professionals be liable for errors in the software they produce? Should companies be allowed to electronically monitor their employees? On the other hand, micro-level questions focus on individuals (in the presence or absence of law or policy). Should I make a copy of this piece of software? Should I lie to my friend? Should I work on a project making military weapons? Sometimes these types of questions are answered by a rule established at the macro level, but other times the macro-level rules are not there or are not adequate and individuals must make decisions for themselves about what they ought to do.

The theories discussed above inform both approaches, but in somewhat different ways, so that it is important to be clear on which type of question you are asking or answering.

A FINAL NOTE

While the focus of our attention now shifts to the ethical issues surrounding computers, the deep questions and general concerns of ethical theories will continue to haunt us. The dialogue is ongoing. Remember that science is never done either. In both science and ethics we look for reasons for the claims that we make, and we tell stories (develop arguments and theories) to answer our questions. We tell stories about why the physical world is the way it is, why human beings behave the way they do, why lying or killing is wrong, and so on. The stories we tell get better over time, broader (more encompassing) and richer, sometimes more elegant, sometimes allowing us to see new things we never noticed before. The stories always lead to new questions. So it is with ethics as well as science.

Computer ethics has to be undertaken with this in mind, for the task of computer ethics involves working with traditional moral concepts and theories but extending them to situations with somewhat new features. The activity brings insight into the situations arising from use of computers, and it may also bring new insights into ethical concepts and theories.

STUDY QUESTIONS

1. How do descriptive (empirical) statements and prescriptive (normative) statements differ?
2. What is ethical relativism?
3. What evidence is often presented to support ethical relativism?
4. What is utilitarianism? What argument might lead one to adopt this theory?
5. What is the traditional criticism of utilitarianism?
6. Why can't happiness be the highest good for humans, according to deontologists?

7. What is the categorical imperative?
8. How can rights be based on deontological theory? How can rights be based on utility theory?
9. What is the difference between macro- and micro-level issues?

EXERCISES/ESSAY QUESTIONS

1. Is ethical relativism implausible? (This is your opportunity to take issue with Johnson's attack on ethical relativism.)
2. Compare and contrast utilitarianism with Kantian theory.
3. How can such different theories as utilitarianism and deontological theory lead to the same conclusions? Illustrate.
4. Go back to the scenarios at the beginning of Chapter 1. Using the theories or concepts described in this chapter, construct arguments defending the rightness or wrongness of the behavior described in the scenarios.

SUGGESTED FURTHER READING

BAIER, KURT. *The Moral Point of View.* Ithaca, N.Y.: Random House, 1965.
BRODY, BARUCH. *Ethics and Its Applications.* New York: Harcourt Jovanovich, 1983.
BOWIE, NORMAN E. *Making Ethical Decisions.* New York: McGraw-Hill, 1985.
FRIED, CHARLES. *Right and Wrong.* Cambridge, Mass.: Harvard University Press, 1978.
RACHELS, JAMES. *Elements of Moral Philosophy.* Philadelphia: Temple University Press, 1986.

CHAPTER 3

Professional Ethics

SCENARIO 3.1: CONFLICTING LOYALTIES

Carl Babbage is an experienced systems designer. He has been working for the Acme Software Company for over three years. Acme develops and sells computer hardware and software. It does this both by designing and marketing general purpose systems and by contracting with companies and government agencies to design systems for their exclusive use.

During the first two years that Carl worked for Acme, he worked on software that Acme was developing for general marketing. A year ago, however, he was reassigned to work on a project under contract with the U.S. Defense Department. The project involves designing a system that will monitor radar signals and launch nuclear missiles in response to these signals.

Carl initially had some reluctance about working on a military project, but he put this out of his mind because the project seemed challenging and he knew that if he did not work on it, someone else would. Now, however, the project is approaching completion and Carl has some grave reservations about the adequacy of the system. He is doubtful about the system's capacity for making fine distinctions (for example, distinguishing between a small aircraft and a missile) and the security of the mechanism that can launch missiles (for example, it may be possible for unauthorized individuals to get access to the controls under certain circumstances). Carl expressed his concern to the project director but she dismissed these concerns quickly, mentioning that Acme is already behind schedule on the project and has already exceeded the budget that they had agreed to with the Defense Department.

Carl feels that he has a moral responsibility to do something, but he doesn't know what to do. Should he ask for reassignment to another project? Should he go to executives in Acme and tell them of his concerns? It is difficult to imagine how they will respond. Should he talk to someone in the Defense Department? Should he go to newspaper or TV reporters and "blow the whistle"? If he does any of these things, he is likely to jeopardize his job. Should he do nothing?

SCENARIO 3.2: SYSTEM SECURITY

After getting an undergraduate degree in computer science, Diane Jones was hired by a large computer company. She initially worked as a programmer, but over the years she was promoted to technical positions with increasing responsibility. Three years ago she quit her job and started her own consulting business. She has been so successful that she now has several people working for her.

At the moment, Diane is designing a database management system for the personnel office of a medium-sized company that manufactures toys. Diane has involved the client in the design process, informing the CEO, the director of computing, and the director of personnel about the progress of the system and giving them many opportunities to make decisions about features of the system. It is now time to make decisions about the kind and degree of security to build into the system.

Diane has described several options to the client, and the client has decided to opt for the least secure system because the system is going to cost more than they planned. She believes that the information they will be storing is extremely sensitive, because it will include performance evaluations, medical records for filing insurance claims, and salaries. With weak security, it may be possible for enterprising employees to figure out how to get access to these data, not to mention the possibilities for on-line access from hackers. Diane feels strongly that the system should be much more secure.

She has tried to explain the risks to her client, but the CEO, director of computing, and director of personnel are all willing to accept a system with little security. What should she do? For example, should she refuse to build the system as they request?

SCENARIO 3.3: CONFLICT OF INTEREST

Marvin Miller makes a living as a private consultant. Small businesses hire him to advise them about their computer needs. Typically, a company asks him to come in, examine the company's operations, evaluate its automation needs, and make recommendations about the kind of hardware and software that it should purchase.

Recently, Marvin was hired by a small, private hospital, which was particularly interested in upgrading the software used for patient records and accounting. The hospital asked Marvin to evaluate proposals they had received from three software companies, each of which offered a system that could be modified for the hospital's use. Marvin examined the offers carefully. He considered which system would best meet the hospital's needs, which company offered the best services in terms of training of staff and future updates, which offered the best price, and so on. He concluded that Tri-Star Systems was the best alternative for the hospital, and he recommended this in his report, explaining his reasons for drawing this conclusion.

What Marvin failed to mention (at any time in his dealings with the hospital) was that he is a silent partner (a co-owner) in Tri-Star Systems. Was this unethical? Should Marvin have disclosed the fact that he has ties to one of the software companies?

WHY PROFESSIONAL ETHICS?

Carl, Diane, and Marvin find themselves in difficult situations. The ethical theory described in the last chapter should help us to figure out what our responsibilities are in situations like these, but we have to be careful. While it is tempting to jump in and see what course of action can be justified using utilitarian or deontological theory, such analyses will not be useful unless we take the contexts in which the individual is acting fully into account. Carl, Diane, and Marvin have each taken a job and this creates responsibilities. We cannot accurately understand their situations if we view them simply as individuals acting in ways that affect other individuals. We must consider what it means to act in a professional or occupational role. What responsibilities or obligations do employees have to their employers? What can employers rightfully expect of their employees? What can clients expect from professionals? What moral responsibility do employed professionals have for the effects of their work?

Having completed the previous chapter on ethical theory, we might have turned to this chapter and had the following sort of response. Why do we need to talk about "professional ethics" at all? If I find myself with an ethical problem, I should think it through using ethical theory, try to understand what rules or principles are at stake, and then act accordingly. That I act as a computer professional, or any other kind of professional, seems irrelevant.

There is some truth to this, for when one acts as a professional, one does not cease to be a moral agent. Nevertheless, the domain of professional ethics is special in several respects. For one thing, professional roles often carry special rights and responsibilities. Doctors, for example, are allowed to prescribe drugs and keep information confidential, and they are expected to respond when individuals are hurt in emergencies. Others (laypersons) are not allowed to do what doctors may do, nor are they expected to behave in the way doctors are expected to.

To be sure, some professional roles are more "strongly differentiated" than others.[1] Strongly differentiated roles are those that involve powers and privileges that are exceptions to ordinary morality. Think, for example, of the lawyer's obligation not to reveal confidential information given to her by a client, even when the information would affect the outcome of a trial; or think of the physical harm that police officers may inflict in the course of their work. These are behaviors that are prohibited by ordinary morality but allowed when performed by certain professionals acting in their professional roles. Other occupational roles are not strongly differentiated in that they do not allow or call upon one to act outside ordinary morality. For example, sales personnel, construction workers, and bus drivers have no special powers or privileges.

Even when an occupational or professional role carries no special powers or privileges, professional ethics can be thought of as a special domain in at least two respects. First, as mentioned at the onset, professionals function in a special context, a context that typically includes relationships with employers, clients, co-professionals, and the public. The context also involves legal, political, and economic constraints. Computer professionals, for example, are often employed by private corporations seeking a profit, constrained by law in a variety of ways, operating in a highly competitive environment, and so on. This context is usually very rich in complexity, and this cannot be ignored in analyzing ethical decision making.

Professional ethics can also be thought of as a special domain because of the "efficacy" of professionals. "Efficacy" refers to the power that professionals have to affect the world. Professionals generally have some skill or knowledge that they use to produce a product or provide a service. Sometimes they do this on their own, for example, when a doctor examines a patient and prescribes a method of treatment. More often professionals contribute their abilities and their activity to a larger enterprise wherein their contribution, together with that of others, leads to a product or service. Thus, for example, an engineer may use her skill to design one component of an airplane or a skyscraper; or a research scientist may work with a team of other scientists to develop the cure for a disease.

Skill and knowledge are an important part of the efficacy of a professional, but not the only part. Simply having skill and knowledge is not enough to produce an effect—one must exercise the skill and use the knowledge, and in most professions this cannot be done in isolation. One needs a business, clients, consumers, equipment, legal protection, and so on. Thus professionals, especially computer professionals, create their own businesses or obtain employment in companies or government agencies. The positions they fill give them the op-

---

[1] Alan Goldman, *The Moral Foundations of Professional Ethics* (Totowa, N.J.: Rowan and Littlefield, 1980).

portunity to exercise their professional skills and in so doing to affect the world in some way, for example, by creating software for missile detection systems, selling a computer that allows others to maintain records, developing software that assists individuals in financial planning, and so on.

So professionals have the capacity to affect the world because their skill and knowledge give them the ability and their jobs give them the opportunity. When they use their abilities and act in their jobs, their actions can directly or indirectly have powerful effects—on individuals and on the social and physical world we live in. Indeed, these effects are sometimes good and sometimes bad, sometimes foreseen and sometimes unforeseen.

Because professionals have this power to affect the world, we think of them as bearing special responsibility. That is, they acquire duties to behave in ways that do not harm individuals or public goods precisely because they have the capacity to do so. (I will say more on this later.)

ARE COMPUTER PROFESSIONALS "PROFESSIONALS"?

So far I have used the term "professional" rather loosely, to refer to individuals who make a living in a particular line of work, but the term has a variety of meanings. In the loose way in which I have been using the term, "professionals" might be thought of as members of an occupational group. Carpenters, truck drivers, and doctors alike would, then, be professionals. However, "profession" and "professional" are also often used in a narrower sense, to refer to a special set of occupations, which have, among other things, higher status.

Although there is no hard and fast definition, sociologists and ethicists often use doctors and lawyers as the paradigms of these special professions, and other occupations are seen as closer or farther from these on a continuum of profession-nonprofession. The following is a list of characteristics often associated with professions in this special sense of the term.

1. Professions require mastery of an esoteric body of knowledge, usually acquired through higher education. Only members of the profession possess this knowledge and it is this that justifies the next characteristic.
2. Members of professions typically have a good deal of autonomy in their work (as compared to other occupations in which one simply takes orders).
3. Professions usually have a professional organization (recognized by state government) that controls admission to the profession and sets standards for practice.
4. Professions fulfill an important social function or are committed to a social good (such as health, in the case of medicine).

Other characteristics sometimes associated with professions include that the profession has a division between those who are practitioners and those who do research (continually improving on the esoteric body of knowledge), members of professions are bound by a code of professional conduct or ethics, and members are seen as making a life commitment to the field of their profession. These characteristics are thought to justify the higher salaries usually associated with these special professions.

Now, are computer professionals "professionals" in this special sense of the term? Certainly computer professionals possess some of the appropriate characteristics. Most of them have, for example, mastered an esoteric body of knowledge and have done so through higher education. Computer professionals have varying degrees of autonomy. Those who own their own consulting firms and those who have worked their way up the ladder in corporate or government agencies may have a good deal of decision-making authority. As well, academic computer scientists and those who manage projects have a good deal of say about which projects are undertaken and how. On the other hand, many computer professionals have little autonomy. Programmers, for example, may simply implement the designs of others. There are professional organizations for computer specialists, but there is no single organization recognized by federal or state government as "the" legal body in charge of admission (by licensing, for example) or standards in the field of computing. As for fulfilling a social function, it seems clear that computing is now a crucial part of our society, but computing is not a good in itself in the way health and justice are. Computing is an activity that supports social institutions and professions, which in turn are aimed at fulfilling a variety of social functions.

Hence, it seems reasonable to conclude that computing does not fit the classic paradigm. That is, it is not a profession in the same way that law and medicine are. On the other hand, computer professionals are much closer to the paradigm of special professionals than, say, stockbrokers or carpenters or mail carriers.

In any case, whether or not the special meaning of the term "professional" applies to computer professionals is probably not so important as is identifying characteristics of the profession and of practice. An understanding of these is essential to understanding issues of professional ethics. Let us now focus on the relationships that computer professionals enter into at work.

PROFESSIONAL RELATIONSHIPS

When they take jobs, computer professionals typically enter into relationships with one or several of the following: (1) employers, (2) clients, (3) co-professionals (or the profession as a whole), and (4) the public.

Employer-Employee

When a person accepts a job in an organization, he or she enters into a relationship with an employer. Although many conditions of this relationship will be made explicit when the employee is hired (job title and associated responsibilities, salary, hours of work), many conditions will not be mentioned. Some are not mentioned since they are specified by law (for example, an employee may not be required to do anything illegal); they are assumed by both parties. Some aspects of the relationship may be negotiated through a union (for example, that employees with more seniority cannot be laid off before employees with less seniority). Yet many other conditions of the relationship will not be mentioned because neither party has an interest in them at the moment, because no one can anticipate all the situations that may arise, and probably because it is better not to press the uncertainties of some aspects of employer-employee relations. For example, when you accept a job, do you, thereby, agree to work overtime whenever your supervisor requests it? If you work for a local government and it gets into financial trouble, will you accept your salary in script? Do you agree never to speak out publicly on political issues that may affect your employer? Do you agree to a dress code?

When one examines the moral foundation of the employer-employee relationship, it appears to be a contractual relationship. Each party agrees to do certain things in exchange for certain things. Generally, the employee agrees to perform certain tasks and the employer agrees to pay compensation and provide the work environment. Since the relationship is contractual in character, we may think of it as fulfilling the requirements of the categorical imperative. Each party exercises his or her autonomy in consenting to the terms of the contract, since each party is free to refuse to enter into the contract.

According to the categorical imperative, each individual should be treated with respect and never used merely as a means; thus it is wrong for either the employer or the employee to exploit the other. This means, among other things, that each party must be honest. An employee must be honest with her employer about her qualifications for the job and must do the work promised. Otherwise, she is simply using the employer to get what she wants without respecting the employer's interests. Likewise, the employer must pay a decent wage and must be honest with the employee about what she will be expected to do at work.

Workplace hazards illustrate the potential for exploitation here. If your employer says nothing about the dangers involved in a job and simply offers you a big salary and good benefits, making the job so attractive that it is hard to turn down, then the employer has not treated you with respect. He or she has not recognized you as an end in yourself, with interests of your own and the capacity to decide what risks you will or will not take. Your employer has kept important information from you in order to ensure that you will do what he or she wants. You are used merely as a means to what your employer wants. On the other hand, if your employer explains that you will be exposed to toxic substances at work and explains that this will increase the likelihood of your developing cancer, then if you agree to take the job, your employer has not exploited you.

For professional ethics, one of the most difficult areas of the employer-employee relationship has to do with what one rightfully owes an employer in the name of loyalty (or what an employer can rightfully expect or demand of an employee). Although loyalty is generally thought to be a good thing, closer examination reveals that it has both a good side and a bad. In her analysis of loyalty, Marcia Baron describes several negative effects of loyalty.[2] Loyalty is bad because (1) it invites unfairness, (2) it eschews reliance on good reasons, and (3) it invites irresponsibility. For example, if I am responsible for hiring a new employee and I, out of loyalty, choose my friend without considering the qualifications and experience of all other applicants, I have not treated the other applicants fairly. I have not used good reasons in making the decision; hence, I have acted irresponsibly in my position.

On the other hand, Baron points out that loyalty is a good thing because it allows us to have special relationships that are extremely valuable. Parenting and friendship are two powerful examples. Being a parent means treating certain people in special ways. If I were obligated to use my time and resources to help all children equally (that is, if "my" children had no special claims to my care and attention), then the idea that I was someone's parent would be without meaning. It is the same with friendship. If I treated my friends exactly as I treat all other persons, it would be hard to understand what it means to have a friend.

Both the good and bad implications of loyalty come into play in employer-employee relationships. Organizations could probably not function unless individuals recognize that they owe something special to their employers. Having individuals that will take orders and make efforts to coordinate their activities with others allows organizations to accomplish things that could not be accomplished otherwise. Hence, a certain degree of loyalty to an employer seems necessary and even worthy.

Nevertheless, we should not jump to the conclusion that employees owe their employers whatever they demand in the name of loyalty. There are limits. The hard part, of course, is to figure out where to draw the line. Clearly employers cannot demand every form of behavior that will serve the interests of the company. For example, companies have been known to pressure employees to vote in public elections for candidates who the company believes will further the company's interests. Such pressure threatens an employee's right as a citizen to vote as he or she sees fit. Indeed, it threatens democracy. Companies have also been known to expect their employees to buy only company products, that is, nothing made by a competitor. This expectation, especially when coupled with sanctions against those who do not comply, seems to overstep the bounds of legitimate employer expectations.

Trade secrecy is one area where the line is particularly difficult to draw. While employers have a legal right to expect their employees to keep trade secrets, it is unclear to what extent they should be allowed to go to protect their legitimate secrets. Trade secrets often involve information about the design of

---

[2] Marcia Baron, *The Moral Status of Loyalty* (Dubuque, Iowa: Kendall/Hunt, 1984).

a new product, a formula, or a computer algorithm. (In Chapter 4, trade secrecy law will be discussed more fully.) Employers fear that employees may reveal these secrets to competitors, especially when they leave the company. Typically, employers have employees sign agreements promising not to reveal secrets.

Sometimes employees are even expected to agree not to work in the same industry for a certain period of time after they leave the company. Needless to say, employees often want to move on to another job and their best opportunities are likely to be, if not in the same industry, at least doing the same kind of work. Employees learn a great deal of what might be called "generic" knowledge while working at a company. It is not considered wrong for employees to take this knowledge with them to their next job. It is this knowledge and experience, in fact, that makes an employee attractive to another company. Still, employers have been known to try to prevent employees from moving on for fear that the employee will inadvertently, even if not intentionally, reveal valuable information to competitors. So the employer's legitimate concern about a trade secret has to be balanced against the right of an employee to work where he or she wants. Employers can abuse their rights by trying to stop their competitors from hiring a good employee.

The employer-employee relationship is more complicated and less well defined than you might expect. Employees do incur special responsibilities to their employers, but there are limits to this. The Carl Babbage scenario at the beginning of this chapter illustrates the point clearly enough. We cannot say that Babbage has no responsibilities to Acme. If he were to blow the whistle, a great deal of damage could be done to the company, and the damage would be done even if his concerns turned out to be wrong. On the other hand, it is hard to say that out of loyalty to the company he should do nothing. What he owes the company and when he should "break ranks" is not easy to figure out. (We will see more on this later.)

Client-Professional

The Carl Babbage scenario can also be understood to involve a conflict between an employee's responsibility to his employer and his responsibility to a client. The client in this case is the Defense Department, and technically it is Acme's client, only indirectly Babbage's. The Defense Department has entrusted its project to Acme, and it would seem that to be true to this trust, Acme should inform its client of the unanticipated problems. The problem here, of course, is that Acme does not appear to be behaving well, which creates the problem for Babbage. Babbage is expected by Acme to use the channels of authority in the organization. One can think of Acme's organizational structure as a mechanism for managing its responsibilities. Babbage has tried to work through this structure but it has not worked.

In both the Diane Jones scenario and the Marvin Miller scenario, the layers of bureaucracy are removed so that there is a more direct client-professional relationship. These are, perhaps, the better cases to use when first thinking through the character of client-professional relationships.

As with the employer-employee relationship, the client-professional relationship can be thought of as essentially contractual. Each party provides something the other wants, and both parties agree to the terms of the relationship: what will be done, how long it will take, how much the client will pay, where the work will be done, and so on. The important thing to keep in mind about client-professional relationships is the disparity in knowledge or expertise of the parties.

The client seeks the professional's special knowledge and expertise, but because the client does not himself possess that knowledge, he must depend on the professional. "Trust" is the operative term here. The client needs the professional to make or help make decisions that may be crucial to the client's business, and he must trust that the professional will use his or her knowledge competently, effectively, and efficiently. This is true of doctor-patient, lawyer-client, architect-client, and teacher-student relationships, as well as in relationships between computer professionals and clients.

Different models have been proposed for understanding how this disparity in professional-client relationships should be handled. Perhaps the most important are (1) agency, (2) paternalism, and (3) fiduciary.[3]

Briefly, on the *agency* model, the professional is to act as the agent of the professional and simply implement what the client requests. Here the implication is that the client retains all decision-making authority. The professional may make decisions but they are minor, that is, they are simply implications of the client's choice. I call a stockbroker, tell her what stocks I want to buy, how many, and at what price and she executes the transaction. She is my agent.

Some client-professional relationships are like this, but the problem with this model is that it does not come to grips with the special knowledge or expertise of the professional. Often the professional has knowledge that reflects back on what the client ought to be deciding. Professional advice is needed not just to implement decisions but to help make the decisions.

At the opposite extreme is the *paternalistic* model. Here the client transfers all decision-making authority to the professional, who acts in the interests of the client, making decisions that he believes will benefit the client. This model clearly recognizes the special expertise of the professional, so much so that the client has little "say." We used to think of the doctor-patient relationship on this model. I would go to a doctor, report my symptoms, and the rest was up to the doctor, who would decide what I needed and prescribe the treatment. I would simply be expected to accept what the doctor prescribed. How could I question the doctor's authority when I didn't have the expert knowledge? The problem, however, with this model of client-professional relation-

---

[3] See Michael Bayles, *Professional Ethics* (Belmont, Calif.: Wadsworth, 1981) for these and other models of the client-professional relationship.

ships is that it expects the client to turn over all autonomy to the professional and cease to be a decision maker. The client must place himself at the complete mercy of the professional.

The third model attempts to understand client-professional relationships as those in which both parties have a role and are working together. Clients retain decision-making authority but make decisions on the basis of information provided by the professional. This is called the *fiduciary* model, fiduciary implies trust. On this model both parties must trust one another. The client must trust the professional to use his or her expert knowledge and to think in terms of the interest of the client, but the professional must also trust that the client will give the professional relevant information, will listen to what the professional says, and so on. Decision making is shared.

On the fiduciary model, computer professionals serving clients will have the responsibility to be honest with clients about what they can and can't do, to inform them about what is possible, to give them realistic estimates of time and costs for their services, and much more. They will also have the responsibility to give clients the opportunity to make decisions about the parameters of the software or hardware they will get. Diane Jones seems to be working on the assumption of this sort of relationship in that she has informed her client of the possibilities and has made a recommendation. The problem now is that she doesn't think they are making the right decision. The fiduciary model would seem to call upon her to go back to her client and try to explain. It is hard to say what she should do if she is unsuccessful at convincing them. What is clear is that she owes her clients the benefits of her judgment.

In the Marvin Miller scenario, we see a computer professional doing something that threatens to undermine the trust that is so important to client-professional relationships. Miller has allowed himself to enter into a conflict-of-interest situation. His client—the hospital—expects him to exercise professional judgment on behalf of (in the interest of) the hospital. Although Miller may think he will be able to evaluate the offers made by each software company objectively, he has an interest in one of those companies that could affect his judgment. If representatives of the hospital find out about this, they might well conclude that Miller has not acted in the hospital's best interest. Even if Miller recommends that the hospital buy software from another company (not Tri-Star), there is the possibility that Miller's judgment has been distorted by his "bending over backward" to treat the other companies fairly. In that case, the hospital would not have gotten the best system either.

Imperative 1.3 of the 1992 Association for Computer Machinery (ACM) Code of Ethics specifies that an ACM member will "be honest and trustworthy." Included in the discussion of this imperative in the Guidelines to the Code is the statement: "A computer professional has a duty to be honest about his or her own qualifications, and about any circumstances that might lead to conflicts of interest." (See Appendix.) Rules of this kind recognize that clients (and the public) will lose confidence in a profession if they observe members abusing their roles. Indeed, in some professions, it is considered wrong for members to enter into any relationship that has even the appearance of a conflict of interest.

Society-Professional

When professionals exercise their skill and act in their professional roles, their activities may affect others who are neither employers nor clients. For example, you may design a computer system that will be used in a dangerous manufacturing process. Use of the system may put workers at risk or it may put residents in the neighborhood of the plant at risk. Or you might simply design a database for an insurance company, where the security of the system has implications for those who are insured. Because the work of computer professionals has these potential effects, computer professionals have a relationship with those others who may be affected.

This relationship is to a certain extent governed by law. That is, regulatory laws setting safety standards for products and construction are made in order to protect the public interest. But the law does not and cannot possibly anticipate all the effects that the work of professionals may have. At the same time professionals, including computer professionals, are often in the best position to see what effects their work will have or to evaluate the risks involved. Carl Babbage, for example, because of his expertise and familiarity with the system being designed, is in a better position than anyone outside of Acme to know whether or not the missile detecting system needs further evaluation.

The relationship between professionals and the individuals indirectly affected by their work can also be understood as contractual in nature, at least if we think of those affected as "society." Some of the sociological and philosophical literature on professions suggests that we understand each profession as having a social contract with society.[4] According to these accounts, we should think of society as granting the members of a profession (or the profession as a whole) the right to practice their profession (sometimes with special privileges) in exchange for their promise to practice the profession in ways that serve society, or, at least, in ways that do not harm society. This means maintaining professional standards and looking out for the public good. On this model, both parties give something and receive something in the exchange. Society gives professionals the right to practice and other forms of support and receives the benefits of having such professionals. Professionals receive the right to practice and other forms of societal support (protection of law, access to educational systems, and so on) and in exchange take on the burden of responsibility for managing themselves so as to serve the public interest. If a profession were not committed to public good, it would be foolish for society to allow members to practice.

[4] Robert F. Ladenson, "The Social Responsibilities of Engineers and Scientists: A Philosophical Approach," in *Ethical Problems in Engineering*, Volume 1, 2nd ed., Albert Flores (Troy, N.Y.: Human Dimensions Center, 1980).

The social contract account provides a useful framework for thinking about the ways in which computer professionals might organize themselves in the future, but it seems somewhat ill suited for understanding the field of computing as it is now constituted. That is, there is presently no single, formal organization of computer professionals that is recognized by government as having the right to issue licenses or set standards in the field of practice, and these are the most salient (and potent) aspects of a social contract.

We might better account for the responsibility of computer professionals to society by returning to the idea of their possessing special knowledge and skills, and the power of positions. What distinguishes computer professionals from others is their knowledge of how computers work, what computers can and cannot do, and how to get computers to do things. This knowledge, one might insist, carries with it some responsibility. When one has knowledge, special knowledge, one has a responsibility to use it for the benefit of humanity or, at least, not to the detriment of humanity. Special knowledge coupled with the power of position means that computer professionals can do things in the world that others cannot. Thus, they have greater responsibility than others.

The only problem with this account is that it simply asserts a correlation between knowledge and responsibility. The correlation is left as a primitive with no explanation. Thus, we cannot help but ask, why does responsibility come with knowledge? Why does it have to be so?

One way to establish this correlation between knowledge and responsibility is to base it on a principle of ordinary morality. Kenneth Alpern argues that the edict "Do no harm" is a fundamental principle of ordinary morality that no one will question.[5] He has to qualify the principle somewhat so that it reads, "Other things being equal, one should exercise due care to avoid contributing to significantly harming others." He then adds a corollary, which he calls the corollary of proportionate care: "Whenever one is in a position to contribute to greater harm or when one is in a position to play a more critical part in producing harm than is another person, one must exercise greater care to avoid so doing."

Focusing on engineers, Alpern then argues that while engineers are no different from anybody else in having the responsibility to avoid contributing to significant harm, they are different in that they are in positions (because of their work) in which they can do more harm than others. Thus, they have a responsibility to do more, to take greater care.

All of this seems to apply to computer professionals—at least, to many of them. Computer professionals are often in positions to use their expertise to contribute to projects that have the potential to harm others, as in the case of Carl Babbage. Since they act in ways that have the potential to do more harm, they have greater responsibility.

So Alpern's account does apply to computer professionals. The only prob-

[5] Kenneth Alpern, "Moral Responsibility for Engineers," *Business & Professional Ethics Journal*, 2, no. 2 (1983), 39–56.

lem is that if he is right, then it is not just computer professionals that bear responsibility but all those who contribute to projects with the potential to harm. Employed computer professionals can argue that they do not have nearly as much power as corporate managers, CEOs, or anyone above them in an organizational hierarchy. Alpern's proportionality thesis implies that the greater one's power, the greater one's responsibility. Of course, this need not be an either/or matter. Everyone, on Alpern's account, bears some responsibility, and so computer professionals bear their share of the responsibility along with managers and executives.[6]

Alpern's account is not exactly, then, an account of professional ethics but simply an account of the social responsibility of persons. Persons are responsible in proportion to their contribution to harm. Computer professionals are more powerful than some—in virtue of their knowledge and positions—and less powerful than others. They may not bear all the responsibility for a project, but they bear responsibility in proportion to their contribution.

Of course, to say that computer professionals have responsibility as persons and not as professionals is not to say that this is how it should be or has to be. Computer professionals might organize themselves in ways that create a stronger social responsibility and make the profession more of a "profession." They might take on a greater burden of responsibility in exchange for greater autonomy, which they might seek both as an organized professional group and as individual practitioners.

Throughout this chapter there have been hints about the kinds of things that computer professionals might do to bring this about. For example, creation of a professional organization with a code of conduct and a set of standards both for admission to the profession and for practice would be enormously helpful. Such an organization might have the power to grant licenses and to expel (or at least censure) individuals who engage in substandard behavior. The code of conduct would have to make clear the profession's commitment to public safety and welfare, and individuals might be required to take an oath to abide by the code before they are admitted to the profession. These actions would define the parameters of the social contract between society and computer professionals and make computing a distinctive, self-regulating field of endeavor.

Professional-Professional

Many professionals believe that they have obligations to other members of their profession. For example, professionals are often reluctant to criticize one another publicly, and they often help one another in getting jobs or in testifying at hearings when one of them is being sued. However, whether or not such behavior can be justified as a moral obligation is controversial.

---

[6] For a fuller analysis of Alpern, see Deborah G. Johnson, "Do Engineers Have Social Responsibilities?" *Journal of Applied Philosophy,* 9, no. 1 (1992), 21–34.

It seems that the special treatment one professional gives to another may at times be good and at other times not. The earlier discussion of loyalty is relevant here. If one of your co-professionals is an alcoholic and, as a result, not doing a competent job, it is good that you try to help the person. On the other hand, if you keep his problem a secret, not wanting to jeopardize his career, this may result in injury to his employer or client. Similarly, when professionals get together to fix prices, this may be good for the professionals in that they can demand higher and higher prices, but it is not good for consumers who might benefit from a free market system.

One can take the cynical view that professionals only unite with one another to serve their self-interest, but even this line of thinking, when extended to long-term interests, leads to some constraints on what professionals should do. Every professional has an interest in the status and reputation of the profession as a whole for this affects how individual members are perceived and treated. Hence, each member of a profession may further her self-interest by forming alliances with other co-professionals and agreeing to constrain their behavior. For example, even though some might benefit from lying about their qualifications, or taking bribes, or fudging test results, in the long run such practices hurt the profession and, in turn, individual practitioners. The trust that clients and society must place in professionals is undermined and eroded when members of a profession behave in this way, so that all members of the profession are hurt. Clients become more reluctant to use computer systems and to rely on computer experts.

One way to think about what professionals owe one another is to think of what they owe each other in the way of adherence to certain standards of conduct, rather than simply to think of what they might do to help and protect one another in the short term. Rules about being honest, avoiding conflicts of interest, giving credit where credit is due, and so on can be understood to be obligations of one member of a profession to other members (in addition to their justification in moral theory).

CONFLICTING RESPONSIBILITIES

Managing one's responsibilities in the relationships just discussed is no small task, and the workplace is not structured to ensure that they will be in harmony. Issues of professional ethics often arise from conflicts between responsibilities to different parties.

Possibly the most common—at least, the most publicized—conflict is that between responsibilities to an employer and responsibility to society. The Carl Babbage case illustrates the typical situation. The employed professional is working on a project and has serious reservations about the safety or reliability of the product. For the good of those who will be affected by the project, the professional believes the project should not go forward yet. On the other hand, the employer (or supervisor) believes that it is in the interest of the company that the project go forward. The professional has to decide whether to keep quiet or do something that will "rock the boat."

To see why this conflict arises, we can return to our discussion of the characteristics of the work life of professionals and compare the situation of a typical employed computer professional with that of a stereotypical doctor. Perhaps the most striking difference is that the typical computer professional employed in a large private corporation has much less autonomy than a doctor in private practice. Computer professionals often work as employees of very large corporations or government agencies and have little autonomy.

Another characteristic of the work of computer professionals in contrast with that of doctors is its relatively fragmented nature. Computer professionals often work on small parts of much larger, highly complex projects. Their authority is limited to the small segment, with someone else having the designated responsibility for the whole project.

In addition, computer professionals are often quite distant from the ultimate effects of their activities. They may work on a project at certain stages of its development and then never see the product until it appears in the marketplace, having no involvement in how it is used, distributed, or advertised. Doctors, on the other hand, see in their patients the direct results of their decisions.[7]

Because of these characteristics of the work of computer professionals, they find themselves in a tension between their need for autonomy and the demands for organizational loyalty made by their employers.[8] On the one hand, they need autonomy because they have special knowledge. If they are to use that knowledge in a responsible manner and for the good of society, they must have the power to do so. However, insofar as they work for corporations with complex, highly bureaucratized organizational structures, and insofar as such large organizations need coordination of their various parts, there must be a division of labor, and they must often simply do what they are told. Carl Babbage's dilemma arises from this tension.

Acts of whistle-blowing arise out of precisely this sort of situation. Whistle-blowers opt against loyalty to their employer in favor of protecting society.[9] Whistle-blowing is, perhaps, the most dramatic form of the problem. Other issues that come up for computer professionals are more subtle aspects of this same tension—between loyalty to employer and social responsibility or pro-

[7] I have identified these same characteristics of the work of engineers in "Do Engineers Have Social Responsibilities?" pp. 22–23.

[8] Edwin Layton, *The Revolt of the Engineers: Social Responsibility and the American Engineering Profession* (Baltimore, Md.: Johns Hopkins University Press, 1971, 1986).

[9] A good deal has been written about whistle-blowing. See, for example, Gene G. James, "In Defense of Whistleblowing," *Business Ethics: Readings and Cases in Corporate Morality,* ed. Hoffman and Mills (New York: McGraw-Hill, 1983); and James C. Petersen and Dan Farrell, *Whistleblowing: Ethical and Legal Issues in Expressing Dissent* (Dubuque, Iowa: Kendall/Hunt, 1986).

fessional responsibility. Should I work on military projects or other projects that I believe are likely to have bad effects? What am I to do when I know that a certain kind of system can never be built safely or securely enough, but I need the money or my company needs the contract? What do I do when a client is willing to settle for much less safety or security than I know is possible?

In the case of computer professionals, because the profession is relatively new and not well organized, the commitment to public safety and welfare is neither well entrenched in everyday practice nor well articulated in professional codes or literature. Nevertheless, the tension between protecting public good or adhering to professional standards and staying loyal to a higher organizational authority is there. It comes into clear focus now and then when cases involving public safety come to public attention. One of the first cases of whistle-blowing to be written about extensively involved three computer specialists working on the Bay Area Rapid Transit (BART) system.[10] The computer professionals in this case were concerned about the safety of the system controlling train speeds. They feared that under certain circumstances trains might be speeded up when they should be slowed. When their concerns were dismissed by their supervisors and then by the board monitoring the project, they went to newspaper reporters. In the same type of situation, more recently, David Parnas, a computer scientist, spoke out against funding for the Strategic Defense Initiative.[11]

CODES OF PROFESSIONAL CONDUCT

The Association for Computer Machinery (ACM) is the largest organization of computer professionals in the United States. It adopted a Code of Professional Conduct in 1973 and revised this code in 1992. Both codes can be found in the Appendix.

In examining professional codes, it is important to consider what the function of a code of conduct is. What should or does it aim to do? Related to this is the question: Who is the code of conduct written for? There are no simple answers, as codes usually aim to do a variety of things and are meant to make statements to the public as well as to members and prospective members of the profession.

A developing profession might use a code of conduct as part of a strategy to win public confidence and stave off external regulation. The code, in effect, says to the public that this profession will serve the interests of the public and will adhere to certain standards of behavior as well as aspire to certain ideals. In making this statement, the profession wants to show that it is worthy of spe-

[10] Robert M. Anderson et al., *Divided Loyalties: Whistle-Blowing at BART* (West Lafayette, Ind.: Purdue University, 1980).

[11] David Parnas, "Professional Responsibility to Blow the Whistle on SDI," *Abacus*, 4, no. 2 (1987), 46–52.

cial status and privileges. In doing this, the code also sets expectations: It informs employers, clients, and the public about what to expect in their dealings with members of the profession.

Insofar as codes of conduct are aimed at the public, they may appear to some to simply be a public relations tool; that is, they aim to make the profession look good. So it is important to remember that regardless of the motive for its creation, if the code contains rules that protect the public and promote worthy practices, their self-serving character is not problematic.

In addition to making statements to the public, codes are clearly statements to and for members of the profession. They can serve several functions in this way. First, a code may be understood to be a statement of the shared commitments of the members. As such we might think of a code as the embodiment of agreed-upon values and concerns. Second, a code may be a statement of agreed-upon rules or standards. In creating a code, a profession may be understood to be saying that these are the standards we all agree to follow. For example, when the 1992 ACM code states in 2.8 that ACM members should "access computing and communication resources only when authorized to do so," it sets a standard of behavior. A third and somewhat different kind of function of a code is that it sensitizes members to issues that they might not be aware of. As new members read the code for the first time (or experienced members reread the code), they may become aware of issues surrounding computing that they had not fully recognized before. The 1992 ACM code, for example, emphasizes special responsibilities of organizational leaders. While organizational leaders will have thought about the special responsibilities of their job, they may not have thought about their importance in terms of setting standards for the profession.

Related to the standard-setting function, a code of professional conduct might be designed to provide guidance to professionals when they find themselves in tough ethical situations. In other words, a professional who finds herself in a tight spot might look to the code to help figure out what she should do.

Finally, a code of conduct could be used as a mechanism for educating or socializing. Here the idea is that those entering the field, when introduced to the code, will quickly learn what the standards in the profession are. Without a code, there is little quality control on what new members of an occupational group learn are the standards in the field. If my first job happens to be in a place where the tone is sleazy, I come to believe that is the way all members behave. I may luck out and land a first job in an environment in which the tone is highly professional, but which situation I get is to some extent "the luck of the draw." A code ensures that all new members will at least be informed about the standards explicated in the code.

Needless to say, it is probably impossible for a code to serve all the functions mentioned above. The process of developing and adopting a code is extremely complex and political. Some functions must give way to others, depending on where a profession is in its development. Nevertheless, the variety of functions that a code might serve is important to recognize in evaluating codes and thinking about how they might be changed.

A FINAL NOTE

It is important in thinking about issues of professional ethics not to fall into the mode of always thinking of them as issues of individual choice. They are also macro-level issues. Indeed, it is very important to ask what changes might be made in the environment in which computer professionals work so as to minimize ethical conflicts, or to make it easier for computer professionals to behave in socially responsible ways. You might try to think of ways to provide more protection for whistle-blowers; for example, professional organizations might provide more support to professionals who find themselves in morally tight spots. Changes in the way professionals are managed could be made to better handle technical dissent. Changes might also be made in the educational requirements for computer science to ensure that future computer professionals are better prepared for the ethical dilemmas in the world of their work.

The bottom line is that all of us will benefit from a world in which computer professionals take responsibility for the computing in our society, at least when it comes to safety, reliability, and security, but also for other effects. Ideally we would have all computer professionals working to shape computer systems for the good of humanity.

STUDY QUESTIONS

1. What is special about professional ethics? What has to be taken into account when reasoning about ethics for professionals as opposed to ordinary persons?
2. What is meant by the "efficacy" of professionals?
3. What are the two different meanings of "profession"?
4. What characteristics are usually associated with the special, higher-status meaning of "professional"?
5. Name the parties with whom computer professionals may have relationships. Can each type of relationship be thought of as contractual in character? Explain how.
6. How does the categorical imperative apply to the employer-employee relationship? What requirements does it impose on how employers treat employees and how employees treat employers?
7. Why is loyalty valued? What is wrong with loyalty?
8. How do the agency, paternalistic, and fiduciary models of client-professional relationships deal with the disparity in knowledge of the client and professional? What is wrong, if anything, with each of these models?

9. On the fiduciary model of client-professional relationships, what might a computer professional owe to a client, and what might a client owe to a computer professional?

10. How would a social contract theory account for the responsibility of professionals to those who may be affected by their work?

11. What is the corollary of proportionate care? How might it apply to computer professionals?

12. Why do professionals have obligations to one another?

13. Why does the issue of whistle-blowing arise for computer professionals?

14. What functions might a code of professional conduct serve?

EXERCISES/ESSAY QUESTIONS

1. Are computer professionals "professionals"? In what sense are they and in what sense not?

2. Compare the 1973 and 1992 ACM codes of conduct (Appendix). Evaluate the 1992 code in terms of the functions it serves. Are there changes you would recommend to make it better?

3. Write an essay in which you explain what Carl Babbage (or Diane Jones, or Marvin Miller) ought to do. Defend your position by giving reasons and using ethical theory or principles of ordinary morality.

4. Consider the following case.

    Jennifer Watson works for one of the major computer hardware and software companies in the country. She works at one of their installations on the West Coast, where she is part of a unit that designs configurations of software and hardware to meet the needs of clients. She is assigned to head up a project designing software for a large national fast-food chain. The chain would like software designed so that it can be used in their cash registers and their accounting system in such a way that each day, data from the cash registers across the country can be uploaded to the central accounting office. Because of her work on other projects, Jennifer is quite familiar with the software and hardware being produced by other major computer companies.

    After discussion with a wide range of representatives from the client company, Jennifer believes she has a good idea of what the client company wants. As she begins figuring out how best to meet their needs, she realizes that the client could get exactly what it wants, very inexpensively, by buying software produced by one of her company's major competitors.

    Jennifer is not exactly sure what to do, but after a few days she decides to mention this to her supervisor. Her supervisor quickly tells Jennifer to forget the idea. While the information would be enormously useful to the client, it would surely mean that Jennifer's unit would not make the sale and, the supervisor tells Jennifer, her unit is down in sales for the year. The unit badly needs this client's business.

    Write an essay in which you describe what Jennifer ought to do and defend your position.

SUGGESTED FURTHER READINGS

ANDERSON, RONALD E., ET AL. "Using the New ACM Code of Ethics in Decision Making." *Communications of the ACM,* 36, no. 2 (1993), 98–105.

BAYLES, MICHAEL. *Professional Ethics.* Belmont Calif.: Wadsworth, 1981.

CALLAHAN, JOAN (ed.). *Ethical Issues in Professional Life.* New York: Oxford University Press, 1988.

GOLDMAN, ALAN. *The Moral Foundations of Professional Ethics.* Totowa, N.J.: Rowman and Littlefield, 1980.

GOTTERBARN, DONALD. "Computer Ethics: Responsibility Regained." *National Forum, Phi Kappa Phi Journal* (Summer 1991), pp. 26–31.

JOHNSON, DEBORAH G. *Ethical Issues in Engineering.* Englewood Cliffs, N.J.: Prentice-Hall, 1991.

JOHNSON, DEBORAH G. "The Social Responsibility of Computer Professionals." *Journal of Computing and Society,* 1, no. 2 (1991b), 107–118.

CHAPTER 4

Property Rights in Computer Software

SCENARIO 4.1: COPYING PROPRIETARY SOFTWARE

John plays the stock market. A year or so ago, he discovered a commercial piece of software that helps individual investors choose penny stocks. Penny stocks are stocks of small companies that sell for a few dollars or less per share. The software requires users to input information about their attitudes towards risk as well as the names of penny stock companies they are interested in. The software does multiple types of analyses and then recommends strategies and evaluates stocks relative to other penny stocks. John has several friends who invest in stocks, and one of his friends, Mary, has been getting more and more interested in penny stocks. At a party, they begin talking about investing in penny stocks and John tells Mary about the software package he uses. Mary asks if she can borrow the package to see what it is like. The software package is proprietary.

John lends the package to Mary. He reasons that if Mary likes the package she will buy her own copy so that she can get the documentation. Mary finds the software extremely useful so she ignores the copyright and licensing information included in the package, and copies the disks and duplicates the manuals. Then she returns the package to John.

SCENARIO 4.2: PIRATING SOFTWARE

Bingo Software Systems, a small company employing fifteen to twenty people, spends three years developing an operating system for networked microcomputers. Over the course of the three years, Bingo invests approximately two million dollars in development of the system. When completed, the new system is successfully marketed for about a year, and Bingo recovers about 25% of its investment. However, after the first year, several things happen that substantially cut into sales. First, a competing company, Pirate Pete's Software, starts to sell a system very similar to Bingo's, but Pirate Pete's system has several features not available in Bingo's system. It appears that Pirate Pete's Software has examined the system developed by Bingo, adopted the same general approach, possibly copied much of the code, and, in any case, produced a modified and improved version. Second, copying of Bingo's system is rampant. Customers, primarily small businesses, appear to be buying one copy of Bingo's system, and then making multiple copies for internal use. It appears that they are giving copies to other businesses as well. As a result, there is a significant reduction in demand for Bingo's system. Bingo is unable to recover the full costs of developing the system and goes into bankruptcy.

SCENARIO 4.3: IMPROVING SOFTWARE

Earl Eniac develops a virus tester. He publishes it in a journal and announces on the Net that it is available to anyone who wants it. Jake Jasper gets a copy and learns how it works. He thinks it is a clever, creative, and useful piece of software; however, he sees several small changes that could be made to make it even better. He makes these changes and sends a copy to Earl. Jake also publishes the improved version (giving credit to Earl for the original) and makes it available to anyone for the asking.

INTRODUCTION

In this chapter we turn to a set of issues that arise because of the very nature of computer technology. Computers are machines. The hardware that constitutes the machine does not differ fundamentally from other electronic devices such as stereos or televisions. However, the hardware of a computer is controlled by software. When software is put into a computer it causes switches to be set and this determines what the computer can do. Software is an entity that did not and could not exist before computers.

Scenarios 4.1, 4.2, and 4.3 suggest some of the problems surrounding the ownership of software. For a start, we can separate the issues into two categories: issues of individual moral choice and policy issues. Scenario 4.1 typifies the individual moral question: Is it morally wrong for an individual to make an illegal copy of a piece of proprietary software? Here the question is one of what is right or wrong for an individual to do *given the law.* Scenario 4.2 points to the policy issues surrounding ownership of software for here we see what happens when software is not protected (or adequately protected) by law. Scenario 4.3 shows a good effect that might result from public domain software; that is, it would be continuously improved upon and made available to others.

In this chapter, I address the policy questions first: Should computer software be private property? Does the present system of copyright, patent, and trade secrecy law adequately protect computer software? Does the system produce good consequences? Only after this analysis do I take up the individual moral question.

We can begin with the situation described in scenario 4.2. On the face of it, there seems something unfair in what happens. The unfairness lies not simply in the fact that Bingo cannot recoup its investment but rather in the fact that Pirate Pete's is able to use the work of Bingo without having to pay for it. Pirate Pete's is able to make a better system more cheaply by building on the work of Bingo. Bingo pays the price, in effect, but gets none of the reward.

At first glance, this might seem a problem with an easy solution. All we have to do is give Bingo a legal right to own the software it creates, a right which excludes others from taking, using, or selling the software without the owner's permission.

There are, however, at least two reasons for not leaping immediately to such a solution. The first is practical. The standard legal mechanisms for granting ownership rights in inventions (copyright, trade secrecy, patent) do not work well for computer software. The second is philosophical. That is, there are, on closer examination, some good reasons for refusing to grant ownership in software, at least certain forms of ownership.

In order to come to grips with these problems, we need to delve more deeply into what the law now specifies and why. After reviewing the present state of the law, I consider the philosophical justifications traditionally given for property rights and what these imply about the ownership of software.

TERMINOLOGY

It will be helpful to make some distinctions at the onset. When we talk about software we are generally talking about programs, but there are several different aspects of a program. Michael Gemignani makes the distinctions very clearly:

> Programs are responses to problems to be solved. First, the problem in issue must be clearly formulated. Then a solution must be outlined. To be amenable to im-

plementation on a computer, the solution must be expressible in a precise way as a series of steps to be carried out, each step being itself clearly defined. This is usually set forth as a flowchart, a stylized diagram showing the steps of the algorithm and their relationship to one another. Once a flowchart has been constructed, it is used as a guide for expressing the algorithm in a "language" that the computer can "understand." This "coding" of the program is almost certain to employ a "high level" computer language, such as BASIC or FORTRAN. When the algorithm is "coded" in a high level computer language, it is called a *source program*. A source program may bear a striking resemblance to a set of instructions expressed in literary form. The source program is fed into the computer by means of an input device, such as a terminal or card reader. The source program is "translated" by the compiler, a part of the operating systems program, into machine language, a language not at all similar to ordinary speech. The program expressed in machine language is called an *object program*. It is the object program which actuates the setting of switches which enables the computer to perform the underlying algorithm and solve the problem.[1]

While Gemignani's account is slightly dated, the distinctions among algorithm, source program, and object program are clear and they are critical to understanding the ownership issues.

LEGAL MECHANISMS TODAY

At present three legal mechanisms are used by those who create software to protect their creations: (1) copyright, (2) trade secrecy, and (3) patent. In the late 1970s and early 1980s, a good deal of concern was being expressed that none of these legal mechanisms would adequately protect computer software. A sizable literature described the extent and impact of software piracy and illegal copying and expressed fear that software development would be significantly impeded because software developers would not be able to recover the costs of development, let alone profit from their creations. The incentive to create would be significantly dampened.

While there is no indication that software piracy has subsided since the early 1980s, the environment for software development has changed. Many more patents on software-related inventions have been issued, and the software industry has found ways to successfully pursue copyright infringement. In the early 1990s there is still dissatisfaction with the legal situation, and added to complaints of inadequate protection for software are concerns that too much has become proprietary. The new concern is that copyright and patent protection get in the way of, rather than facilitate, software development.[2]

[1] Michael C. Gemignani, "Legal Protection for Computer Software: The View from '79," *Journal of Computers, Technology and Law*, 7 (1980), p. 272.

[2] Brian Kahin, "The Software Patent Crisis," *Technology Review*, 93 (April 1990), 52–58.

Copyright

Though the Copyright Office had been accepting computer programs for registration since 1964, in 1980 Congress amended the 1976 Copyright Act to explicitly extend copyright protection to computer programs. Programs are considered copyrightable as "literary works," and as such are considered formal expressions of ideas. The term computer program is defined in 17 U.S.C. 101 as "a set of statements or instructions used directly or indirectly in a computer in order to bring about a certain result."

While case law pertaining to copyright has become very complicated in recent years, generally the classification of computer programs as literary works has meant that the algorithm is not copyrightable. It is considered the idea of the program, while the source program and the object program are considered expressions of the idea.

Copyright protection can be thought as a weak form of protection for several reasons. First, because the algorithm is not protected, someone may look at a copyrighted program, grasp the idea being implemented, and write a different source program (perhaps in another computer language) using essentially the same algorithm, and this would not violate the copyright. Second, copyright does not give the owner a monopoly on the program. If someone independently designs essentially the same program, there is nothing in the first person's copyright that will prohibit the second person from using or selling what he or she has created. And, the burden of proof is always on the copyright holder to show infringement. The copyright holder must show that the program was copied and that the copying was of such a nature as to constitute an improper appropriation.

To establish that the program was copied, the copyright holder can rely on there being a "striking resemblance" which can only be explained by copying. Although this may be difficult to show since "striking resemblance" is such an imprecise notion, it has been used in a number of important cases. Perhaps the most famous is the *Apple v. Franklin* case (decided by the Supreme Court in 1983) in which Apple was able to show that Franklin copied Apple's operating system (the object code of their operating system) by showing line after line of identical code.[3] Franklin had not even bothered to delete segments of code that included Apple's name.[4]

Where there is a resemblance but not a "striking resemblance," the copyright holder must show that the defendant relied heavily on the copyright holder's program *and* that the defendant's independent contribution was insignificant. You are entitled to draw on a copyrighted work as long as you create something new. "Improper appropriation" is not a precise notion, but it is meant to define the line between "taking" another's work and "building on"

---

[3] *Apple v. Franklin* 714 F.2d 1240 (3rd Cir. 1983).

[4] This case established that copyright applies to programs expressed in object code and that it applies to operating systems programs as well as applications programs.

someone else's work. You may use another's work in some ways, but you have to add something significant to it. Needless to say, proving improper appropriation can be tricky.

A copyright holder pursuing a case of infringement must also show that the defendant had access to the program. This casts doubt on the possibility that the defendant created the program on his or her own. Access may be easy to prove when software has been widely marketed, but when a company keeps its software out of the marketplace, access may be difficult to prove. The software may have been accessed electronically over telephone lines at long distances, without leaving a trace.

In recent years, lawyers in the computer industry have tried to broaden and strengthen the reach of copyright through case law. In a sense, it is still unclear exactly how copyright applies to software; that is, it is unclear what aspects of a piece of software are owned. Attention has focused, for example, on the "structure, sequence and organization" of programs and on the "look and feel" of user interfaces.

The important, precedent-setting case involving "structure, sequence, and organization" was *Whelan Associates, Inc. v. Jaslow Dental Laboratory, Inc.*[5] Whelan had developed a program for Jaslow (for the business activities of his dental office) with the understanding that she (Whelan) would own the rights in the program. A few years after the program had been completed, Jaslow decided that there would be a market for a program like the one Whelan had developed for him, but in a different language and for use on a personal computer. Jaslow developed such a program. While he did not use any of the code written by Whelan, he, evidently, studied how Whelan had organized the program. Whelan sued Jaslow for copyright infringement. The court found infringement based on "comprehensive nonliteral similarity." That is, it found that "copyright protection of computer programs may extend beyond a program's literal code to its structure, sequence and organization."

Since this case was decided, however, new cases have qualified and limited the significance of the Whelan decision by pointing to other factors relevant to copyright infringement. For example, in *Plains Cotton Cooperative Ass'n v. Goodpature Computer Serv., Inc.* the court held that the similarities in two programs designed to perform the same task within the agricultural cotton market, were necessitated by the externalities of the market.[6] That is, both programs attempted to provide the same information to users, and the court determined that the design of the programs was determined by the market; therefore, one program did not infringe the other.

Both Lotus and Apple have sued competitors for copyright infringement

[5] *Whelan Assocs., Inc. v. Jaslow Dental Laboratory, Inc.*, 609 F. Supp. 1307 (E.D.Pa. 1985), aff'd, 797 F.2n 1222 (3d Cir. 1986), cert.denied, 479 U.S. 1031 (1987).

[6] See U.S. Congress, Office of Technology Assessment, *Finding a Balance: Computer Software, Intellectual Property, and the Challenge of Technological Change*, OTA-TCT-527 (Washington, D.C.: U.S. Government Printing Office, May 1992), p. 71.

of their interface designs. Lotus, for example, has filed against both Mosaic Software and Paperback Software claiming that their programs have the same "look and feel" as Lotus 1-2-3 and that their user interfaces are substantially similar to the Lotus 1-2-3 interface.

The look and feel issue arises because of the many layers of what software is. When we drew the distinction among algorithm, source program, and object program, we thought of the algorithm as the idea of a program, and the object and source programs as two different expressions of the idea. If we stay with that way of thinking, we might be led to think of what appears on a computer screen as yet another expression of the underlying idea. Hence, we might be lead to think that the arrangement of data on a screen page is copyrightable. However, it also seems plausible to argue that the screen display or graphic arrangement of data on a screen is the idea—it is what the designer aims to produce—and the source and object programs are expressions of that idea in particular languages. In other words, the object and source code are processes to produce (express) the idea. On this way of conceptualizing, the graphic arrangement of data on the screen should be unownable, i.e., non-copyrightable.

While several cases involving the structure, sequence and organization of software and the look and feel of user interfaces have now been decided, the meanings of these decisions are unclear and probably will remain so for awhile.[7] This in itself makes copyright problematic for use by those who want to protect software. They are uncertain about whether the protection will work.

Trade Secrecy

Trade secrecy laws vary from jurisdiction to jurisdiction but in general what they do is give a company the right to keep certain kinds of information secret. The laws are aimed specifically at protecting companies from losing their competitive edge. Thus, for example, a company can keep secret the precise recipe of foods that it sells or the formula of chemicals it uses in certain processes.

Trade secrecy laws were not, of course, designed with computer technology in mind, and their applicability to the computer industry has been somewhat unclear. Nevertheless, this form of protection has been used extensively.

To hold up in court, what is claimed as a trade secret typically must (1) have novelty, (2) represent an economic investment to the claimant, and (3) have involved some effort in development. As well, (4) the company must show that it made some effort to keep the information a secret. Much software would seem to qualify for such protection; that is, much software will be novel, involve some effort in development, and have required significant investment. Software companies will try to keep their software secret by using nondisclo-

---

[7] Pamela Samuelson, "How to Interpret the Lotus Decision (And How Not To)," *Communications of the ACM*, 33, no. 11 (November 1990), 27-33.

sure clauses in contracts of employment and by means of licensing agreements with those who use their software. Nondisclosure clauses require employees to refrain from revealing secrets that they learn at work. An employee promises not to take copies of programs or reveal the contents of programs owned by the firm, even when he or she ceases to be employed by the firm. With licensing agreements, companies do not actually sell their software but license its use. Those who want such licenses are required to agree not to do anything that will reveal the "secret"; that is, they agree not to give away or sell copies of the software that has been licensed.

In addition to employment contracts and licensing agreements, program developers have employed a variety of technical devices to protect their secrets. Such devices include limiting what is available to the user, that is, not giving the user access to the source program, or building into the program identifying codes so that illegal copies can be traced to their source.

Though this form of protection is used by the computer industry, many complain that even with improved technical devices for maintaining secrecy, the protection offered is not adequate. For one thing, the laws are not uniform throughout the United States and this makes it difficult for businesses that operate in many jurisdictions. Also, the protection provided is still uncertain because the laws were not designed for computer technology. Thus, companies have to take a risk that the courts will support their claims when and if they are ever tested in the courts. Most important, however, is the problem of meeting the requirement of maintaining secrecy. Enforcing employment agreements and licensing agreements is a tricky business. Violators can be caught taking or selling direct copies of programs, but there is nothing to stop an employee of one firm from taking the general knowledge and understanding of the principles used in a program to a new job at another firm. Likewise someone who works with licensed software may grasp general principles that can be used to create new software. Thus, while agreements can be made, there will always be ambiguities in what one agrees not to reveal.

Of course, these problems are not unique to computer software. In a competitive environment, many forms of information are better kept secret. What is somewhat unusual about computer software is that often a company must reveal the "secret" in order to sell the software. That is, in order to provide a licensee with software she can use, the software must be modifiable for the customer's unique needs, and the only way to give a user this facility is to give her access to the source code. The user can then alter the source code to fit her special situation. But once the source program is available, the secret is less likely to remain secret and trade secrecy laws may not apply.

In the typical case described in scenario 4.2, trade secrecy laws would have been helpful to Bingo, but only to a point. Bingo could have kept the design of its new operating system secret during its development by means of nondisclosure clauses in employment contracts. Once the system was ready for marketing, however, keeping it a secret would have been more difficult. In showing the system to potential users, some information would be revealed, and once the system was in widespread use, Bingo's control of the situation would weaken significantly. Companies that have licenses to use the system cannot police their employees, that is, they cannot entirely control what they see or even what they copy and, of course, the general principles used in the system would become known to many users even without malicious intent.

Many companies try to counter this problem by themselves making all modifications to the system for each customer and doing all repairs and maintenance. Provisions for this can be built into the licensing agreement, which minimizes the licensees' exposure to the source code. It works to some extent, though there are still problems in the gray areas of employment agreements and, of course, it is not at all practical for small, less complicated programs, where it is impractical for the vendor to modify each copy for each individual customer. Thus, while trade secrecy promises a rather strong form of protection—by allowing the owner to keep the program out of the public realm—it is not always practically possible to use since the owner may have to put the program in the public realm in order to sell it or license its use.

Patent

Patent protection is the strongest form of protection for software in that a patent gives the owner a monopoly on the use of an invention:

> A patent is a grant of the right to exclude others from making, using or selling one's invention, and includes the right to license others to make, use or sell it. It is a legitimate monopoly . . . .[8]

Patents are granted for a term of 17 years and for certain utility patents, the term may be extended for an additional 5 years. Patent is precisely the kind of protection that program developers claim they need. That is, a patent would have given Bingo, in scenario 4.2, the power to prevent Pirate Pete's from marketing its system. The problem with patent protection is not in the kind of protection it provides to the patent holder but rather in the effects on society of allowing patents on software. In order to understand the problem here, it is helpful to consider the aims and purposes of the patent system.

The aim of the patent system is *not* simply to ensure that individuals reap rewards for their inventions. Rather, the ruling principle behind the patent system is the advancement of the useful arts and sciences. The objectives are to foster invention, to promote disclosure of inventions, and to assure that ideas already in the public domain remain there for free use. The furthering of these objectives is, in turn, expected to improve the economy, increase employment, and generally make better lives for citizens.

---

[8] *Valmont Ind., Inc. v. Yuma Manuf. Co.*, 296 F. Suppl. 1291, 1294 16D. Colo. 1969:17.

One way to encourage invention is to have a system that rewards it. Patent protection does not guarantee that individuals will be rewarded, but it provides a form of protection that is a precondition of reward. If you have a monopoly *and* if your invention has commercial value, then you (and no one else) will be in a position to market the invention. By assuring the possibility of reaping rewards, patent protection thus encourages innovation and invention. Allowing inventors to profit from their inventions is a means, not an end.

The patent system recognizes that inventions brought into the public realm are beneficial not just in themselves but also because others can learn from and build on these inventions. If new ideas are kept secret, progress in the useful arts and sciences is impeded. Patent protection encourages the inventor to put her ideas in the public realm by promising her protection that she wouldn't have if she simply kept her ideas to herself. That is, if you choose not to patent your invention but to keep it secret, then you will not be protected. If someone else comes up with the same ideas, or takes yours, there is nothing to prevent this person from patenting and/or marketing the invention.

These two arguments—that patents encourage invention and encourage the bringing of inventions into the public realm—also lead, however, to an important restriction. Ideas, mathematical algorithms, scientific principles, laws of nature, and mental processes can not be patented. To give someone the exclusive right to use these kinds of things would inhibit further invention rather than fostering it. Laws of nature, abstract ideas, mathematical algorithm, etc. are the building blocks of invention. It is this restriction that has caused problems for the patenting of software.

A patent claim must satisfy a two-step investigation before a patent is granted. The claim must (1) fall within the category of permissible subject matter and (2) satisfy three separate tests: It must have utility and novelty and it must be nonobvious. The latter three tests are not easy to pass, but, as one might imagine, they are not impossible for much computer software; that is, a good deal of software is useful, novel, and not so simple as to be obvious to the average person. Software has faced a problem in the courts primarily in passing the first step and qualifying as appropriate subject matter for a patent.

The subject matter of a patent is limited to "a process, machine, manufacture or composition of matter or . . . an improvement thereof." Generally software has been considered a process or part of a process.

> That a process may be patentable, irrespective of the particular form of the instrumentalities used, cannot be disputed . . . A process is a mode of treatment of certain materials to produce a given result. It is an act, or a series of acts, performed upon the subject matter to be transformed and reduced to a different state or thing. If new and useful, it is just as patentable as is a piece of machinery.[9]

---

[9] *Cochrane v. Deener,* 94 U.S. 780, 787–788:161876:17.

There has been some difficulty in specifying what subject matter is transformed by software: data? the internal structure of the computer? This problem is, however, secondary to a larger issue.

In the 1970s and 1980s, there was reluctance to grant patents on software or software-related inventions for fear that in granting ownership of software we might, in effect, grant ownership of mental processes. Each of the steps which make up an algorithm is an operation that a human can, in principle at least, perform mentally. If we allowed a series of such steps to be owned, then we might end up interfering with freedom of thought. That is, the owner of an algorithm might be able to require that her permission or a license be sought before one performed those operations mentally.

More recently attention has focused away from the problem of mental operations, to the issue of computer algorithms and mathematical algorithms. In granting a monopoly on the use of a software invention, we might be granting a monopoly on the use of a mathematical algorithm and this is explicitly prohibited in patent law, as inappropriate subject matter. What is a software invention if not the order and sequence of steps to achieve a certain result? The issue goes to the heart of what one owns exactly when one has a patent on a piece of software.

Before the *Diamond v. Diehr* case was settled in 1981, very few patents had been granted on computer software.[10] There had been a struggle between the Supreme Court, the Patent Office, and the Court of Customs and Patent Appeals (CCPA), with the former two resisting granting of patents and the latter pressing to extend patent protection to software. In *Diamond v. Diehr,* the Supreme Court, with only a 5 to 4 vote, granted a patent to Diehr. Even though it was a close and disputable decision, the Patent Office and especially the CCPA interpreted the court's reasoning so as to justify granting patents on a broad range of software inventions. Although only a handful of software-related patents had been granted before *Diamond v. Diehr,* several thousand have been granted since. Daniel Browning reports that over 9,000 software patents were granted between late-1960s and the end of 1992, and 1300 were issued in 1992 alone.[11]

As mentioned earlier, concerns are now being expressed that too much is being patented and that patents are getting in the way of development in the field. These concerns go to the heart of the patent system's aim, for they suggest that because so much is owned, invention is now being inhibited. The subject matter limitation on what can be patented aims to insure that the building blocks of science and technology should not be owned so that continued development will flourish, yet complaints suggest just that, the building blocks may now be owned.

The situation can be described roughly as follows: Because so many patents have been granted, before putting new software on the market one must do an

---

[10] *Diamond v. Diehr* 101 S. Ct. 1048 (1981).

[11] Daniel Browning, "Setting the Record Straight on Patents" ACM Forum *Communications of the ACM,* 36 (1993), 17–19.

extensive and expensive patent search. If overlapping patents are found, licenses must be secured. Even if no overlapping patents are found, there is always the risk of late-issuing patents. Patent searches are not guaranteed to identify all potential infringements because the Patent Office has a poor classification system for software. Hence, there is always the risk of lawsuit due to patent infringement. One may invest a great deal in developing a product, invest more in a patent search, and then find at the last minute that the new product infringes on something already claimed. These factors make software development a risky business and constitute barriers to the development of new software. The costs and risks are barriers especially for small entrepreneurs.

A number of important legal scholars have argued that the Patent Office and the CCPA have overextended the meaning of the Supreme Court's decision in *Diamond v. Diehr.*[12] The League for Programming Freedom (LPF) proposes that we pass a law that excludes software from the domain of patents.[13] The situation seems to call for change. Yet, at this point, change may be difficult simply because the computer industry has grown and solidified in an environment structured by these forms of protection.

Summary of Legal Mechanisms

What we have presently, then, is a situation in which there are three forms of legal protection available to software developers, but there are drawbacks to the use of each. *Copyright* does not give the program developer a monopoly on the program, and there is still a good deal of uncertainty about what you own when you have a copyright on computer software. *Trade secrecy* (together with employment contracts and licensing agreements) protects all aspects of software by keeping the software out of the public domain. However, trade secrecy is not always useful to software developers because often they cannot market the software without revealing the secret, and once the secret is out, the law may not apply. Moreover, trade secrecy has the disadvantage that in the long run society does not receive the benefit of exposure to the ideas in the software. *Patents* provide a strong form of protection (a monopoly) but the process of acquiring a patent is long, expensive, and fraught with uncertainty. Moreover, extensive use of patent protection may do as much harm as good for software development.

This unsatisfactory situation arises because computer software does not fit neatly into the traditional categories employed in property law. Computer software seems to defy the distinction between idea and expression and the distinction between patentable and unpatentable subject matter. Neither copyright nor patent protect what appears to be most valuable in software—the algorithm, the structure, sequence and organization, and the "look and feel." At

---

[12] Pamela Samuelson, "Benson Revisited: The Case Against Patent Protection for Algorithms an Other Computer Program-Relted Inventions" *Emory Law Journal,* 39 (1990), 1025–1154.

[13] See The League for Programming Freedom, "Against Software Patents," October 24, 1990 (LPF, 1 Kendall Square #143, P.O. Box 9171, Cambridge, MA 02139).

this point, it may be helpful to stand back from the present situation and take a look at the philosophical roots of our ideas about property.

THE PHILOSOPHICAL BASIS OF PROPERTY

Property is by no means a simple notion. Property is created by law. Laws specify what can and cannot be owned, how things may be acquired and transferred. Laws define what counts as property and create different kinds of property. The laws regulating ownership of an automobile, for example, are quite different from those regulating ownership of land. In the case of land, there are rules about how far the land goes down into the ground and how far up into the air space above, about what can and cannot be constructed on the land, when the land may be confiscated by the government, and so on. With automobiles, the laws are quite different. You may have to show proof of insurance in order to buy a car, and even if you own one, you cannot drive it on public roads unless you have a license. Thus, how you come to own something and what it means to own something are rather complex matters.

As already explained, software has challenged our traditional notions of ownership in that the system of laws created specifically to deal with invention in the useful arts and sciences in the U.S. does not seem to grant property rights in software that are comparable to the property rights of inventors in other fields. In discussing this situation we often implicitly or explicitly make assumptions about or argue for moral (and not just legal) rights in property. These assumptions and arguments need to be fully articulated and critically examined. Drawing on the analysis made in Chapter 2 on philosophical ethics, we can identify theories of property that seem to fit consequentialist and natural rights frameworks.

The reasoning behind both the patent and copyright systems is consequentialist in that the system's primary aim is to create property rights which will have good effects. Invention is encouraged and facilitated so that new products and processes will be made available. Nevertheless, many discussions of property rights assume that property is not a matter of social utility, but rather a matter of justice or natural right. We will consider this approach first, as it applies to the ownership of software.

Natural Rights Arguments

The strongest natural rights argument that can be made for private ownership of software is based on the idea that a person has a natural (and, therefore, moral) right to what he or she produces and this natural right ought to be protected by law. John Locke's labor theory of property bases the natural right of ownership on the labor one puts into a thing in creating it.

According to this theory, a person acquires a right of ownership in something by mixing his labor with it. Thus, in a state of nature (that is, before laws and civilized society), *if* an individual were to come upon a piece of land that looked suitable for cultivation, and *if* this person were to cultivate the land by planting seed, tending to the crops daily, nourishing them and so on, *then* the crops would belong to the person. The person has a strong claim to the crops because his labor produced them and they would not exist without this labor. It would be wrong for someone else to come along and take the crops. The intruder would, in effect, be confiscating the creator's labor.

On the face of it, this Lockean account seems plausible. Locke's theory is tied to the notion of individual sovereignty. A person cannot be owned by another and since a person's labor is an extension of her body, it cannot be owned by another. If an individual puts her labor in something and then someone else takes it, the laborer has been rendered a slave.

Using a Lockean theory of property, a software developer could argue that the program she developed is rightfully "hers" because she created it with her labor. Similarly, the unfairness we feel when we hear Scenario 4.2 seems to arise from our sense that Bingo is entitled to the products of its labor. Pirate Pete's has rendered Bingo its slave.

Critique of moral rights in software.   Now, while this argument seems plausible, it can be countered in several ways. First, we can imagine a just world in which we did not acquire rights to what we created. To be sure, it would be unjust if others acquired rights to what we created, but if there were no property rights whatsoever, then there would be no injustice. Those who created things would simply create things. If one mixed one's labor with something, one would simply lose one's labor. Robert Nozick alludes to the possibility of such an arrangement when he questions Locke's theory in *Anarchy, State and Utopia:*

> Why does mixing one's labor with something make one the owner of it? Perhaps because one owns one's labor, and so one comes to own a previously unowned thing that becomes permeated with what one owns. Ownership seeps over into the rest. But why isn't mixing what I own with what I don't own a way of losing what I own rather than a way of gaining what I don't? If I own a can of tomato juice and spill it in the sea so that its molecules (made radioactive, so I can check this) mingle evenly throughout the sea, do I thereby come to own the sea, or have I foolishly dissipated my tomato juice?[14]

A second counter to the Lockean theory applies only to intellectual or nontangible things, such as computer software. Though software's primary function is for use in computers, software is intelligible as a nontangible entity. The software designer can describe how the software works and what it does. Another person can comprehend, and even use this information as instructions—without the software ever being put into a machine.

The point is that with intellectual things, many people can "have" or use them at the same time. If a second person eats or sells food that I have grown,

[14] Robert Nozick, *Anarchy, State and Utopia,* (New York: Basic Books, 1974), pp. 174–5.

I have lost the products of my labor altogether. But one can continue to have and use software when others have and use it. So, when a person copies a program that I have created, she has not taken it from me. I am not deprived of it by her act. Rather, what is usually the case is that by copying my program, the person has taken my *capacity to profit from my creation,* either by making it difficult for me to sell it (since it becomes available at no cost), or by taking my competitive advantage in using the program (since my competitors can now also use it).

Once this difference between intellectual and tangible things is recognized, the natural rights argument appears much weaker than at first sight. The claim of software developers turns out *not* to be a claim to their creations (this they still have when others have their software), but a claim to a right to profit from their creations. However, to show that a person has a right to profit from his creation requires more than showing that he has created it. If he ever has a right to profit, it would seem that such a right would be socially created. It would be defined by an economic system with laws about what can be owned, what can be put into the marketplace, under what conditions, and so on. In other words, the right would derive from a complex set of rules structuring commercial activity.

The natural rights argument is, therefore, not convincing on its own. To be sure, there is a moral issue when it comes to confiscation for profit. It is unfair for one person (or company) to take a program written by someone else, and sell it. However, from a moral point of view software need never enter the commercial realm. It might be declared unownable or public property.

So, the claims of software developers must be understood not to be claims to a natural or moral right, but rather to a social right. Deciding whether or not such a social right should be created is a consequentialist issue. In a moment we will explore the consequentialist reasons for creating property rights in software, as already suggested by the rationale of the patent and copyright. For now it may be useful to point out that a natural rights argument could be made against private ownership of software.

Against ownership.   Some of the early legal literature on ownership of programs and some of the court cases focused on the idea that a patent on a program might violate "the doctrine of mental steps." This doctrine states that a series of mental operations like addition or subtraction cannot be owned. Discussion of the doctrine was based on the possibility that computers, in effect, perform, or at least duplicate, mental steps. It is acknowledged that the operations are performed quickly on the machine so that in a short time a large number of steps can take place. Still, it might be argued, the operations performed by the computer are in principle capable of being performed by a person. If this is so, then ownership of programs could be extremely dangerous for it might interfere with freedom of thought. Those who had patents on programs would have a monopoly on mental operations and might be able to stop others from performing those operations in their heads.

If this is right, then we have the basis of a natural rights argument against ownership of computer software. The argument would be that individuals have a natural right to freedom of thought, and ownership of software will interfere with that right. The argument is worthy of further reflection, especially in light of research in artificial intelligence.

This concern disappeared from the debate about ownership of software. Perhaps as we have become more familiar with computers, we are more confident in distinguishing operations performed by a computer from those performed mentally by a person.

The natural rights arguments for and against the ownership of software are mentioned here primarily because they are so often implicit in discussions of proprietary rights in software. The natural rights framework is, however, not the right framework in which to think through issues of software ownership.

Consequentialist Arguments

As suggested earlier the claims of software developers make most sense as arguments for a social right to ownership. They can and do claim that good consequences result from ownership and bad consequences result when there is no or inadequate protection. Unless individuals and companies have some proprietary rights in what they create, they will not invest the time, energy, and resources needed to develop and market software. Without protection, they can never make money at producing software. Why develop a new program if the moment you introduce it, others will copy it, produce it more cheaply, and yours will not sell? If we, as a society, want software developed, we will have to give those who develop it the protection they need; otherwise society will lose because the great promise of computers will not be realized. There must be an incentive to create programs and that incentive is profit—so the argument goes.

Objections can be made to this very important argument. In particular, we can argue that there are incentives other than profit to create software. For one thing, people will create software because they need it for their own purposes: they can use it and make it available to others or keep it to themselves, as they choose.

Another possibility is that we could create a credit system similar to what we have now with scientific publications, in which individuals are given credit and recognition for new knowledge they create when they publish it and make it available to others. (Admittedly, credit may not be enough of an incentive to encourage the development of expensive and elaborate programs, and it may lead to more secrecy.)

Along these lines, we might consider how "shareware" has fared and/or how to improve the environment for proliferation of shareware. Shareware is software that is made readily available. You are encouraged to make copies for yourself. Often it is distributed on networks or electronic bulletin boards. The developers of such software try to make money by encouraging users, if they like the software, to voluntarily pay a small price. Sometimes the developer offers to support the software and provide printed documentation to those who register and pay a fee. A fair amount of shareware is now available, though some argue that the quality is generally not as good as commercial software.

Another possible incentive on which we might rely, if software were not ownable, would be the incentive of hardware companies to create software to make their computers marketable. A company's computers are useless without good software to go with them. Indeed, the better the software available for a type of computer, the better the computer is likely to do in the marketplace.

The point is that if ownership of software were disallowed, software development would not come to a complete standstill. There would be other incentives for creating software. So, while the consequentialist argument for ownership is a good argument—ownership does encourage development—it is not such an overwhelming argument that we should reject all other considerations.

Indeed, as already explained, both the copyright and the patent system recognize reasons for limiting ownership. Both recognize that the very thing we want to encourage—development of the technological arts and sciences—will be impeded if we fail to limit ownership. Both the copyright and patent systems recognize that invention will be retarded if ideas and other building blocks of science and technology are owned.

This gets us to the dilemmas that we presently face in both copyright and patent law: How can we draw a line between what can and cannot be owned so that software developers can own something of value but not something which will interfere, in the long run, with development in the field.

This is no easy dilemma. It is precisely the same dilemma that leads to tough and related questions about the benefits and disadvantages of standardization in the computer industry. Up until recently the field of computing was wide open for new invention. More recently, it has begun to appear that in the realm of personal computers, the market has selected essentially two types, IBM or IBM compatible and Apple or Apple compatible. There is some indication that we may even be moving in the direction of compatibility between these two types. On the one hand, standardization will have great advantages for computer users; with some basic skills they will be able to use any computer and run any software. The debate about the ownership of look and feel is related to this. If look and feel is not ownable then a good deal of software might come to employ the same interface (possibly with continuous improvement). Consumers would benefit from this in that they would not have to learn a new system each time they bought new software.

On the other hand, standardization reduces innovation because once standardization takes place, there is greater resistance to change. Creative new computers and computer systems are still possible, but it takes much more to convince users to spend the money and take the time to learn a whole new way of doing things.

Conclusions from the Philosophical Analysis
of Property

The preceding philosophical analysis of property rights in software supports a consequentialist framework for analyzing the property rights issues surrounding software (and not a natural rights framework). The consequentialist framework puts the focus on deciding ownership issues in terms of effects on continued creativity and development in the field of software. This framework suggests that we will have to delicately draw a line between what is ownable and what is not ownable when it comes to software, along the lines already delineated in patent and copyright law.

A number of authors have suggested that we might develop a special form of legal protection specifically applicable (sui generous) to software and software related inventions. While this is an idea worth considering, the preceding analysis would seem to suggest that any form of legal protection will have to draw distinctions in different aspects of software, and will have to decide which aspects should be ownable and which not, in terms of the long term effects. Removing the process from the context of patent and copyright law may not may this any easier to do.

IS IT WRONG TO COPY PROPRIETARY SOFTWARE?

We must now turn our attention to the individual moral issue: Is it wrong for an individual to make a copy of a proprietary piece of software? You will see that the answer to this question is somewhat connected to the preceding discussion of policy issues.

To begin, it will be helpful to clarify the domain of discussion. First, making a back-up copy of a piece of software, which you have purchased, for your own protection is generally not illegal, and is, in any case, not at issue here. Second, while I have labeled this the "individual" moral issue, it is not just an issue for individuals but applies as well to collective units such as companies, agencies, and institutions. The typical case is the case in which you borrow a piece of software from someone who has purchased it and make a copy for your own use, as in scenario 4.1. This case does not differ significantly from the case in which a company buys a single copy of a piece of software and makes multiple copies for use within the company in order to avoid purchasing more.

We can begin with the intuition (which many individuals seem to have) that copying a piece of software is *not wrong* (that it is morally permissible). This intuition seems understandable enough at first glance. After all, making a copy of a piece of software is easy, and seems harmless, and the laws aimed at preventing it seem illsuited for doing the job. Nevertheless, when we examine the arguments that can be made to support this intuition, they are not very compelling. Indeed, after analysis, it seems difficult to deny that it is morally wrong to make an illegal copy of a piece of software. The key issue here has little to do with software per se and everything to do with the relationship between law and morality.

Perhaps the best way to begin is by laying out what seem to be the strongest arguments for the moral permissibility of individual copying. The strongest arguments claim: (1) the laws protecting computer software are bad, and either: (2a) making a copy of a piece of software is not intrinsically wrong, or (2b) making a copy of a piece of software does no harm, or (2c) *not* making a copy of a piece of software actually does some harm.

Premise (1) was partially dealt with in the preceding sections of this chapter, but it is important to be clear on what could be claimed in it. Here are some of the possibilities: (1a) All property law in America is unjust and the software laws are part of this; (1b) all intellectual property laws are unjust and software laws are part of this; (1c) most property law in America is just, but the laws surrounding computer software are not; and (1d) while the laws surrounding the ownership of software are not unjust, they could be a lot better. The list could go on and just which position one holds makes much of the difference in the copying argument.

We will not be able to analyze each of the possibilities here, but it should be clear from the preceding sections that I believe that the system of intellectual property rights in America (in particular patent, trade secrecy, and copyright laws) may not be the best of all possible laws in every detail but they are roughly just. That is, copyright and patent laws aim at a utilitarian system of property rights and aim essentially to draw the right kind of line between what can and cannot be owned. I recognize that there are problems in extending these laws to software, and I recognize the system could be improved. Nevertheless, I do not believe that the system is blatantly unjust or wholly inappropriate for software.

Now, the next step in my argument is to claim that an individual has a prima facie obligation to obey the law of a roughly just system of laws. ("Prima facie" means "unless there are overriding reasons.") The prima facie obligation to obey the law can be overridden by higher-order obligations or by special circumstances that justify disobedience. Higher-order obligations will override when, for example, obeying the law will lead to greater harm than disobeying. Higher-order obligations may even require civil disobedience—that is, if the law is immoral, then disobedience is morally obligatory. Special circumstances can justify disobedience to an otherwise good law when harm will come from obeying the law this one time. For example, the law prohibiting us from driving on the left side of the road is a good law but we would be justified in breaking it in order to avoid hitting someone.

So I am not claiming that people always have an obligation to obey the law; I claim only that the burden of proof is on those who would disobey roughly good laws. Given that extant laws regarding computer software are roughly good and given that a person has a prima facie obligation to obey roughly good laws, the second premise carries the weight of the argument for the moral permissibility of copying. In other words, the second premise must provide a reason for disobeying roughly just laws.

Premises (2a)–(2c) must, then, be examined carefully. Premise (2a) to the effect that there is nothing intrinsically wrong with making a copy of a piece of software is true, but it doesn't make the argument. The claim is true in the sense that if there were no laws against copying, the act of copying would not be wrong. Indeed, I argued earlier that property rights are not natural or moral in themselves but a matter of social utility. They acquire moral significance only when they are created by law and only in relatively just systems of law. Still, premise (2a) does not support copying because copying has been made illegal and as such is prima facie wrong: There have to be overriding reasons or special conditions to justify breaking the law.

According to premise (2b), making a copy of a piece of software for personal use harms no one. If we think of copying taking place in a state of nature, this premise is probably true; no one is harmed. However, once we are in a society of laws, the laws create legal rights, and it seems that a person harms another by depriving him of his legal right. When a person makes a copy of a piece of *proprietary* software, she deprives the owner of his legal right to control use of that software and to require payment in exchange for the use of the software. This is a harm. (Those who think this is not a harm should think of small software companies or individual entrepreneurs who have gone into the business of developing software, invested time and money, only to be squeezed out of business by customers who would buy one copy and make others instead of buying more.) So premise (2b) is false. Making a copy of a piece of proprietary software in our society harms someone.

Premise (2c) has the most promise as an argument for copying in that if it were true that one was doing harm by obeying the law, then we would have a moral reason for overriding the law, even if it were relatively good. Richard Stallman[15] and Helen Nissenbaum[16] have both made arguments of this kind. Both argue that there are circumstances in which not making a copy or not making a copy *and* providing it to a friend does some harm. However, in their arguments, the harm referred to does not seem of the kind to counterbalance the effects of a relatively just system of property rights. Both give examples of how an individual might be able to help a friend out by providing her with an illegal copy of a piece of proprietary software. Both argue that laws against copying have the effect of discouraging altruism.

Still, this argument ignores the harm to the copyright or patent holder. Even if I were to grant that not providing a copy to a friend does harm, we have to compare that harm to the harm to the owner and chose the lesser.

[15] Richard Stallman, "Why Software Should Be Free," Free Software Foundation, Inc., 1990.

[16] Helen Nissenbaum, "Should I Copy My Neighbors Software?" *Computers and Philosophy* 2 (forthcoming).

Given what I said above about the prima facie obligation to obey the law, it follows that there may be some situations in which copying will be justified, namely when some fairly serious harm can only be prevented by making an illegal copy of a piece of proprietary software and using it. In most cases, however, the claims of the software owner to her legal rights would seem to be much stronger than the claims of someone who needs a copy to make her life easier.

If the position I have just sketched seems odd, consider an analogy with a different sort of property. Suppose I own a private swimming pool and I make a living by renting the use of it to others. I do not rent the pool every day and you figure out how to break in undetected and use the pool when it is not opened and I am not around. The act of swimming is not intrinsically wrong, and swimming in the pool does no obvious harm to me (the owner) or anyone else. Nevertheless, you are using my property without my permission. It would hardly seem a justification for ignoring my property rights if you claimed that you were hot and the swim in my pool made your life easier. The same would be true, if you argued that you had a friend who was very uncomfortable in the heat and you, having the knowledge of how to break into the pool, thought it would be selfish not to use that knowledge to help your friend out.

Of course, there are circumstances under which your illegal entry into my pool might be justified. For example, if someone else had broken in, was swimming, and began to drown, and you were innocently walking by, saw the person drowning, broke in, and jumped in the pool in order to save the other. Here the circumstances justify overriding my legal rights.

There seems no moral difference between breaking into the pool and making a copy of a proprietary piece of software. Both acts violate the legal rights of the owner—legal rights created by reasonably good laws. I will grant that these laws do prevent others from acting altruistically, but this, I believe, is inherent to private property. Private property is individualistic, exclusionary, and, perhaps, selfish. So, if Stallman and Nissenbaum want to launch an attack on all private property laws, I am in sympathy with their claims. However, I would press them to explain why they had picked out computer software law when private ownership of other things, such as natural resources or corporate conglomerates, seems much more menacing.

I conclude that it is prima facie wrong to make an illegal copy of a piece of proprietary software because to do so is to deprive someone (the owner) of their legal rights, and this is to harm them.

A FINAL NOTE

The issues discussed in this chapter are among the most fascinating and important. Our ideas about property are tied to deeply ingrained notions of rights and justice—economic justice. Law and public policy on the ownership of various aspects of computer software will structure the environment for software development and, thereby, shape its future development. The issue of the permissibility of making personal copies of proprietary software is also fascinating and important but for different reasons. Here we are forced to clarify what makes an action right or wrong. We are forced to come to grips with our moral intuitions and to extend these to entities with unique characteristics.

The thrust of this chapter has been to move discussion of property rights in computer software away from the idea that property rights are given in nature, and towards the idea that we can and should develop property rights which serve us all.

STUDY QUESTIONS

1. Explain the differences among copyright, trade secrecy, and patents. What are the advantages and disadvantages of each for developers of computer software?
2. What are the differences among object programs, source programs, and algorithms?
3. What is meant by improper appropriation in copyright law?
4. Why is it sometimes difficult for employees to keep company information secret?
5. What is Locke's "labor theory" of property? Why doesn't it necessarily apply to ownership of computer software?
6. What natural rights arguments can be made for or against ownership of software?
7. What would happen to the development of computer software if software were declared unownable?
8. What are the premises of an argument for the moral permissibility of copying software, according to Johnson?
9. What are Johnson's criticisms of these premises?

ESSAY QUESTIONS

1. Choose one of the scenarios at the beginning of this chapter. Write an essay criticizing or defending the behavior of the person described in the scenario.
2. Should the look and feel of computer software be copyrightable? Give your reasons. Anticipate arguments on the other side. How would you respond?
3. Should computer algorithms be patentable? Give your reasons. Anticipate arguments on the other side. How would you respond?
4. Is it wrong to make a copy of a piece of proprietary software? Explain your position in relation to Johnson's and defend your arguments.
5. In order to understand the impact of ownership issues on the development of computer software, and the trade-offs between standardization and innovation, explore another technology and how ownership has affected its development. For example, consider what developments in automobile technology have been

ownable (steering wheels, brakes, etc) and how this has affected innovation. Draw parallels with software.

SUGGESTED FURTHER READINGS

JOHNSON, DEBORAH G. "Should Computer Programs Be Owned?" *Metaphilosophy*, 16, No. 4 (1985), 276–88.

SAMUELSON, PAMELA. "Why the Look and Feel of Software User Interfaces Should Not Be Protected by Copyright Law" *Communications of the ACM*, 32, No. 5 (1989), 563–72.

SAMUELSON, PAMELA. "Benson Revisted: The Case Against Patent Protection for Algorithms and Other Computer Program-Related Inventions," *Emory Law Journal*, 39, No. 4 (Fall 1990), 1025–1154.

U.S. Congress, Office of Technology Assessment. *Finding a Balance: Computer Software, Intellectual Property, and the Challenge of Technological Change*, OTA-TCT-527 (Washington, D.C.: U.S. Government Printing Office, 1992).

CHAPTER 5

Computers and Privacy

SCENARIO 5.1: DOWNLOADING PERSONAL INFORMATION

Max Brown works in the Department of Alcoholism and Drug Abuse of a northeastern state. The agency administers programs for individuals with alcohol and drug problems and maintains huge databases of information on the clients who use their services. Max has been asked to take a look at the track records of the treatment programs. He is to put together a report that contains information about such factors as number of clients seen in each program each month for the past five years, length of each client's treatment, number of clients who return after completion of a program, criminal histories of clients, and so on.

In order to put together this report, Max has been given access to all files in the agency's mainframe computer. It takes Max several weeks to find the information he needs because it is located in a variety of places in the system. As he finds information, he downloads it to the computer in his office; that is, he copies the information from the mainframe onto the hard disk of his office microcomputer.

Under pressure to get the report finished by the deadline, Max finds that he is continuously distracted at work. He decides that he will have to work at home over the weekend in order to finish on time. This will not be a problem. He copies the information (containing, among other things, personal information on clients) onto several disks and takes them home. He finishes the report over the weekend and decides to send it to his office computer by telephone. He leaves the disks at home and forgets about them.

Was Max wrong in moving personal information from the mainframe to his office computer? In moving personal information from his office computer to his home computer? In leaving the disks containing personal information at home? What might happen as a result of Max's treatment of the data? Should the agency for which Max works have a policy on use of personal information stored in its system? What might such a policy specify?

SCENARIO 5.2: MONITORING TELEVISION VIEWING

With two children, two cars, a dog, and a house in the suburbs, the Crawford family is a fairly typical American family. Six months ago Mr. Crawford was laid off, and since then the family has been struggling financially while trying to live on Mrs. Crawford's salary. Today they have received good news. They have been offered an opportunity to participate in a television rating system. They will be paid every month by a television rating firm and will receive free cable television service in exchange for their participation. The firm proposes to install computerized television viewer scanning machines in the Crawford's family room and master bedroom, the two rooms in which they presently have televisions. The scanning machine learns, and then is able to identify, human faces. It scans the room every two seconds and records who is facing the television, what channel the television is set at, and so on. This information provides a complete record of the television viewing habits of all family members (and visitors). The rating firm sells this information to television stations and advertisers.[1]

Should the Crawfords say "yes" to this opportunity?

SCENARIO 5.3: MONITORING WORK

Estelle Cavello was recently hired to supervise a large unit of a medical insurance company. Estelle will be in charge of a unit responsible for processing insurance claims. When she was hired, the vice president made it clear that he expects her to significantly increase the efficiency of the unit. The company has targets for the number of claims that should be processed by each unit, and Estelle's unit has never been able to meet its target.

---

[1] Devices of this kind have already been developed and are expected to appear in the next few years. See Erik Larson, "Watching Americans Watch TV," *The Atlantic Monthly* (March 1992), pp. 66–80.

One of the first things Estelle will do when she starts this job is to install a software system that will allow her to monitor the work of each and every claims processor. The software will allow Estelle to record the number of keystrokes made per minute on any terminal in the unit. It also will allow her to bring the work of others up on her computer screen so that she can watch individual work as it is being done. As well, Estelle will be able to access copies of each employee's work at the end of each day. She will find out how much time each worker spends with the terminal off; she will see what correspondence the person prepares; she will review e-mail that the worker sends or receives; and so on.

Is Estelle doing the right thing by using this software?

INTRODUCTION

These scenarios depict several of the ways that information can be created, gathered, moved, and used as a result of computer technology. Of all the social and ethical concerns surrounding the use of computers, the impact of computerized record-keeping on personal privacy was probably the first to capture public attention. Privacy continues to be of public concern: We read about it frequently in the popular media; major studies have been undertaken;[2] and many laws have been passed to regulate computerized information.[3] Later in the chapter, I will discuss the value of privacy in our society; for now, it is important to ask why computers are causing such concerns about personal privacy.

In Chapter 1 I suggested that computers, like other new technologies, create new possibilities; they create possibilities for behavior and activities that were not possible before. Public concern about computers and privacy arise for precisely this reason. Computers make it possible (and, in many cases, easy) to gather detailed information about individuals to an extent never possible before. Federal, state, and local government agencies now maintain extensive records of individual behavior, including such things as dealings with criminal justice agencies, income taxes, Social Security, and use of human services agencies. Private organizations maintain extensive databases of information on individual purchases, credit worthiness, television viewing, employment, and so on, as well.

---

[2] Alan Westin and Michael Baker, *Databanks in a Free Society,* New York: Quadrangle Press/The New York Times Book Company, 1972; Secretary's Advisory Committee on Automated Personal Data Systems, *Records Computers, and the Rights of Citizens,* U.S. Department of Health, Education, and Welfare, DHEW Publication (OS) 73–94 (Cambridge, Mass.: MIT Press 1973); Privacy Protection Study Commission, *Personal Privacy in an Information Society,* Washington, D.C.: U.S. Government Printing Office, 1977.

[3] Fair Credit Reporting Act of 1970; Family Educational Rights and Privacy Act of 1974; Privacy Act of 1974; Right to Financial Privacy Act of 1978.

We have the technological capacity for the kind of massive, continuous surveillance of individuals that was envisioned in such frightening early twentieth-century science fiction works as George Orwell's *1984*[4] and Zamyatin's *We*[5] The only differences between what is now possible and what was envisioned then are that much of the surveillance of individuals that is now done is by private institutions (marketing firms, insurance companies, credit agencies), *and* much of the surveillance now is via electronic records instead of by direct human observation or through cameras.

Of course, record-keeping is not a new phenomenon. Corporations and government agencies have been keeping records for thousands of years and using this information in a variety of ways. Nevertheless, computer technology has changed these activities in a number of undeniable and powerful ways. First, the *scale of information gathering* has changed, second, the *kind of information* that can be gathered has changed, and third, the *scale of exchange* of information has changed.

The mere fact that paper records are paper and are stored in file cabinets imposes some limitations on the amount of data gathered, who has access, how long records are retained, and so on. Electronic records do not have these limitations. One can collect, store, manipulate, exchange, and retain practically infinite quantities of data. The point is that technology no longer limits what can be done; now only time and money and, perhaps, human capabilities impose limits on the quantity of information that can be gathered.

The kind of information that it is now possible to create is also new. Think, for example, of the workplace monitoring example in which an employer can keep a record of every keystroke an employee makes. Before computers, finger movements of this kind would not have been thought to be important, let alone the kind of thing that could be recorded. Think also of the enormously large and complex calculations used to launch space shuttles. Those calculations are a kind of knowledge that could only have existed in principle before. And think of the television viewer scanning device. Information has been gathered about television viewing habits since television's infancy, but the directness and detail of information that computerized mechanisms make possible is unprecedented. Computer technology creates information—knowledge—that couldn't exist before.

Typically, information of one kind will be gathered and stored separately from information of another kind; for example, marketing firms will gather and store information on buying habits, one government agency will record income tax information, another government agency will record criminal justice activities. With computers, however, it is technically possible to combine all this information. In the private sector this is done routinely. Within government it has been slower to occur, but already matching of information from

---

[4] George Orwell, *1984* (New York: Harcourt, Brace & World, 1949).

[5] Y. Zamyatin, *We* (Originally published in Russia, 1920). (Harmondsworth: Penguin Books, 1972).

separate agencies has been done. Matches have been made, for example, between federal employee records and records of the Aid to Families with Dependent Children program, to investigate fraud; and between IRS records of taxpayer addresses and lists of individuals born in 1963 (supplied by the Selective Service System), to locate violators of the draft registration law.[6] Matching of records can produce a profile of an individual which, before computers, would only have been available to those who knew the individual intimately.

Even without matching, records from various sectors can be combined to follow a person wherever she or he goes. As you buy airlines tickets, rent a car, make telephone calls, eat at restaurants, and so on, you may leave "an electronic trail" of your activities.

Add a further element to these changes in the scale and kind of information gathered with computer technology. Because computerized information is electronic, it is easy to copy and distribute. Before computers were connected by telephone lines, information could be fairly easily copied using tapes or disks. Now that computers are connected via telephone lines ("data lines"), information can go anywhere in the world where there are telephone lines. Hence, the extent to which information can be exchanged is now practically limitless. Once information about an individual is recorded in a machine or on a disk, it can be easily transferred to another machine or disk. It can be sold, given away, traded, and even stolen. The information can spread instantaneously from one company to another, from one sector to another, and from one country to another.

This exchange happens when you subscribe to a magazine and your name and address are sold to a marketing firm, which infers from the subscription that you have certain tastes and begins sending you a variety of opportunities to buy the things you like. Forester and Morrison report the case of a woman who took her landlord to court after he refused to do anything about the pest problem in her apartment.[7] He did not show up for court but evicted her shortly after the court date. When she went looking for another apartment, she found that she was repeatedly turned down by landlords. She would look at an apartment, notify the landlord that she wanted it, and within a few days hear back that the apartment was already rented to someone else. It turned out that a database of names of individuals who take landlords to court is maintained and the information is sold to landlords. Your medical records (say you have psychiatric problems, or you are HIV positive) can be transferred to your employer; records of your videotape rentals can be transferred to the press; records of your contributions to an on-line forum can be made available to law enforcement agencies; and so on.

---

[6] John Shattuck, "Computer Matching Is a Serious Threat to Individual Rights," *Communications of the ACM,* Inc., 27, no. 6. (June 1984), 538–41.

[7] Tom Forester and Perry Morrison, *Computer Ethics: Cautionary Tales and Ethical Dilemmas in Computing* (Cambridge, Mass.: MIT Press, 1990), p. 91.

What I have just described is what is technically possible. Some of these exchanges and uses of information are now illegal. For example, a special law was passed to protect records of video rentals.[8] The point for now is that computer technology makes an unprecedented scale of distribution of information *possible.*

As far as the technology goes, the distribution of information can take place with or without the knowledge of the person whom the information is about, and it can take place intentionally as well as unintentionally. There is an unintentional distribution when records are provided that contain more information than is requested. As well, when information is stolen, the exchange is unintentional from the point of view of the agency that gathered or maintained the records. Think also of the Max Brown scenario; Brown's wife, children, or friends might (while using his home computer) inadvertently access the data on individuals in the state's treatment programs and see the name of someone they know.

If all of this were not cause enough for concern, there is more. Information stored in a computer can be erroneous and, at the same time, can be readily distributed. The effect of a small error can be magnified enormously. Information can be erroneous due to unintentional human error or because someone has intentionally altered it to harm a competitor or enhance his own records. It is important to remember that databases of information are not always as secure as we would like them to be. When computers are connected via telecommunications lines, the possibilities of data being tampered with or stolen are increased.

For example, suppose a person is turned down for a loan on the basis of erroneous information. John A. Smith's file was inadvertently combined with John B. Smith's. John A. has never failed to pay his debts, has a good job, and has a sizable holding of stocks, while John B. has a low-paying job, declared bankruptcy three years ago, and is once again deeply in debt. John A. Jones is wronged when he is turned down for a loan. Moreover, suppose that, after a series of inquiries and complaints by John A., the error is discovered, and John A.'s file is corrected. (This is not always as easy as it sounds. Companies are often very slow in responding to complaints about errors in records.) John A. asks his bank to send for the updated report, and the bank changes its mind about the loan when it sees the accurate information. It would appear that the injury to John A. has been remedied. Not necessarily. The inaccurate information may have been given to other companies before it was corrected, and they, in turn, may have given it to others. As a result, it may be difficult, if not impossible, to track down all the databases in which the error is now stored. It may be impossible to completely expunge the erroneous information from John A.'s records.

---

[8] In 1988 Congress passed a bill protecting privacy of video rental records in response to an incident in which a reporter had obtained copies of the video rental records of Judge Robert Bork, while he was up for confirmation for the U.S. Supreme Court.

When information is stored in a computer, there is little incentive to get rid of it; hence, information may stay with an individual permanently. Information stored in a computer takes up very little space and is easy to maintain and transfer. Something insignificant that happened to an individual when he was ten years old may easily follow him through life because the information has been recorded once and there is little motivation to delete it. In the past, the inconvenience of paper served to some degree as an inhibitor to keeping and exchanging apparently useless information.

Because it is so easy to keep information, some fear that individuals will become categorized and stigmatized at early stages in their lives. One way to see this is to imagine what it would be like if elementary and secondary school records were put into a national database where prospective employers, government agencies, or insurance companies could get access. We might find decisions being made about us on the basis of testing done when we were in elementary school or on the basis of disciplinary incidents in our teenage years.

When decision makers are faced with making decisions about individuals, they want data, both to ensure a good decision and to justify their decision to others. When they must choose between making a decision on the basis of little or no data and making it on the basis of lots of data known to be unreliable, many prefer the latter. Hence, information tends to be used if it is available even though it may not be relevant or reliable.

In summary, while record-keeping is by no means a new activity, it appears that computers have changed record-keeping activities in the following ways: (1) They have made possible a new scale of information gathering, (2) they have made possible new kinds of information, (3) they have made possible a new scale of information distribution, (4) the effect of erroneous information can be magnified, and (5) information about events in one's life may stay in one's records for life.

As an aside here, you may be tempted to say that computers are not really "the problem" or "the cause" of the problem. It is individuals and organizations that are creating, gathering, exchanging, and using information. Computers simply facilitate these activities. Computers, according to this line of argument, are simply tools; if there is a problem, the problem is the people who use computers, not the computers themselves. Although there is a good deal of truth to this, it is important to remember that computers facilitate certain kinds of activities, and because of this, individuals and organizations are more likely to engage in those activities. For example, in scenario 5.3, Estelle would not monitor employees to the extent she will or in quite the way she will if the workers weren't working on computers and the monitoring software were not available. Individuals opt to engage in activities because computers make these activities possible. Hence, computers are very much a factor in determining what people do and in shaping the kind of society we have.

USES OF INFORMATION

Information about individuals would not exist if organizations did not have an interest in using it. Information is created, collected, and exchanged because people and organizations can use it to further their interests and activities. Information about individuals is used to make powerful decisions, often decisions that profoundly affect the individuals the information is about. Information about you that is stored in a database may be used to decide whether or not you will be hired by a company; whether or not you will be given a loan; whether or not you will be called to the police station for interrogation, arrest, or prosecution; whether or not you will receive education, housing, Social Security, unemployment compensation, and so on.

The standard way to frame "the computers and privacy issue" is as an issue calling for a balancing of the needs of those who use information about individuals (typically government agencies and corporations) *against* the needs or rights of those individuals whom the information is about. In general, those who want information about individuals want it because they think it will allow them to make better decisions. Several examples quickly illustrate this point. Banks believe that the more information they have about an individual, the better they will be able to make judgments about the individual's ability to pay back a loan or about the size of the credit line the person can handle. The FBI's National Crime Information Center (NCIC) provides criminal histories of individuals to all the states. Law enforcement agencies justify the existence of this database on grounds that the more information they have about individuals, the better they will be able to identify and capture criminals. We might also bring in examples from the insurance industry where decisions are made about which individuals to insure at what rate, or from the Department of Health and Human Services where decisions are made about who qualifies for various welfare and medical benefits. In theory, the better the information these organizations have, the better their decision making will be.

In addition to these sorts of needs for information, marketing firms claim that they need information in order to better serve their customers. If a marketing firm knows what I buy at the grocery store, it can use that information to send me coupons for the items I will buy; if television stations know what I watch on television and when I change the channel, they can use that information to develop programming more suited to my tastes; if marketing companies know about my income level and my tastes in clothes, food, sports, books and magazines, the ages of my children, and so on, they can send me catalogues or special offers for products and services that fit my precise tastes.

Information is now big business. Indeed, many believe that we will never be able to stop the onslaught of personal information gathering that now takes place. Whether or not this is true, we have to ask the prior questions: Should we try to stop it? Should we monitor and control it? If so, how?

On one side of the computers and privacy issue we have, then, public and private institutions that want information about individuals. On the other side, we have the individuals whom the information is about. Many of us are uncomfortable with the amount of information that is gathered about us and the fact that we do not know who has what information about us and how it is being used. Why are we so uncomfortable? What do we fear? Can we make the case for limiting the amount of information that public and private institutions gather about us? Can we make the case for giving individuals control over their personal information? Let us now consider the case for personal privacy.

PERSONAL PRIVACY

Privacy is a broad and, in many ways, elusive concept. A variety of arguments have been put forth in defense of the value of personal privacy, and it will be useful to begin by distinguishing privacy as an instrumental good (a means to some end) from privacy as an intrinsic good.

Charles Fried appears to claim that privacy is instrumentally valuable when he argues that privacy is necessary for relationships of intimacy and trust.[9] In a society in which individuals have no privacy, he argues, friendship, intimacy, and trust cannot develop. If we want such relationships, we must have privacy. Others argue that privacy is necessary for democracy.[10] Individuals will not say what they think and vote as they believe unless they have the opportunity to do so in private. Yet others argue that privacy is necessary for autonomy. Not unrelated to the democracy argument, on this argument it is claimed that one cannot exercise autonomy unless one has privacy. You'll remember from the discussion of Kantian theory that autonomy is not just one among many values; autonomy is fundamental to what it means to be human, to our value as human beings.

While these arguments cast privacy as an instrumental value, other arguments tie privacy more tightly to autonomy, respect, and democracy. In the latter arguments privacy is understood to be not just a means to autonomy, respect, or democracy but a part of the very meaning of these terms. We don't seek privacy in order to get autonomy, for example; rather, autonomy is inconceivable without privacy.

It will take us too far afield to explore these arguments. The analysis I want to propose here begins by suggesting that privacy is necessary for a diversity of relationships, moves to privacy as an essential aspect of autonomy, and concludes that privacy might best be understood as "power" in modern, democratic societies.

[9] Charles Fried, "Privacy," *Yale Law Journal,* 77 (1968), 477.
[10] Westin and Baker, *Databanks in a Free Society.*

In a seminal article, "The Right to Privacy," Samuel D. Warren and Louis D. Brandeis argued that there is a right to privacy that is recognized in the common law.[11] Warren and Brandeis were primarily concerned about the publication of photographs, portraits, or gossip in newspapers.[12] Nevertheless, their attempt to protect the facts of one's life from being publicized might be thought to establish a principle for dealing with personal information stored in a computer. Warren and Brandeis suggested a connection between information about oneself and what they called one's inviolate personality. They argued that common law recognizes an individual's right to his or her inviolate personality and that this would encompass facts about the individual's life.

This right to an inviolate personality is closely related to Kant's idea of humans as autonomous beings and the respect due to such beings. The connection between autonomy and information about oneself becomes clear when we focus on social relationships.

Information Mediates Social Relationships.   Information is the basis for establishing a social relationship and determining the character of the relationship. Perhaps this can be made clear with a short tangent. James Rachels has argued that people need to control information about themselves in order to maintain a diversity of relationships.[13] His insight is that individuals maintain a variety of relationships, for example, with parents, spouses, employers, friends, casual acquaintances, and so on, and each of these relationships is different because of the different information that each party has. Think, for example, about what your best friend knows about you as compared with what your teacher, your employer, or your dentist knows about you. These diverse relationships are a function of differing information.

Take your relationship with your dentist. Suppose she has been your dentist for five years but she knows relatively little about you. Now suppose you need extensive work done on your teeth, and you begin to go to her office regularly at a time of the day when she is not rushed. You strike up conversations about your various interests. Each time you talk to her, she learns more about you and you learn more about her. Suppose you discover you have several hobbies and sports interests in common. She suggests that if you schedule your appointment next week so you are her last appointment, you could go out and play tennis afterward. The story can go on about how this relationship might develop from one of patient-professional to being good friends, perhaps to one of being life-long, intimate friends. The changes in the relationship will in large measure be a function of the amount and kind of information you acquire about one another.

---

[11] *Harvard Law Review*, IV, no. 5 (1890), 193–220.

[12] Of course, in 1890 they were not thinking of computerized records, which admittedly are different from information published in newspapers. Among other things, information stored in a computer can be protected from public access and may actually be seen by very few individuals.

[13] James Rachels, "Why Privacy Is Important," *Philosophy and Public Affairs*, 4 (Summer 1975), 323–33.

Rachels uses this insight to argue that privacy is important because it allows us to maintain a diversity of relationships. If everything were open to all (that is, if everyone knew the same things about you), then, he claims, diversity would not be possible. You would have similar relationships with everyone.

Rachels is certainly right about the way information affects relationships. We control relationships by controlling the information that others have about us. When we lose control over information, we lose significant control over how others perceive and treat us. However, while Rachels seems right about this, he seems to go wrong in putting the emphasis on the diversity of relationships, rather than simply staying with loss of control.

Individual-Organization Relationships.   Of course, Rachels was thinking primarily about individual-to-individual relationships, and for our purposes in trying to understand the implications of abundant personal information being stored in computers, the important relationship is that between *an individual and a formal organization.* When it comes to relationships between individuals and formal organizations, what is important to the individual is that the individual have some power or control in establishing or shaping the relationship (not that he or she have a diversity of such relationships). Information about us is what allows an organization such as a marketing firm, a credit card company, or a law enforcement agency to establish a relationship with us. And information determines how we are treated in that relationship. You are sent an offer to sign up for a credit card when the credit card company gets your name and address and finds out how much you earn or own. How much credit is extended depends on the information. Similarly, a relationship between you and your local police force is created when the police force receives information about you; the nature of the relationship depends on the information received.

The twentieth century has seen an enormous growth in the size of formal organizations, both public and private. Instead of dealing with small, local, family-owned businesses wherein one might know or come to know the decision makers personally, most of us now deal almost exclusively with large national or international organizations operating with complex rules and regulations. Indeed, it is often a computer that makes the decision about our credit line or loan application. We shop at grocery stores, department stores, or franchises that are local units of national companies; we deal with banks that are national or international; we go to large impersonal agencies for government services such as driver's licenses or building permits; we attend colleges of 10,000–40,000 students; and so on. Although our dealings with these organizations may have the most powerful effects on our lives, we may know little about them and the people who own or manage them; certainly we know nothing on the order of what they know about us.

Moreover, we have very little say in the character of the relationships we have with these organizations. We may have legal rights created by such legislation as the Fair Credit Reporting Act of 1970 and the Privacy Act of 1974.

However, the laws dealing with personal privacy and computerized information generally *only* give us access to our records upon request and a means of recourse in the event that we discover errors in records; they do not give us the power to decide who obtains and uses what information.

The report of the Privacy Protection Study Commission recognized much of the above already in 1977. Contrasting face-to-face relationships with relationships to record-keeping organizations, the report explains:

> What two people divulge about themselves when they meet for the first time depends on how much personal revelation they believe the situation warrants and how much confidence each has that the other will not misinterpret or misuse what is said. If they meet again, and particularly if they develop a relationship, their self-revelation may expand both in scope and detail. All the while, however, each is in a position to correct any misrepresentation that may develop and to judge whether the other is likely to misuse the personal revelations or pass them on to others without asking permission. Should either suspect that the other has violated the trust on which the candor of their communication depends, he can sever the relationship altogether, or alter its terms, perhaps by refusing thereafter to discuss certain topics or to reveal certain details about himself. Face-to-face encounters of this type, and the human relationships that result from them, are the threads from which the fabric of society is woven. The situations in which they arise are inherently social, not private, in that the disclosure of information about oneself is expected.
>
> An individual's relationship with a record-keeping organization has some of the features of his face-to-face relationships with other individuals. It, too, arises in an inherently social context, depends on the individual's willingness to divulge information about himself or to allow others to do so, and often carries some expectation as to its practical consequences. Beyond that, however, the resemblance quickly fades.
>
> By and large it is the organization's sole prerogative to decide what information the individual shall divulge for its records or allow others to divulge about him and the pace at which he must divulge it. If the record-keeping organization is a private-sector one, the individual theoretically can take his business elsewhere if he objects to the divulgences required of him. Yet in a society in which time is often at a premium, in which organizations performing similar functions tend to ask similar questions, and in which organizational record-keeping practices and the differences among them are poorly perceived or understood, the individual often has little real opportunity to pick and choose. Moreover, if the record-keeping organization is a public-sector one, the individual may have no alternative but to yield whatever information is demanded of him[14]

It would seem, then, that while private and public organizations are powerful actors in the everyday lives of most individuals in our society, we (individuals) have very little power in our relationships to them. One major factor making this possible is that these organizations can acquire, use, and exchange information about us, without our knowledge or consent.

[14] Privacy Protection Study Commission, "Personal Privacy in an Information Society," pp. 13–14.

REJOINDERS TO CONCERNS ABOUT PERSONAL PRIVACY

Several rejoinders to the analysis just presented seem worth considering.

Rejoinder #1

Someone might argue that the situation is not so bad, that individuals who have done nothing wrong have nothing to fear. If I haven't broken the law, if I am doing a good job at work, if I pay my debts, and so on, then I have nothing to worry about. "Privacy only protects people who have something to hide."

Unfortunately, this rejoinder is quite misleading; there is cause for concern even if you have nothing to hide. For one thing, erroneous information can dramatically affect your life. Suppose you are traveling away from your home and the police begin chasing your car. They point guns and rifles at you and force you to get out of your car. They frisk you. If you panic and respond suspiciously, you could be beaten or killed. The police officers believe you are driving a stolen vehicle and disregard your explanation and evidence that the car is *yours,* that it *had* been stolen, but was found last week and returned to you by the police in the city where you live. When you reported the car stolen, the information was put into a database available to patrol cars in several bordering states. Evidently, however, the information that the car was found never made its way into the database. It takes these police officers a day to confirm the error, while you are sitting in jail. Even though you have done nothing wrong, you have been harmed as a result of inaccurate information in a database.

You can also be harmed by irrelevant information. Imagine databases containing information about the race, ethnic background, or political affiliations of individuals. Such databases could be sold to decision makers and used by them even though the information is irrelevant (and often illegal to use) for the decision being made. As a result, you, who have done nothing wrong, could be turned down for insurance, for a job, for a loan, and so on.

So the computers and personal privacy issue cannot be written off as only of concern to those who have something to hide. The way in which personal information is gathered, exchanged, and used in our society affects all of us.

Rejoinder #2

A second possible rejoinder to the account of personal privacy given above is to argue that individuals in our society do have some power to control their relationships with private and public organizations. Many individuals, it might be argued, have simply opted to give up their privacy. "After all, individuals can refuse to give out personal information."

This argument contains an ounce of truth but hides a much more complicated situation. In particular it hides the fact that the way things now work, the price of privacy is extremely high. Yes, I can choose not to use credit cards (using only cash) so that there is no information gathered about my buying activities. I can choose not to subscribe to magazines so that no company ever identifies my interests and sells my name and address to a marketing firm. I can choose not to buy a home until I have saved enough to pay for it in cash, so that I do not have to ask a bank for a mortgage loan. I can choose not to have a checking account with a bank, not to have health insurance, and so on. These choices will reduce the amount of information that private organizations have about me. Notice, however, that I will have to give up many useful services; hence, I have to pay a high price for my privacy.

When it comes to public organizations, what I have to give up in order to get privacy is even more precious. Citizens are entitled to many benefits, such as Social Security, Medicare, driver's licenses, as well as rights to due process, protection from law enforcement agencies, and so on. However, the moment I request these benefits, information is created about me, stored in a computer, and becomes a matter of public record. For example, in many localities when one purchases or sells property, the transaction becomes a matter of public record and may subsequently be published in a local newspaper. Soon after I perform such a transaction I will begin to get an onslaught of telephone calls and mail offering me services appropriate to new homeowners. The information may now be matched as well with other records on me in other government agencies. Remember also the case of the database of tenants who sued their landlords. In order to avoid my name being put into such a database, I would have to give up my right to take my landlord to court; in other words, I would have to give up participating in a process that protects my rights as a citizen.

So, while there are many things an individual can do to protect his or her personal privacy, there is a cost to the individual and the cost is high. It seems counter to the idea of democracy that we should have to give up rights and benefits in order to achieve personal privacy.

LEGISLATIVE BACKGROUND

How, you may ask, have we gotten here? Why is our personal privacy so poorly protected? Does it have to be this way? What can we do to change things? Answers to these questions are crucial to understanding what any of us should do (as citizens, consumers, or computer professionals) to bring about change. I will only be able to begin to answer these questions here.

As mentioned earlier, not all of the activities made possible by computers are allowed by law. It seems important now to discuss some of the legislation that has been developed in the United States to protect personal privacy and to balance it against the needs of public and private organizations. Only a sketch can be provided, for the first thing to note about the American approach is that it has been piecemeal. We have a patchwork of legislation dealing separately with personal information in different domains or sectors. Table 1 (taken from

TABLE 1

Fair Credit Reporting Act of 1970 (Public Law 91-508, 15 U.S.C. 1681) requires credit investigation and reporting agencies to make their records available to the subject, provides procedures for correcting information, and permits disclosure only to authorized customers.

Crime Control Act of 1973 (Public Law 93-83) requires that State criminal justice information systems, developed with Federal funds, be protected by measures to insure the privacy and security of information.

Family Educational Right and Privacy Act of 1974 (Public Law 93-380, 20 U.S.C. 1232(g)) requires schools and colleges to grant students or their parents access to student records and procedures to challenge and correct information, and limits disclosure to third parties.

Privacy Act of 1974 (Public Law 93-579, 5 U.S.C. 552 (a)) places restrictions on Federal agencies' collection, use, and disclosure of personally identifiable information, and gives individuals rights of access to and correction of such information.

Tax Reform Act of 1976 (26 U.S.C. 6103) protects confidentiality of tax information by restricting disclosure of tax information for nontax purposes. The list of exceptions has grown since 1976.

Right to Financial Privacy Act of 1978 (Public Law 95-630, 12 U.S.C. 3401) provides bank customers with some privacy regarding their records held by banks and other financial institutions, and provides procedures whereby Federal agencies can gain access to such records.

Privacy Protection for Rape Victims Act of 1978 (Public Law 95-540) amends the Federal Rules of Evidence to protect the privacy of rape victims.

Protection of Pupil Rights of 1978 (20 U.S.C. 1232(h)) gives parents the right to inspect educational materials used in research or experimentation projects, and restricts educators from requiring intrusive psychiatric or psychological testing.

Privacy Protection Act of 1980 (Public Law 96-440, 42 U.S.C. 2000 (a)(a)) prohibits government agents from conducting unannounced searches of press offices and files if no one in the office is suspected of committing a crime.

Electronic Funds Transfer Act of 1978 (Public Law 95-630) provides that any institution providing EFT or other bank services must notify its customers about third-party access to customer accounts.

Intelligence Identities Protection Act of 1982 (Public Law 97-200) prohibits the unauthorized disclosure of information identifying certain U.S. intelligence officers, agents, informants, and sources.

Debt Collection Act of 1982 (Public Law 97-365) establishes due process steps (notice, reply, etc.) that Federal agencies must follow before they can release bad debt information to credit bureaus.

Cable Communications Policy Act of 1984 (Public Law 98-549) requires the cable service to inform the subscriber of: the nature of personally identifiable information collected and the nature of the use of such information; the disclosures that may be made of such information; the period during which such information will be maintained; and the times during which an individual may access such information. Also places restrictions on the cable services' collection and disclosures of such information.

Confidentiality provisions are included in several statutes, including: the Census Act (13 U.S.C. 9214), the Social Security Act (42 U.S.C. 408(h)), and the Child Abuse Information Act (42 U.S.C. 5103 (b)(2)(e))).

Note: All statutes embody the same scheme of individual rights and fair information practices.

Sources: Robert Aldrich, Privacy Protection Law in the United States (NTIA Report 82-98, May 1982); Sarah P. Collins, Citizens Control over Records Held by Third Parties (CRS Report No. 78-255, December 8, 1978); and the Office of Technology Assessment.

the 1986 Office of Technology Assessment report *Electronic Record Systems and Individual Privacy*) lists and describes U.S. statutes providing protection for information privacy.

Many American statutes have been modeled after the Privacy Act of 1974, which in turn was modeled after the "Code of Fair Information Practices." A brief look at these reveals the general characteristics of the U.S. approach.

The "Code of Fair Information Practices" was developed and recommended for implementation in the 1973 Report of the Secretary of Health, Education, and Welfare's Advisory Committee on Automated Personal Data System (titled "Records, Computers and the Rights of Citizens"). The code itself was never made into law. Rather it has been (and continues to be) used as a standard and model for legislation. It consists of five principles:

1. There must be no personal data record-keeping system whose very existence is secret.
2. There must be a way for an individual to find out what information about him or her is in a record and how it is used.
3. There must be a way for an individual to prevent information about him or her that was obtained for one purpose from being used or made available for other purposes without his or her consent.
4. There must be a way for an individual to correct or amend a record of identifiable information about him or her.
5. Any organization creating, maintaining, using, or disseminating records of identifiable personal data must assure the reliability of the data for their intended use and must take precautions to prevent misuse of data.

These principles constitute the core of the Privacy Act of 1974. The Privacy Act stipulates that federal agencies meet six major requirements.

1. Permit an individual to determine what records pertaining to him are collected, maintained, used, or disseminated
2. Permit an individual to prevent records pertaining to him obtained by such agencies for a particular purpose from being used or made available for another purpose without his consent
3. Permit an individual to gain access to information pertaining to him in federal agency records, to have a copy made of all or any portion thereof, and to correct or amend such records
4. Collect, maintain, use, or disseminate any record of identifiable personal information in a manner that assures that such action is for a necessary lawful purpose, that the information is current and accurate for its intended use, and that adequate safeguards are provided to prevent misuse of such information
5. Permit exemptions from the requirements with respect to records provided in the act only in those cases where there is an important public policy need for such exemption as has been determined by specific statutory authority
6. Be subject to civil suit for any damages which occur as a result of willful or intentional action which violates any individual rights under the Act.[15]

[15] U.S. Congress, Office of Technology Assessment, *Federal Government Information Technology: Electronic Record Systems and Individual Privacy*, OTA-CIT-296 (Washington, D.C.: U.S. Government Printing Office, June 1986).

There are several important things to notice about these requirements. First, they do not give individuals *control*. Individuals do not have the right to give or withhold information, so the act does not give individuals the power to protect themselves. Rather, it provides protection for individuals by constraining what record-keepers can do. Individuals have rights after the fact. That is, individuals have the right of access to their personal information; they have the right to have information corrected or amended; and they have the right to civil damages if their rights are willfully or intentionally violated. This, in large measure, explains why it is that individuals have so little control in their relationships with federal agencies. Personal information is gathered, used, matched, and so on and the individual is never informed. If you can figure out which agencies have your name in which databases, you can write and request a copy of your file. If you discover errors in these files, you can request that the information be corrected. If you find evidence of intentional or willful violation of your rights, you can sue.

It is also important to note that exceptions to a number of the requirements of the Privacy Act have weakened the act's impact. The third requirement permitting individuals to gain access to information pertaining to them in federal agency records allows exemptions for records that include investigatory material compiled for law enforcement purposes or for the purpose of determining suitability, eligibility, or qualifications for federal civilian employment, military service, or federal contracts. The fourth requirement, that an individual be permitted to prevent records pertaining to him or her obtained by such agencies for a particular purpose from being used or made available for another purpose without consent, has been significantly weakened in recent years by interpretations of the requirement permitting the matching of databases from different agencies, mentioned earlier.

The Office of Technology Assessment (OTA) report, *Electronic Record Systems and Individual Privacy* (mentioned earlier) also points out that new electronic technologies make possible activities that are not covered by the Privacy Act, and these activities may lead to a national database:

> Overall, OTA has concluded that Federal agency use of new electronic technologies in processing personal information has eroded the protections of the Privacy Act of 1974. Many applications of electronic records being used by Federal agencies, e.g., computer profiling and front-end verification, are not explicitly covered either by the act or subsequent OMB guidelines. Moreover, the use of computerized databases, electronic record searches and matches, and computer networking is leading rapidly to the creation of a de facto national database containing personal information on most Americans.[16]

Finally, it is important to note that the Privacy Act pertains only to records in federal agencies, not to private organizations nor to state and local government agencies. Record-keeping in these organizations is regulated by other

[16] U.S. Congress, Office of Technology Assessment, *Federal Government Information Technology*, p. 99.

statutes. The Code of Fair Information Practices has also been the model for many of these statutes so that in many of these as well, individuals have been given the right of access, but their consent need not be sought before information about them is entered into a database, changed, or exchanged.

WHAT CAN BE DONE?

The tension between the need/desire of public and private organizations for information about individuals and individual interests in personal privacy is deeply embedded in our society. We now have a massive information industry and many secondary industries that rely heavily on information about individuals. At the same time, as individuals we have expectations of and desires for a good deal of personal privacy. Change will not be easy to bring about. In the remaining pages of this chapter, a variety of ways to make changes will be briefly discussed. For a problem so woven into the fabric of our society, a many-pronged approach will be necessary.

Broad Conceptual Changes

As mentioned before, the United States has taken a piecemeal, ad hoc approach, with information privacy being dealt with separately sector by sector. We might do better to think about more comprehensive legislation, for both public and private sector organizations.

Issues in the private sector are especially worrisome in the United States because they are not covered by the constitutional tradition. Our legal notions of privacy can be traced back to two of the amendments to the Constitution. The First Amendment addresses freedom of speech and the press, and the Fourth Amendment proscribes unreasonable search and seizure and ensures security in person, houses, papers, and effects. These two amendments deal respectively with the relationship between the government and the press and the government and the individual. Our American forefathers were concerned about protecting us from the power of government (as they should have been). They did not envision the enormous power that private organizations might have over the lives of individuals. Corporations are treated, in law, as persons in need of protection from government, rather than as powerful actors that need to be constrained in their dealings with individuals. We need to consider broad changes that would address this gap in our tradition.

We might be better served if we treated personal information as part of the infrastructure of our society. Infrastructure activities are those that facilitate commerce and affect so many aspects of our lives that they serve us better when managed outside the marketplace. We ought, at least, to explore whether a better system might be one in which personal information were *not* treated as a commodity to be bought and sold but instead managed as part of a public utility. This way of thinking about information might lead us to adopt a system similar to those in some European countries. Sweden, for example, has a system in which a Data Inspection Board (DIB) has the responsibility for licensing all automated personal information systems in both the public and private sectors. The DIB has the authority to control the collection and dissemination of personal data and has the power to investigate complaints, to inspect information systems, and to require information from organizations. It is responsible for designing detailed rules for particular systems and users, including what information may be collected and the uses and disclosures of this information.[17]

Legislation

If we fail to adopt new and more comprehensive legislation, we must continue to improve upon the statutes we now have. We will have to adapt existent statutes to new technological developments as well as create statutes in areas where none exist.

Computer Professionals

Computer professionals can play an important role, individually and collectively. First and foremost, individual professionals must not wash their hands of privacy issues. Actions to be taken depend on a person's job and circumstances. For example, a computer professional can point out privacy matters to clients or employers when building databases containing sensitive information. Whether or not computer professionals should refuse to build systems that they judge to be insecure is a tough question but certainly one that ought to be considered an appropriate question for a "professional."

Individually and collectively, computer professionals can inform the public and public policy makers about privacy and security issues, and they can take positions on privacy legislation as it pertains to electronic records. As mentioned in Chapter 3, computer professionals are often in the best position, because of their technical expertise, to evaluate the security of databases and the potential uses and abuses of information.

The original ACM Code of Professional Conduct specified that an ACM member, whenever dealing with data concerning individuals, shall always consider the principle of the individuals' privacy and seek the following:

To minimize the data collected
To limit authorized access to the data
To provide proper security for the data
To determine the required retention period of the data
To ensure proper disposal of the data

These continue to be useful general guidelines for computer professionals.

---

[17] U.S. Congress, Office of Technology Assessment, *Federal Government Information Technology*, pp. 150–1.

One of the General Moral Imperatives of the 1992 ACM Code of Ethics and Professional Conduct is that an ACM member will "respect the privacy of others." The guidelines explain: "It is the responsibility of professionals to maintain the privacy and integrity of data describing individuals. This includes taking precautions to ensure the accuracy of data, as well as protecting it from unauthorized access or accidental disclosure to inappropriate individuals."

Institutional Policies

Where no law applies or the law is unclear, private and public organizations can do a great deal to protect privacy by adopting internal policies with regard to the handling of personal information. Computer professionals working in such organizations can recommend and support such policies. For example, organizations such as banks, insurance companies, registrars' offices of universities, marketing agencies, and credit agencies should have rules for employees dealing with personal information. They ought to impose sanctions against those who fail to comply. It is not uncommon now to hear of employees who casually reveal interesting information about individuals, which they discovered while handling their records at work. Remember the case of Max Brown in the scenario at the very beginning of this chapter. His agency should have had a policy prohibiting employees from moving personal information out of an agency computer without special authorization.

Personal Actions

As suggested above, it will not be easy, and may be quite costly, for individuals to achieve a significant degree of personal privacy in our society. Gary Marx (1991) has provided a list of steps that individuals can take. (1) Don't give out any more information than is necessary. (2) Don't say things over a cellular or cordless phone that you would mind having overheard by strangers. (3) Ask your bank to sign an agreement that it will not release information about your accounts to anyone lacking legal authorization and that in the event of legal authorization, it will contact you within two days. (4) Obtain copies of your credit, health, and other records and check for accuracy and currency. (5) If you are refused credit, a job, a loan, or an apartment, ask why (there may be a file with inaccurate, incomplete, or irrelevant information). (6) Remember that when you respond to telephone or door-to-door surveys, the information will go into a databank. (7) Realize that when you purchase a product or service and file a warranty card or participate in a rebate program, your name may well be sold to a mailing-list company.[18]

---

[18] Gary Marx, "Privacy and Technology," *Whole Earth Review* (Winter 1991), pp. 91–95.

A FINAL NOTE

Change, as mentioned before, is not going to be easy to bring about and will most likely come about through a many-pronged approach. One thing is for sure: The use of electronic records is not going to diminish of its own accord. Information about individuals is extremely valuable both in the private and in the public sector. This issue is not going to go away until we do something about it.

STUDY QUESTIONS

1. How have computers changed record-keeping?
2. Is the computers and privacy issue a new issue? an old issue in a new guise?
3. Why is information about individuals so important to organizations? Give examples of the uses of personal information by private and public organizations.
4. Why is personal privacy important?
5. What does Johnson mean when she claims that personal privacy is costly in our society?
6. Describe cases in which individuals would be harmed by inaccurate and/or irrelevant information.
7. Who should be concerned about the threat to personal privacy? Why?
8. What kinds of changes might be made in our society to better protect our personal privacy?
9. What could you do as a computer professional to protect personal privacy?
10. What can you do to protect your own privacy?

ADDITIONAL EXERCISES/PRODUCTS

1. Individually or in a small group, choose one of the federal statutes listed in Table 1 or find a state statute dealing with personal privacy. Find out what the law specifies, that is, what rights and responsibilities it assigns to data subjects and to information gatherers. Report this to the rest of the class.
2. Individually or in a small group, choose another country and find out what laws or system that country has to protect personal privacy? How does this compare to protection in the United States?
3. To further develop a sense of what computer professionals can do to effect privacy, discuss the following situations:

Situation 1. Choice of Project

For many years George has worked as a software designer for a major computer company. Over the course of time, he has worked on a variety of types of systems, for example, computer games, simulation systems, spreadsheets.

He has nearly finished the project he has been working on for the last two years and has begun to discuss with his supervisor what his next project will be. The company seems to want George to work on a new surveillance system that will be particularly good for monitoring electronic bulletin board activity. The company expects to make this project one of its highest priorities, so George's position in the company would be greatly enhanced by his involvement. The new software will use data processing techniques with which George is familiar but which have never before been used in this kind of software. Should he work on this project or ask for other options?

Situation 2. Merging Files

A psychology professor learned that two different kinds of data on essentially the same type of subjects were contained in two files stored in the university's computer. He believed that there would be significant scientific value in merging the files and reanalyzing the data. The data consisted of information on the use of drugs by students. Individual students were not identified by name in these files but by number. Presumably a key with student names and numbers was kept by the original researchers. The psychology professor asked Sally von Neumann, a programmer employed as a consultant in the university computing center, to access the data, merge the files, and analyze the data as he indicated. Sally understood what she was being asked to do and found that, in fact, both files were accessible with the password that the psychologist had given to her. Thus, she did as he requested. Should she have done this?

SUGGESTED FURTHER READING

FLAHERTY, DAVID. *Protecting Privacy in Surveillance Societies.* Chapel Hill: University of North Carolina Press, 1989.

HOFFMAN, L.J. (ed.). *Computers and Privacy in the Next Decade.* New York: Academic Press, 1980.

LAUDON, KENNETH. *Dossier Society, Value Choices in the Design of National Information Systems.* New York: Columbia University Press, 1986.

SCHOEMAN, FERDINAND. *Philosophical Dimensions of Privacy: An Anthology.* Cambridge, England: Cambridge University Press, 1984.

CHAPTER 6

Crime, Abuse, and Hacker Ethics

THE ROBERT MORRIS CASE

Around 6 P.M. EST on Wednesday, November 2, 1988, a computer "worm" was discovered in a system in Pennsylvania. Soon the worm was spreading itself across Internet, which connects many research and university systems. By 10 P.M. the worm had managed to infect the Bay Area Research Network (BARnet), which is one of the fastest and most sophisticated in the nation. At this time, the worm exploded quickly throughout Internet, and teams of computer wizards combined forces to stop the threat.

The worm attacked the system in three different ways. First, it simply cracked various passwords by force. Next, it attacked the core of UNIX, a program widely used in the network, by attacking a main function known as "sendmail" and adjusting its commands. Finally, it overstacked data into a status report function known as "finger demon" or "fingerd." The worm did this without attracting notice by making itself look like legitimate commands. After completing infection of a site, the worm replicated itself and went to another system. When a site was successfully infected, the worm sent a signal to "Ernie," a popular computer system at Berkeley. In order to avoid quick detection, the worm program rolled a fifteen-sided die to see if it could infect a new system. A positive roll, a one-in-fifteen chance, instructed the worm to go ahead.

Unfortunately, the program was faulty and was infecting on a fourteen-in-fifteen chance instead. This caused systems to slow down and operators to take notice.

The infector was eventually identified as Robert T. Morris, Jr., a Cornell computer science graduate student. Within forty-eight hours, the worm had been isolated and decompiled, and notices had gone out explaining how to destroy the pest. Although the worm did no permanent damage, it slowed systems to a standstill and acquired passwords into these systems.

Morris was suspended from Cornell by a university board of inquiry for irresponsible acts, and he went to trial in January of 1990. A federal court in Syracuse charged him with violating the Federal Computer Fraud and Abuse Act of 1986. The Morris case was unprecedented in United States courts; it was the first to test the 1986 act. During the trial, Morris revealed that he had realized he had made a mistake and tried to stop the worm. He contacted various friends at Harvard to help him. Andrew Sudduth testified at the trial that he had sent messages out with the solution to kill the program, but the networks were already clogged with the worm.

Morris was found guilty, placed on three years' probation, fined $10,000, and ordered to perform 400 hours of community service. He could have been jailed up to five years and fined $250,000.

During the trial, the seriousness of Morris's behavior was debated in newspapers and magazines. On one side, some said that his crime was not serious and that release of the worm had managed to alert many systems managers to the vulnerability of their computers. Those who thought this also thought that no jail time was appropriate, but community service was. On the other side, some argued that Morris should go to jail. The argument put forth was that a jail sentence would send a clear message to those attempting similar actions on computer systems.[1]

THE CRAIG NEIDORF CASE

Gaining interest in computers through video games, Craig Neidorf began his career as a hacker at age fourteen. Donning the title "Knight Lightning," Neidorf established the electronic newsletter *Phrack*, which detailed both illegal and legal activities involving computer systems and telecommunications lines. Published from 1985 through 1989, *Phrack* was seen by law enforcement

---

[1] This case summary was written by Dave Colantonio based on the following: "The Worm's Aftermath," *Science*, November 11, 1988, p. 1121; "Hacker's Case May Shape Computer Security Law," *The Washington Post*, January 9, 1990, p. A4; "Student Testifies His Error Jammed Computer Network," *The New York Times*, January 19, 1990, p. A19; "From Hacker to Symbol," *The New York Times*, January 24, 1990; "Revenge on the Nerds," *The Washington Post*, February 11, 1990; "U.S. Accepts Hacker's Sentence," *The New York Times*, June 2, 1990; "No Jail Time Imposed in Hacker Case," *The Washington Post*, May 5, 1990; p. A1; "Computer Intruder Is Put on Probation and Fined $10,000," *The New York Times*, May 5, 1990, p. 1.

officers as a potential threat, and it was used over and over again as evidence against computer criminals. On January 18, 1990, the U.S. Secret Service asked Neidorf about an Enhanced 911 (E911) emergency system document, which he turned over to the officers. On the following day, Neidorf was asked to contact the U.S. attorney's office in Chicago by the officers and University of Missouri campus police, who possessed a search warrant. (Neidorf was a student at the University of Missouri.) By January 29, he arrived in Chicago with a lawyer and continued to cooperate by giving information while being interrogated. Four days earlier, however, evidence had been presented to a federal grand jury. On February 1, additional evidence was given to the jury, who in turn charged Neidorf with six counts in an indictment for wire and computer fraud and interstate transportation of stolen property valued at $5,000 or more.

Eventually, the grand jury reconvened to issue a new indictment that added new counts of wire fraud but dropped the computer fraud charges. Neidorf was finally charged with ten felony counts, which could mean up to sixty-five years in prison. Centered on the E911 text file, the government claimed that the file was highly sensitive and belonged to Bell South at the value of $23,900. Supposedly, the document was considered a road map to the 911 system, and anyone possessing the file could find a way to disrupt 911 service.

The government further claimed that Robert Riggs stole the document to publish it in *Phrack* as a scheme to inform other hackers about how to break into computer systems. "Hacker" was defined as an individual "involved with the unauthorized access of computer systems by various means."

On July 24, Assistant U.S. Attorney William Cook began the prosecution by weaving a conspiracy tale involving Neidorf, Riggs, and other members of the Legion of Doom who had broken into Bell South computers. Sheldon Zenner, Neidorf's attorney, defended Neidorf as an exchanger of free information protected by constitutional law and other civil liberties. As the trial proceeded, with testimony from Bell South employees, it became increasingly clear that the E911 document was not highly sensitive and secret and that Bell South had not treated the document as though it were. Eventually it was revealed that the material was actually available in the public domain, and the government dropped all charges.[2]

INTRODUCTION

In Chapter 1, I suggested that we think about computer technology as a new territory, not yet inhabited, and that we think carefully and cautiously about the rules, if any, we would want to create for settling and inhabiting the terri-

---

[2] This case summary was written by Dave Colantonio based on "The *United States v. Craig Neidorf,* A Debate on Electronic Publishing, Constitutional Rights and Hacking," Dorothy E. Denning, comments by Donn B. Parker, Steven Levy, Eugene Spafford, Paula Hawthorn, Marc Rotenberg, J.J. Buck BloomBecker, Richard Stallman, and rebuttal by Dorothy E. Denning. *Communications of the ACM,* 34, no. 3 (March 1991), pp. 23–43.

tory, so that it would become and remain a good place, a place that promotes human well-being. Each chapter of this book might be thought of as a contribution to that undertaking (each chapter deals with a different aspect of the new territory), and in this chapter we turn to "Cyberspace" and how it ought to be settled and inhabited. I use the term "Cyberspace" here to refer to the network or web of telephone lines that potentially connects every computer in the world with every other.[3]

We can ask such questions as the following: Who should have access to Cyberspace? Should Cyberspace be considered private or public? What should count as authorized (or unauthorized) access? What should be considered criminal behavior? Should First Amendment rights be extended to Cyberspace? and so on. Of course, the fact of the matter is that many claims have already been staked out in this new territory. The communication lines are privately owned; courts have decided that precomputer laws apply in the new territory; where old laws haven't worked, new laws have been created to define on-line criminal behavior; and so on. There seems no doubt that more new laws and legal precedents are in the works.

The debate about Cyberspace has, in effect, already taken shape; the Morris and Neidorf cases illustrate several dominant themes. A major part of the debate has to do with activities that begin with unauthorized access to systems and files. Once access is obtained, the intruder may just look around, or may alter files or systems, plant viruses or worms, or makes copies of proprietary information.

Such activities have received a good deal of public attention. The press and the public have been shocked and fascinated by so-called "hackers," what they do, and what they reveal about the vulnerabilities of computer technology. The Robert Morris case is probably the most well-known case. News coverage demonstrated to the public just how vulnerable our nationwide web of computers is—so vulnerable that a young, knowledgeable individual, not in a particularly powerful position, acting essentially on his own, could wreak havoc on powerful and critical computer systems across the world. Media coverage of the incident revealed a degree of social ambivalence about such activities, as some saw Robert Morris as a hero in drawing attention to a serious problem, while others saw him as a common criminal.

The second part of the debate that has come into focus is related to the first but raises a different set of issues. The case of Craig Neidorf involved unauthorized access, but it drew the attention of the computing community because of the activities of law enforcement officials in pursuit of Neidorf. Law enforcement agencies watched on-line activities, covertly observed a convention of hackers, searched facilities, confiscated computers and software, and so on. These activities brought to the fore the potential for law enforcement interference in the free flow of information on-line. The case forced those who fol-

---

[3] This term comes from William Gibson's science fiction novel, *Neuromancer* New York: Ace Science Fiction Books, 1984.

lowed it to come to grips with a tenet of hacker philosophy, the belief that information should be free. This tenet touches a complex and powerful set of beliefs in our society about where and how to draw the line between individual liberty and state control. What is at stake here is freedom of expression on-line and how much power the government, or anyone, should have to patrol and control on-line activities.

Many fear that law enforcement officials, in the name of protecting Cyberspace, will severely diminish the great potential of the technology for enhanced communication and exchange of ideas. The Neidorf case was particularly important to law enforcement officials, not just because it involved unauthorized access and not just because it involved copying of information thought to be proprietary but because the information would assist others in gaining access to private systems, and because Neidorf distributed this information to others on-line.

The law enforcement response to Neidorf's activities makes clear the potential for surveillance and censorship on-line. We can imagine a Cyberspace in which everything you "say"or do is monitored by law enforcement officials, so that you must anticipate that anything you say on-line may some day come back and haunt you. Or we can imagine a Cyberspace that realizes the dream of democracy, in which individuals freely exchange information of importance to them, without fear of repercussions, so that they are able to learn from one another and openly debate the issues of the day.

With these two themes (unauthorized/disruptive access and freedom of expression) shaping the debate about what should and will become of Cyberspace, the following sorts of questions arise. How should we view unauthorized access and disruptive activities such as virus planting? How seriously should we punish these activities? Should malicious intent play a role in determining guilt or innocence or amount of punishment? Should the victim's lack of efforts to protect a system or files play a role in diminishing the responsibility of the criminal? Should we constrain what law enforcement officials can do in pursuit of computer crimes? What should we do if it turns out that in protecting freedom of speech on-line, we are protecting viruses and worms?

THE PROBLEM

At base, the set of issues surrounding hackers, viruses, and the flow of information on-line could be understood to be a classic problem of balancing the freedom, needs, and interests of some individuals against the freedom, needs, and interests of others. We can easily imagine many individuals in a "state of nature" wanting to develop and enforce rules having to do with access to caves or tools. They might want to be able to use territory and tools in ways that require that these be left alone when not being used by their "owners."

Furthermore, the individuals who want this kind of control over "things" might believe that they have a claim to these territories and tools because they obtained them in a certain way. At the same time, we can imagine others in this "state of nature" who have no such desires. They do not like rules and do not like ownership. They prefer a more open, less structured social world, with less privacy and, perhaps, more public ownership. They think it would be terrible to live in a world in which an individual couldn't use spaces or things that they find not in use, when they need them. Now, if each set of people acts as it chooses, it interferes with the other's freedom to act as it chooses.

Most in the computing community would say that what they want is a computing system that is reliable; one that works without interruptions; one that has privacy and integrity so that you can store and send information from one place to another, without fear that it will be seen by others or that it will be tampered with. Such users want to be able to function without fear of being infected with a virus, and without fear that the system will be brought down.

The problem, as they would see it, is simply that there are other users who do just those things that are unwanted. They snoop around trying to see what they are not authorized to see. They plant viruses and worms that make the technology unreliable, they bring down the system, they copy and distribute proprietary information, they violate privacy, and so on.

Ten or twenty years ago, Cyberspace was close to a state of nature, and we might have described the situation, using Moor's idea, as a vacuum of policies. All we needed then were laws and rules to fill the vacuum. Of course, the vacuum has since been filled, and it is still in the process of being filled. For the most part this has been done by extending old laws through new interpretations and creating new laws to cover Cyberspace.

For the most part, Cyberspace has been filled with rules based on preexisting rights and laws. For example, since Cyberspace exists in telephone lines, and since telephone lines are privately owned, this system (in which users rent from common carriers) has simply been extended to computer communications. Because we have extended a preexisting system to the new domain, we have never had much public discussion or debate about how Cyberspace might best be set up. We have never, as a society, engaged in a discussion on such topics as whether Cyberspace should be public or private; whether there should be one or many separate systems; whether use should be encouraged for commercial, educational, personal, or government use; and so on. Yet the rules that come to operate in this territory will make all the difference in what kind of place it becomes. If there are no rules, for example, it may be that individuals will not use the on-line aspects of the technology much, or will use them only for inconsequential activities. If the rules privatize *and* commercialize all activities, Cyperspace will become one sort of place; if we declare Cyberspace public domain—part of the infrastructure of our society, like the road system—it will become quite another sort of place.

The problem has been characterized so far as a human problem, but some characterize it as technological: They argue that what we need is not (or not only) rules or policies but better technology. According to this approach, the problem is that the technology is built or set up in ways that make it too *vulnerable,* so we must add more technology or improve upon the present technology to make it more secure. The field of endeavor known as security aims at this. Of course, to take this approach exclusively is to presume that we already know what Cyberspace should look like; we just need to figure out how to implement it.

The social or human approach may also presume that we already know what Cyberspace should look like. Because this approach focuses on rules and laws, however, it seems more likely to lead to open discussion about the character of the world we should create in Cyberspace. The human or social approach proposes that we solve Cyberspace problems by changing the legal and social environment of computing—by changing user attitudes and beliefs about computing. This approach calls for laws making undesirable behavior a crime, for education, and for creation of social conventions surrounding the use of computers.

The distinction between the two approaches is not hard and fast; for example, specialists in security will often be involved in promoting legislation and education, and those who know about the human side can and do inform security experts. The two approaches are certainly not mutually exclusive—they can and are both used together. Indeed, when one reads the literature on this topic, one finds that each side concludes that its approach *cannot* do the job. Those involved with security admit that they cannot anticipate and plug up every vulnerability. As quickly as security techniques are developed, they become known to those who figure out how to overcome them. On the other hand, those who take the human approach recognize that while a good deal can be done to change attitudes and conventions, this approach cannot encompass *all* computer users. There will always be a few who will find the challenge of breaking in irresistible.

DEFINITIONS AND DISTINCTIONS

It is difficult to list all the behaviors that might be encompassed in the discussion of this chapter, but it may be helpful to clarify some terms.

Hacker/Cracker

"Hacker" is used in a variety of ways. When the term was first coined, it referred to those who were computer enthusiasts. Hackers love computers and have the expertise to use them in very clever ways. Hackers form computer clubs and user groups, circulate newsletters, attend trade shows, and even have their own conventions.

More recently, the term has acquired a negative connotation referring to those who use computers for illegal, unauthorized, or disruptive activities. In order to emphasize this difference, some use the term "cracker" to refer to the latter and "hacker" as it originally was used. I am going to use "hacker" in its more recent and more popular meaning to refer to those who engage in illegal or unauthorized and disruptive behavior.

Software Pirate

Pirates make unauthorized copies of copyrighted software, and they will go to great lengths to do so. They may or may not distribute copies to others. Software pirates are often hackers, and vice versa. (Since illegal copying of proprietary software was dealt with in Chapter 4, my focus in this chapter will be on other types of computer abuse and crime.)

Viruses and Worms

I include definitions of viruses and worms to assist those who are less familiar with the problems of computer crime and abuse. Those who are more familiar with computers will be able to specify a more elaborate taxonomy of terms for various kinds of intrusions, including Trojan horses, ants, and so on.

The term "virus" was first used to refer to any unwanted computer code, but the term now generally refers to "a segment of machine code (typically 200–400 bytes) that will copy its code into one or more larger 'host' programs when it is activated. When these infected programs are run, the viral code is executed and the virus spreads further."[4]

Technically, Robert Morris did not use a virus but rather a worm. Worms are "programs that can run independently and travel from machine to machine across network connections; worms may have portions of themselves running on many different machines."[5]

Intentional and Unintentional Abuse

In addition to these definitions, it may be helpful to mention two distinctions that are often employed in thinking about computer crime. First, it is tempting to try to distinguish unintentional or accidental acts from those that are intentional. Users may accidentally gain unauthorized access or disrupt a system, and these cases do not seem so condemnable as cases in which the abuse was intentional. Hence, this distinction might be thought to be important in developing responses to computer crime.

Nevertheless, we have to be extremely careful in drawing this distinction. In the case of Robert Morris, for example, while he admitted to intentionally

---

[4] Eugene H. Spafford, Kathleen A. Heapy, and David J. Ferbrache, "A Computer Virus Primer," in Peter J. Denning (ed.), *Computers Under Attack* (New York: ACM Press/Addison-Wesley, 1990), p. 316.

[5] Spafford, et. al. "A Computer Virus Primer," p. 317.

planting the worm, he claimed that he did not intend for it to do the kind of damage it did. The fact that he did not intend the degree of damage he caused may mitigate his responsibility, but it cannot absolve him entirely of responsibility. Generally we hold those who are engaged in risky activities to a higher standard of care. We expect, for example, truck drivers who carry toxic chemicals to be more cautious than ordinary drivers. When the risky activity is illegal, the person generally bears even greater responsibility for ill effects. Take the case of a burglar who uses dynamite to break into a building, believing that no people are in that section of the building. Suppose a guard just happens to be walking through and is killed by the explosion. The burglar did not intend to kill the guard, but he engaged in a dangerous activity, and the guard would not have died if the burglar had refrained.

The point is that we cannot think of hacker behavior simply as intentional or unintentional. There is a range of behaviors with various degrees of intentionality and recklessness.

Abuse for Fun and Abuse for Personal Gain

Another distinction that might be employed in dealing with computer crime is that between intrusions for fun and intrusions for criminal purposes. We might try to separate out cases in which a person uses computers and computing lines to steal, embezzle, do industrial espionage, sabotage competitors, and so on, from cases in which the individual is not interested in personal gain. For example, the United Kingdom's Computer Misuse Act of 1990 distinguishes unauthorized access, unauthorized access in furtherance of a more serious crime, and unauthorized modification of computer material. The first offense has a lesser penalty than the second and third.

While these are important distinctions, again we have to be very careful here. It is misguided to assume that acts done purely for fun, without the motive of personal gain, or with no criminal intent beyond unauthorized access are, thereby, all right. We are quite likely to encounter cases in which we cannot be sure what the person's motives are. Moreover, even when the motives are noble, the effect of the behavior may be devastating. The behavior may be reckless. Imagine, for example, a case where a hacker finds a flaw in the security of a database of information about women who have had abortions. The hacker contacts the state agency that maintains the database and tries to get the agency to make the database more secure. He is unsuccessful. Out of frustration, the hacker discusses what he has found in an electronic bulletin board and thus tells others about the weakness in the system. A few of those who hear this decide to see if they, too, can get access. One person gets access and uses the information to find women who can be blackmailed—many of the women do not want their families or friends to know that they have had an abortion. Or suppose a newspaper reporter "listens" in on the bulletin board and decides to write a piece so that the agency will do something about the weakness in the system. The reporter writes a story about the situation and to make the piece powerful, she includes some of the data she was able to access. The names of several women who have had abortions are published. In both these cases, significant harm is done with quite noble intentions.

These examples make clear that actions cannot always be evaluated simply by their motives. Hence, when it comes to hacking, we may well want to assign different penalties for unauthorized access with and without intent to commit another, more serious crime, but it would be a shame if this were understood to imply that the one kind of behavior is more tolerable than the other.

HACKER ETHICS

As suggested above, most people in the computing community want computing that is reliable and private. Let us now consider the other side of this by looking at what hackers say about what they do. Are the things hackers do so wrong? How does their behavior look when the justification for it is examined critically? The important thing for our purposes is not who hackers are (they are generally intelligent teenage males) and what they are like as persons. What is important for our purposes is whether hacker behavior is good or bad, justifiable or unconscionable, and whether it should be prohibited or tolerated, punished or condoned. This we can determine by asking whether hacking can be justified in a coherent, consistent ethical analysis. What arguments can be given in defense of hacker behavior?

A number of authors have identified the arguments that hackers generally give in defense of their behavior.[6] I have sorted these into four arguments: (1) All information should be free, and if it were free there would be no need for intellectual property and security. (2) Break-ins illustrate security problems to those who can do something about them; those who expose flaws are doing a service for the computing community. (3) Hackers are doing no harm and changing nothing; they are learning about how computer systems operate. (4) Hackers break into systems to watch for instances of data abuse and to help keep Big Brother at bay. Now let us consider each one of these arguments separately.

(1) All information should be free and if it were free there would be no need for intellectual property and security. This is a most interesting and important argument. First let us divide it into its two parts, the claim that all information should be free and the claim that if it were free, there would be no need for intellectual property and security. The second claim, a conditional, is true: *If* all information were free, *then* it follows that there would be no need

[6] Eugene H. Spafford, "Are Computer Hacker Break-ins Ethical?" *The Journal of Systems and Software* 17 (January, 1992), pp. 41–47; Dorothy Denning, "Hacker Ethics," presented at the National Conference on Computing and Values at Southern Connecticut State University, New Haven, August 1991; Peter Denning (ed.), *Computers Under Attack.* (New York: ACM Press/Addison-Wesley, 1990).

for intellectual property and security. To say that all information is free is to say that it is unownable, and if it were unownable, there would be no need for intellectual property and security. The only catch here is that at the moment all information is *not* free. Hence, the important part of this hacker argument is the first claim, that all information *should* be free.

This claim has a strong intuitive appeal, especially when we contemplate the fundamental role that information plays in the lives of all individuals. Human beings, as autonomous, self-determining creatures, form desires and plans for their lives, and they make decisions about how to pursue their desires and goals. Individual goals and decisions are always based on beliefs, and beliefs are formulated on the basis of information. Here are some examples. (1) Suppose I enjoy traveling and have decided to save money for a trip to the Caribbean. Perhaps I know from personal experience that I enjoy traveling. My desire to go to the Caribbean is based on a multitude of information about the Caribbean—what it is like there, how much it will cost while I am there, what the weather is like, and so on. (2) Suppose I plan to undergo surgery. My consenting to the surgery is based on a multiplicity of beliefs, beliefs that are formed around information. The information upon which my decision is based has come to me in a variety of ways: My doctor has given me a good deal of information, I have beliefs about doctors and hospitals and their reliability, I have done some reading, I have talked to people who have undergone surgery, and so on. We need information to do most things in life, and the more and better information we have, the better our decisions are likely to be.

Add two other points to this analysis of the role of information in personal decision making. First, remember from Chapter 4 on property that intellectual property rights have the potential to interfere with freedom of thought. If we aren't careful about what we allow to be owned, we could create a situation in which we would be violating property rights by having certain thoughts, using certain information. Moreover, ownership of information can significantly constrain its availability. Imagine my wanting to go to the Caribbean but being unable to obtain information about it because the information is proprietary and the owner is unwilling to sell it, or is willing to sell it but only for a price I cannot afford. So, access to information is important to living.

Second, consider the role of information in a democratic society. Access to information seems especially crucial in a democratic society, for in democracies individuals make decisions not only about their own lives but about the shape of their society. How could I vote for candidates in a public election if information about them was unavailable or extremely expensive. Democracy requires that individuals vote on the basis of accurate information, otherwise, the outcome of democratic elections has little to recommend it. If only a select few have access to the relevant information, then that makes a strong case for letting the select few decide, and, of course, this is antithetical to democracy. Given the role of information in decision making, given the dangers of ownership of information, and given the importance of information in a democratic society, therefore, freedom of information is extremely desirable. We would not want to give it up or diminish it lightly.

Nevertheless, these arguments for freedom of information are very general. They do not show that we need freedom of *all* information; they do not show that freedom of information is the highest of all values; they do not show that freedom of information should never be traded off against other values. In the United States, and other countries as well, we have traded off freedom of information in certain domains for the sake of other values. I cannot argue here that this is the best or only way for a society to go, for we can imagine societies in which there is more freedom of information than exists in the United States. Still, we seem to have chosen to constrain the free flow of certain kinds of information for the sake of other things that we value.

Here are three areas in which we have traded off freedom of information in order to achieve valuable ends. First and foremost, in developing a capitalist economy, we have recognized that information can play a critical role in competition and we have allowed individuals (and corporations) to own and control information in the form of, for examples, patents and trade secrets (as we saw in Chapter 4). The argument for this is utilitarian: By allowing individuals to own information, information is created and used for beneficial purposes. If it were not allowed to be owned, it might not be created or used in quite the way that it is.

A second area in which we have traded off freedom of information is national security. Given what I said above about the important role of freedom of information in a democracy, this area is extremely delicate. On the one hand, government officials claim that there is a great need for keeping some information top secret so that our country can carry on covert activities in international affairs. This, however, has to be balanced against the accountability of government to its citizens.

A third area has to do with individual privacy. In recognizing that individuals have a right to privacy, at least in certain domains of their lives, we have, in effect, restricted the free flow of information. For example, information about such things as sexual preference, political or religious affiliation, and so on are protected in the sense that they cannot be used in certain contexts, information about what we do in the privacy of our homes can only be acquired with a search warrant.

I do not mean to defend each of these trade-offs; rather, I point out that our society has adopted policies that constrain the free flow of information in order to promote, facilitate, or protect activities considered very valuable. It can be argued that many businesses could not exist without trade secrets, that our national security would not be as strong as it is without secret information, and that individuals would not enjoy as much personal happiness without the privacy they now have.

This is not to say that hackers are all wrong about the issue. The importance of the hacker claim that information should be free is reinforced if we think about the system of public libraries that has been established in the United States. Our public libraries exist because we recognize the importance of information being available to every citizen without cost. Hackers see the enormous potential of computer technology to bring the equivalent of libraries and much more into our homes. Computer technology with telecommunications lines connecting libraries to one another and connecting libraries to users can equalize the smallest and largest libraries and can bring any library into every home. Equipped with computers and data lines, every citizen can have endless information placed at his or her fingertips.

This is a powerful and significant potential of computer technology that ought to be pursued. The free flow of information is crucial in a democracy. Where the hacker argument goes wrong, however, is in claiming that *all* information should be free, without addressing differences between kinds of information, and in presuming that there are no other values that might be balanced against the value of freedom of information. We need a system that distributes information broadly while at the same time allowing certain kinds of information to be private.

(2) Break-ins illustrate security problems to those who can do something about them; those who expose flaws are doing a service for the computing community. With this argument, hackers, in effect, claim that their behavior does some good. Robert Morris has been defended on such grounds. On careful examination, however, this seems a weak argument, for a number of reasons. First, if an individual finds a flaw or weakness in a computer system, it would seem that she should first try nondisruptive and nondestructive means to get the problem fixed.

The hacker argument suggests that on-line break-ins should be seen as a kind of whistle-blowing, but the literature on whistle-blowing suggests that whistle-blowers should try internal channels first. Yes, we can imagine cases in which an individual is frustrated in his attempts to get a flaw fixed, and we can imagine cases in which the flaw is serious enough for severe action (as we saw in the case of Carl Babbage in Chapter 3). Still, such cases are going to be rare, not the typical motive for a break-in or use of a worm.

Spafford argues against the claim that hackers are doing a service by using an analogy. When hackers say this, he writes, it is like saying that "vigilantes have the right to attempt to break into the homes in my neighborhood on a continuing basis to demonstrate that they are susceptible to burglars."[7] Since we would never accept this argument made in defense of burglars, we should not accept it for hacking. Spafford also points out that on-line break-ins, even when done to call attention to flaws in security, waste time and money and pressure individuals and companies to invest in security. Many do not have the re-

---

[7] Spafford, "Are Computer Hacker Break-ins Ethical?" pp. 43–44.

sources to fix systems or implement tighter security, yet the "vigilante behavior" forces upgrades.

The analogy with automobile security also seems relevant here. We used to be able to leave our automobiles on the streets without locking them. Now, in many parts of the country, owners not only must lock their automobiles but must invest in elaborate security devices to protect against stealing. All the resources put into automobile security (the owner's money, the police force's time, the automobile manufacturer's expertise) could be invested elsewhere if so many individuals were not trying to steal automobiles. Analogously, those who attempt to gain unauthorized access, plant worms and viruses, and so on force the computing community to put energies and resources into protecting systems and files when they could be using their energies and resources to improve the technology in other ways, for example, making it more accessible, making new applications, and so on. It is important to see that this argument applies as much to the energies and resources of the designers and manufacturers of computer technology as to computer center directors and individual users.

So this defense of hacker behavior does not seem to have force. There is no doubt that it is a good thing for those who become aware of flaws and weaknesses in computer systems to inform those who are affected, and even to urge appropriate persons to fix these flaws. We can imagine cases in which flaws in security are serious and an individual is frustrated in her attempts to get them fixed, but it is much more difficult to imagine cases that would justify bringing a system down or accessing private files.

(3) Hackers are doing no harm and changing nothing; they are learning about how computer systems operate. The first part of this argument can be dismissed fairly quickly, for it seems quite clear that people have been harmed by hacking activities. After all, nonphysical harm is harm nonetheless. If individuals have proprietary rights and rights to privacy, then they are harmed when these rights are violated, just as individuals are harmed when they are deprived of their right to vote or their right to due process. Moreover, hackers can do physical harm. It is possible for hackers to get access to systems used in hospitals where patients are at risk or systems running industrial processes in which workers are at physical risk from dangerous chemicals or explosions. Think, for example, of a case in which a hacker plants a worm that slows down a system. Suppose the system is being used to match donated organs with those who need transplants. Timing is critical: A slowdown in the system can make the difference between finding a match or not, between life and death.[8]

The hackers' defense that they are learning about computer systems seems inadequate. Hackers do learn a great deal about computer systems from their hacking activities and from one another, however, this hardly shows that hacking is a good thing. Is any activity that promotes learning thereby a good ac-

[8] I am grateful to Paul Doering for suggesting this example to me.

tivity? Is hacking the only way to learn about computing? Is hacking the best, or even a good, way to learn about computer technology?

A few examples make it easy to say "no" to the first of these questions. Giving electric shocks to learners when they make mistakes may promote learning, but this does not make it a good teaching method. Allowing children to stick things in electric outlets might result in their learning the dangers of the outlets, but this hardly seems a good thing. Therefore, hackers learning by hacking does not make hacking a good thing.

Hacking is certainly not the only way to learn about computing. Aside from the standard ways a person learns in the classroom (by reading, listening to a teacher, doing problems), we can imagine a variety of creative ways to teach people about computers. These might include challenging games and tournaments that encourage learners to be creative and clever in their use of computers.

Even when it comes to learning about security, hacking is probably not the best way to learn, but, frankly, there is no evidence to tell us one way or another. For those interested in security, there may be something important to be learned from imagining oneself a hacker trying to break into a system. Such an exercise can, of course, be set up in computer classes by first obtaining the permission of those who own and run a computer system, so that no rights are violated and no harm is done. Still, I am reluctant to recommend such exercises because they tend to encourage the attitude that it is "fun" to break into systems. The point is that even if hacking did promote learning about computers, the good created would have to be weighed against the negative consequences. The good of hacking would hardly seem to counterbalance the harm done to others when their privacy and property rights are violated.

So this defense of hacking behavior is also not successful. A case can be made for the importance of learning about computers and computing, indeed, a case can be made for such education being available to all. Still, this end hardly seems to justify the means chosen by hackers.

(4) Hackers break into systems to watch for instances of data abuse and to help keep Big Brother at bay.[9] This argument returns us to the problem of civil liberties on-line, a problem not to be dismissed lightly. With this argument it would seem that hackers present themselves, again, as vigilantes: They protect us where we are not being adequately protected by formal authorities. We can imagine cases where government agencies are gathering (or matching) information that they are not authorized to use. Suppose, for example, that a law enforcement agency is monitoring bulletin boards on a certain topic, tracking participants, and recording what each participant says in the interest of identifying individuals likely to commit crimes. We can imagine companies, as well, maintaining secret databases of information that is prohibited by law from be-

[9] For those unfamiliar with the phrase "Big Brother," it comes from the novel *1984* by George Orwell. "Big Brother" refers to the government, which watched over every move of every citizen.

ing collected or used. For example, suppose a database of information about religious affiliation or voting record is being sold to employers.

Hackers argue that they can provide us with some protection against this. By gaining unauthorized access to government or commercial systems, they can see when abuse is occurring and reveal it to the public. They will thus be able to alert us to covert abuses.

Hackers are right that we need protection against data abuse and Big Brother, as discussed in Chapter 5. Nevertheless, we must ask if hackers can provide the kind of protection we need, and whether the cost of tolerating hackers will be worth what we gain in protection. In other words, do hackers solve the problem or make it worse?

If we step back from the hacker argument and ask about the best way to monitor such things as data abuse and government surveillance on-line, it would seem that we have several options. We might create a national data protection commission, which would have the authority to monitor databases and prosecute violators. We might also impose on computer professionals a special obligation to report their suspicions or evidence of data abuse and covert surveillance. This would be consistent with the analysis provided in Chapter 3. Yet another possibility is development of a set of social conventions surrounding computing that would encourage users to "keep watch" without abusing systems and files.

This hacker argument is important because it points to a problem in Cyberspace that is not being adequately addressed. Nevertheless, it seems counterproductive to gain protection by tolerating or condoning hacking. We get rid of one problem by creating another, for what would Cyberspace be like with vigilantes roaming around? While we might have to worry less about data abuse and covert surveillance by government and by commercial interests, we would have to fear the vigilantes, who might decide to take a look at our files or wander through systems in the name of protection. On reflection, it seems a crude and costly method for dealing with a problem for which there are other solutions.

WHAT SHOULD BE DONE?

What can and should be done to minimize crime and abuse on-line and ensure that Cyberspace is structured in ways that are beneficial to citizens and users? At the beginning of this chapter, I mentioned that two approaches have generally been undertaken to deal with computer crime and abuse, the technological approach (which emphasizes improving the technology so as to prevent crime and abuse) and the human approach (which emphasizes changing human behavior on-line). The emphasis here will be on the human approach, which encompasses a range of activities.

The human approach includes better legislation, changing informal so-

cial attitudes and conventions, changing the professions responsible for computer technology, and education. Chapter 3 discussed changes in the profes-
sion(s) of computing. More needs to be said about legislation, changing social
attitudes and conventions, and, finally, education.

Legislation

Law is one of the primary ways we have begun to respond to problems
created by hacking. The law used in the prosecution of hackers has become extremely complex in a relatively short period of time. Federal and state legislation dealing specifically with computer crime has been created and many traditional statutes have been extended to prosecute computer crimes. As a recent
legal scholar explained:

> In just over ten years, the number of states that have enacted computer crime
> statutes has grown to forty-eight. On the federal level, Congress has responded
> by enacting the Counterfeit Access Device and Computer Fraud and Abuse Act
> in 1984 and amending it with the Computer Fraud and Abuse Act in 1986.
>   There are forty federal statutes and eleven areas of traditional law that can be
> used to attack computer crime. The areas of state law include: arson, burglary,
> embezzlement, larceny, theft of services or labor under false pretenses, and theft
> of trade secrets.[10]

The Computer Fraud and Abuse Act of 1986 (CFAA) was the legislation
used to prosecute Robert Morris, as discussed earlier. The CFAA is the major
federal legislation in this area and prohibits six types of computer abuse:
(1) knowingly accessing a computer without authorization or in excess of authorized access and obtaining information related to national defense, foreign
relations, or information restricted by Section 11 of the Atomic Energy Act of
1954, with the intent or reason to believe that the information will be used to
injure the United States or assist a foreign nation; (2) intentionally accessing
a computer without authorization or exceeding authorized access, and thereby
obtaining information contained in a financial record of a financial institution;
(3) intentionally, without authorization, accessing any computer of a department or agency of the United States; (4) knowingly and with intent to defraud,
accessing a federal interest computer (without authorization, or in excess of
authorization) and by means of such conduct furthering the intended fraud,
obtaining anything of value, unless the object of the fraud and the thing obtained consists only of the use of the computer; (5) intentionally accessing a
federal interest computer without authorization, and by means of one or more
instances of such conduct altering, damaging, or destroying information if
losses surpass $1,000, during a one-year period, or if such action interferes with
any medical care of one or more individuals; and (6) knowingly and with in-

[10] Christopher D. Chen, "Computer Crime and the Computer Fraud and Abuse Act of 1986,"
Computer/Law Journal, x (1990), 71–86.

tent to defraud trafficking in any password or similar information through which a computer may be accessed without authorization if it affects interstate or foreign commerce or if the computer is used by the government of the United States.[11]

Although I have tried to simplify the language of the law, you can see that it is complex and deals primarily with government computers and financial institutions. It has already been criticized for having loopholes and ambiguities. Many argue that the CFAA and other new legislation is still not adequate to deal with computer crime and abuse.[12] Better laws will assist in the prosecution of computer crime, but we cannot help concluding that other approaches are necessary.

Good Neighbor Conventions

Computer users develop attitudes toward computer technology that subtly affect how they behave with the technology. These attitudes develop from observations and interactions with other users, their peers, teachers, vendors, the media, and so on. We are often unaware of the attitudes we are conveying. The college teacher, for example, who challenges students to find a way into a new security system may be unaware of conveying a sense that it is fun and not a serious offense to try to get into systems and files. The secondary school teacher who accepts pirated software from a student condones unauthorized copying even when he accepts the copy reluctantly and only because the school cannot afford to buy the software. A news reporter who glamorizes a hacker as a hero "sticking it to" the big, bad guy—a big corporation—may not acknowledge that the story encourages hacking.

Attitudes and social conventions surrounding computing must make it clear to users that certain forms of behavior are unacceptable. One way this might happen is to develop what I will call a "good neighbor policy" in the community of computing. The idea of such a policy arises from thinking about hackers on the analogy of "burglars and snoops." As suggested before, those who continuously try to crack passwords and get unauthorized access are analogous to individuals who walk down a quiet street testing the doors to see which houses are unlocked. (Perhaps a more accurate analogy would be of a person targeting a house and standing in front of the door with a large key ring, trying one key after another to see if any will let him in.) We can imagine a range of different criminal types who do this: those that stop at finding an unlocked door (they find a key that works but do not enter); those that enter the house and steal; those that enter the house and simply look around, but take nothing; those that enter, take nothing, but move things about so that the owner knows someone has been there; those that enter, take nothing, but set booby traps;

---

[11] Computer Fraud and Abuse Act of 1986, Pub. L. No. 99–474, 100 Stat. 1213.

[12] Daniel J. Kluth, "The Computer Virus Threat: A Survey of Current Criminal Statues," *Hamline Law Review*, 13 (Spring 1990), 297–312.

and so on. The parallels with various types of hackers should be clear. Some crack passwords, period; some crack passwords, go into the system, and look around; some crack passwords, go in, and take information; some crack passwords, go in, and plant worms or viruses; and so on.

You can debate whether the analogy is useful or misleading. No doubt, there are some differences between hackers and off-line trespassers and burglars. For example, when a burglar steals a television or jewelry, the owner no longer has those items, but when people steal on-line, they do not deprive the owner of information; they simply make a copy. This difference disappears, of course, if what is copied was proprietary and intended for the marketplace.

In any case, one of the practices that often works in protecting against snoops and burglars in a residential neighborhood is the detection of the burglar by a neighbor who happens to be home and sees something suspicious. If your neighbor notices a stranger trying keys at the door to your house, or notices activity in your house when you are away on vacation, *and* if the neighbor takes the trouble to contact the police, then you have been protected. If you live in a neighborhood in which neighbors will do this, you have a measure of safety that you would not have otherwise. You are much safer in that environment than in an environment in which neighbors look the other way.

You would have the same increased measure of protection in computing if the convention was to report suspicious activities to individuals or systems operators. In both the neighborhood and the computing environment case, members of the neighborhood might get together periodically to talk about problems they see developing, patterns of behavior they have observed, measures that might be taken jointly, and so on.

Neighborhoods function to a large extent on the basis of trust. Members trust one another to follow the rules and live up to their obligations. This trust is further enhanced when individuals do more than just abide by the rules; they take responsibility for the community as a whole and are willing to help one another. In some residential neighborhoods, the neighbors get together now and then to talk about common problems they might be able to do something about collectively. The same might go on in communities of Cyberspace. Users should take note when they see suspicious-looking behavior and report it to appropriate individuals—individual users or systems operators. Users of a system should periodically discuss what is happening on-line and how to make the system work better. They need not come up with new rules enforced by authorities, but they may develop informal agreements.

Just as it would be a tragedy for Cyberspace to become a police state, it would be a tragedy for it to be settled as a place in which citizens did not care what happens to one another. A sense of citizenship in the community of computer users would go a long way toward reducing the amount of hacking that goes on. Rules enforced by authorities can only do so much; in the end, what is needed most is responsible users.

Education

Education has a large role to play in changing the attitudes and, ultimately, the behavior of computer users. Given the preceding analysis, it seems that what is needed most is for users to understand the connection between their behavior on-line and its impact on other users. These connections need to be made explicit so that a user cannot deceive herself about the significance of unauthorized access, planting a worm, making an unauthorized copy, and so on. It would probably be naive to believe that this alone will stop all hackers, but it would go a long way toward sensitizing the majority of users.

A whole range of types of education is needed. Users can be reached through formal and informal programs in elementary and secondary schools, as well as in their college years. Computer professionals can be reached through special courses in degree programs, and through continuing education programs. In addition to users and professionals, we need to educate the legal community. We need legislators, lawyers, and judges who understand computers well enough to see the potentials for abuse and to develop effective new legislation or make use of extant law effectively, in combatting dangerous and disruptive behavior. In addition, we need a public educated enough about computer technology to see both its potential for good and the parameters of abuse.

A FINAL NOTE

There is no doubt that hacker behavior causes harm to others in the sense that it violates legitimate privacy and property rights, and it compels others to invest in security when they might prefer to spend their time and money on other activities. At the same time, hacker arguments point to values that may be pushed aside too easily in the development of computer technology. I have suggested in the chapter on property that there are some signs that too much may be owned when it comes to computer software. In the chapter on privacy I have suggested that we might think of better ways to protect and manage personal information. The concerns that are implicitly expressed by hacking behavior about Big Brother on-line and constraints on the free flow of information are important. Cyberspace could be ruined by too much interference and too much ownership.

Hence, in criticism of hacker behavior, we should not slip into blindly condemning, for while hacking is disruptive, dangerous, and unjustified, there is no doubt that improvements are needed in the way that Cyberspace is developing. Computers have great potential for making information more available than ever before and for facilitating communication in a way never possible before. At the same time, Cyberspace could be carved up by commercial interests; more information could become proprietary, meaning less individual autonomy, diminished civil rights, and so on.

STUDY QUESTIONS

1. What is "Cyberspace"?
2. What two themes arise in the debate about what Cyberspace should be like?
3. Problems in Cyberspace can be characterized as human or as technological. Explain these two approaches. What sorts of solutions does each propose?
4. Define the following: hacker, software pirate, virus, worm.
5. What four arguments might hackers give in defense of their behavior? Can you think of other arguments they might give?
6. Take each of the hacker arguments that Johnson mentions and explain how she responds. Is her analysis of each argument adequate? Can you think of other criticisms of the hacker arguments or other defenses?
7. What is the "good neighbor policy"?
8. What does the Computer Fraud and Abuse Act prohibit?
9. What kinds of education will be useful in discouraging computer crime?
10. Which of the human approaches to computer crime do you think will be the most effective? Why?

SUGGESTED FURTHER READINGS

BRANSCOMB, ANNE W. "Rogue Computer Programs and Computer Rogues: Tailoring the Punishment to Fit the Crime" *Rutgers Computer & Technology Law Journal*, 16 (1990), 1-16

CHEN, CHRISTOPHER D. "Computer Crime and the Computer Fraud and Abuse Act of 1986." *Computer/Law Journal*, X (1990), 71–86.

CLUKEY, LAURA L. "The Electronic Communications Privacy Act of 1986: The Impact on Software Communications Technologies." *Software Law Journal*, 2 (Spring 1988), 243–63.

DENNING, P.J. (ed.) *Computers Under Attack: Intruders, Worms, and Viruses.* Reading, Mass.: ACM Books/Addison-Wesley, 1991.

KLUTH, DANIEL J. "The Computer Virus Threat: A Survey of Current Criminal Statutes." *Hamline Law Review,* 13 (Spring 1990), 297–312.

SPAFFORD, EUGENE H. "Are Computer Hacker Break-Ins Ethical?" *Journal of Systems and Software,* 17, no. 1 (1992), 41–47.

CHAPTER 7

Responsibility and Liability

SCENARIO 7.1: WHO IS RESPONSIBLE?

Civil engineers employed by a state agency were engaged in numerous construction design projects, such as flood control, where safety of humans is a factor. They were held personally responsible for their work, under a professional and business responsibility law. In their design activities, the engineers increasingly relied on computer programs designed by systems analysts and implemented by computer programmers. The engineers specified the problems requiring solution and, to various degrees, specified the methods of solution and test cases for demonstrating that the computer programs functioned correctly. Several of the computer programs included logic where decisions were based on engineer-specified criteria and where the program output selected types and quantities of construction materials and stated how deliverable end products were to be constructed.

The engineers complained to their management that they were not able to determine the correctness and integrity of the computer programs, and the results of their work relied heavily on those qualities. Therefore, an error in a computer program or an error in operation of the computer (that could be detected by the programmer) could result in a serious design flaw that could cause harm to people. The engineers wanted the systems analysts and computer programmers to share the responsibility for any losses under the professional and business law.

The systems analysts and programmers stated that they were merely providing tools and had no involvement in their use. The engineers could test and analyze the programs to assure themselves of their accuracy. Therefore, the systems analysts and programmers should not be held responsible.[1]

SCENARIO 7.2: ACCOUNTABILITY AND COMPUTER DECISION MODELS

Rosemary Martin works for an investment company that manages several pension funds. Martin has been managing pension accounts for ten years and has been increasingly successful. She is now in charge of one of the company's largest accounts, the pension fund of a major automotive company.

A year ago, her company purchased an expert system for investment decisions. Each week a manager can input current figures on key economic indicators and the system will produce a set of recommended actions. This week Martin is quite nervous about the stock market. All the indicators she has come to trust point in the direction of a serious and long-term downswing, so she believes it would be best to reduce the pension fund's holdings in stocks. However, the expert system recommends just the opposite. She rechecks the figures she has put into the system, but the output continues to recommend that the percentage of holdings in stocks be increased to 90 percent of the portfolio.

Martin does not understand the reasoning that is built into the expert system; hence, she does not know whether the system's reasoning is better or worse than her own. It is even possible that the system is malfunctioning. If she goes with the advice of the expert system, the account could lose heavily, so much so that income to retirees would have to be adjusted downward. On the other hand, if she goes against the expert system and she is wrong, the account could be jeopardized and she would be in serious trouble for diverging from the recommendation of the expert system. What should she do?

SCENARIO 7.3: LIABILITY IN ELECTRONIC BULLETIN BOARDS

Sam Simpson is a free-lance journalist. One of the ways he keeps up to date on the topics on which he writes is by subscribing to a computer service that gives him access to bulletin boards on a variety of topics. The bulletin boards are set up so that participants can enter information and ideas, comment on one another's ideas, reference articles, and so on.

Simpson has been away on an assignment for the last month, and upon

---

[1] Donn B. Parker, Susan Swope, and Bruce N. Baker, *Ethical Conflicts in Information and Computer Science, Technology, and Business* (Wellesley, Mass.: QED Information Sciences, 1990).

his return he signs on to the bulletin board about South American politics, a field in which he has a growing reputation. As he reads through various comments, he is outraged to find that someone has attacked him by claiming that he is involved in illegal drug operations and that his stories are filled with lies to protect others who are involved.

After the shock subsides, Simpson enters his denial of the accusations into the bulletin board. Even with his denials, however, the accusations will harm his reputation. Simpson decides to call the computer service and find out who entered the defamatory comment (the accuser used a name that was obviously a pseudonym). The computer service refuses to give out any information on its subscribers.

Since the accusations are completely false, Simpson wants to sue the person who made them. Because he can't identify the individual, he decides to sue the computer service company. After all, the service could have monitored entries to the bulletin board and filtered out irresponsible and slanderous comments. Should the computer service be liable for the contents of the bulletin board?

INTRODUCTION

Because computers and computer systems are powerful tools, they have powerful effects. When they fail, serious harm can be done. Humans may be physically harmed, money may be lost, reputations destroyed, time wasted, and so on, and when this happens, we want to know who is accountable. We want to know what went wrong, why it went wrong, and who will pay for the damages.

The responsibility issues surrounding computers are diverse and can be organized in different ways. We can distinguish the issues in terms of different parts of the technology: hardware, software, and information or data. The issues surrounding hardware generally have to do with who is responsible for defects in computers and what exactly should be guaranteed by the manufacturer. From a legal point of view these issues are not unique—computers are treated like other products that are bought and sold. Software is another matter, for software is a type of entity that did not exist before computers. Software has challenged our legal and moral notions of responsibility in a number of ways. It has not always been clear whether those selling software should be understood to be providing a service to users or selling a product, and in the American legal system this distinction determines which body of law applies. Moreover, some software is so complex (involving millions of lines of code) that no single individual can fully understand it; hence, some would say that no one can be responsible for it. Indeed, as mentioned in Chapter 1, some have suggested that a unique feature of software is its inherent unreliability. This unreliability arises from complexity.

Data and information pose yet another set of issues. As explained in Chapter 5 on privacy, erroneous personal information can have a significant effect on a person's life. Inaccurate information in an expert system might lead to financial losses. Defamatory comments are another form of information; when such information is electronic it can have much broader and more detrimental effects because it can be instantaneously distributed around the world.

Another way to sort out the responsibility issues surrounding computers is to organize them around the individuals involved in the production and distribution of software and electronic information. The primary parties here are the software creators and software users. (I am going to use the words "manufacturer" and "producer" to refer to those who create software.) The relationship between creators and users is rarely simple or direct and often involves intermediaries. More often than not, that is, the creator of the software is not a single individual but a team (or several teams) that are part of a company or agency, as in scenario 7.1. In addition to the primary parties, there are often intermediaries such as software vendors, consultants hired to assist in the purchase of software, managers of projects to develop a system for a unit in a company, and so on. In addition to producers and users there often are third parties who are affected (harmed or helped) by the software. For example, when an investment company uses an expert system as described in scenario 7.2, the company is the user, but retirees or future retirees will be affected by an error in or poor quality of the software. Hence, while the core relationship is that between producer and user, the lines of accountability are more complex, extending to intermediaries and third parties.

In this chapter, we will be concerned with liability for errors or malfunctions in software, and later with liability for information distributed in electronic bulletin boards. We will focus first on the relationship between the producer of software and the buyer. The analysis here will provide the basis for discussions later in the chapter of the liability issues that arise in scenarios 7.1 and 7.3. All of these issues are still being worked out in law, and they are likely to be around for awhile as our world becomes more and more dependent on computer technology.

DIFFERENT SENSES OF RESPONSIBILITY

Before we embark on these issues, it will be useful to clarify the meanings of the cluster of words that are used in addressing these issues: "accountable," "responsible," "responsibility," and "liable" and "liability." I am going to use "accountable" as the broadest of these terms. To say that someone is accountable for an event or mishap is simply to say that he is the appropriate person to respond when something undesirable happens. Just what he is accountable to do depends on a whole variety of factors that will become clearer later on.

Sometimes he is accountable simply to find out what happened and explain; other times he is accountable to go to jail or to pay compensation.

The terms "responsible" and "responsibility" are used to express a variety of ideas. At least four different uses must be distinguished. First, someone may be said to be "responsible" in the sense that she has "role-responsibility." A person has role-responsibility when she has a duty (or duties) in virtue of occupying a certain role. Parents are responsible for their children in this way. Police officers are responsible for the safety of a neighborhood. In Disciplinary Rule 4.2.1 of the old ACM Code, members were told not to "maliciously injure the professional reputation of any other person." This rule indicates a "responsibility" (a duty) to refrain from certain kinds of behavior because of one's role as a member of ACM.

A second important use of "responsible" is related to causality. Sometimes when we say that someone is responsible, we mean that he did something (or failed to do something) and this caused something else to happen. We say "John is responsible for the accident" meaning John did something that led to the accident. Causal responsibility is also attributed to nonpersons, that is, to natural events or conditions; for example, when we say, "the wind is responsible for the damage to the roof," we are picking out the wind as the factor that caused the damage.

Attributions of causal responsibility are rarely simple. In almost any situation we can imagine, an event or effect will be the result of a multitude of factors. We single out some element as making the crucial difference and consider this "the cause." Often it is a person's action or inaction that is singled out as the element that made the difference. So we say such things as: "John is responsible for the fire; he lit the match that started it" or "Her alarming speech is responsible for the panic." Any number of factors contribute to these events, and we assume most as normal conditions (e.g., oxygen was present when the fire started.) We find what we consider the non-normal factor and identify this as causally responsible for what happened.

A third use of "responsible" and "responsibility" is equivalent to "blameworthy." When we use "responsible" in this way, we claim that a person did something wrong, which led to the event or circumstance. For example, we might say of someone who has written defective code for a computer program, "He is responsible; it was his fault," And here we mean not just that he did something that caused something else; we mean that he did something he shouldn't have done and that is what caused the untoward event.

Blame is often correlated with causality and sometimes with role-responsibility as well. If you fail to smother your campfire and the smoldering embers lead to a forest fire, your blameworthy act causes an untoward event. You can become blameworthy for failing to fulfill a role-responsibility (except of course when there are extenuating circumstances). For example, we would think parents blameworthy if their child is malnourished (as long as there were no extenuating circumstances, such as poverty). The parents would be blame-worthy because they failed to fulfill their role-responsibility and their actions or inactions were the cause of the malnutrition.

Finally, a person may be responsible in the sense that she is liable. You are liable when you are the one that must pay damages or compensate those who are harmed by an event or action. There are two very important things to remember about legal liability. First, legal liability is often tied to one of the other senses of responsibility. A person may be legally liable for failure to fulfill a role-responsibility. For example, if a software vendor deceives a customer about the software being sold, the vendor may be liable to refund the price of the software and compensate the customer for losses incurred from the software failing to do what the vendor said it would do. Of course, the buyer may have to prove causal responsibility in order to establish the vendor's liability. For example, in the example just mentioned, the buyer would have to show that the losses incurred were the result of the software and not something else, such as poor management or employees who didn't know how to use the software.

The second important thing to keep in mind about legal liability is that it is not always tied to blameworthiness. The law often imposes what is called strict liability, which means liability "without fault." When strict liability is used, individuals or companies are liable (to pay damages or compensation) even though they did nothing wrong. This is particularly important to consider for software because, as mentioned above, some software is so complex that errors may slip through even though everyone did everything reasonable to test it. In some sense, no one is "at fault."

Although the focus here will be on legal liability, it is important to keep all the different senses of responsibility in mind.

HONESTY

We can begin to examine the accountability issues surrounding computers by examining the foundation of a relationship in which one person sells and another buys. The categorical imperative entreats us never to treat a human being merely as a means, and it may seem, at first glance, that when someone sells something to another, he is doing just that. In selling something, it would seem that you use the buyer as a means to making money. Remember, however, that the categorical imperative requires that we never treat another person *merely* as a means. By selling something to another person you may actually be doing something beneficial for her by providing her with something she wants or needs.

In a sense the categorical imperative constrains how we use others, rather than prohibiting it. Whenever we do anything to others, we must always recognize the others as ends—beings with needs, desires, their own plans, and the ability to make their own decisions. There is nothing wrong with selling something to others as long as you are honest with them about what they are getting and don't force them to buy. If you get people to buy something by deceiving them about what they are getting, or if you manipulate them into buying what they don't really want, then you are merely using them for your own ends. If, on the other hand, you give your customers accurate information—information that they need to decide whether or not to buy your product—and you don't pressure them, then you are recognizing your customers as beings with the capacity to decide for themselves. You are treating them with respect.

There is nothing inherently wrong, therefore, with selling computer software, or anything else, it all depends on how it is done. The vendor has a duty to be honest and not to coerce. (Duties also fall to the buyer, for example, to pay the amount promised, but we will not discuss these here.) This sounds very straightforward, but a little reflection reveals that neither honesty nor coercion are simple notions. Both admit of degrees.

Take honesty first. Yes, software vendors should not lie to their customers, but how much must they tell? We cannot expect them to tell everything—every detail of what is in the software. If this were carried to the extreme, prospective customers could simply go home and make the software themselves. Moreover, most customers don't want to know every detail. On the other hand, if we say that vendors need only answer questions asked by the customers, then there is some chance that the customers will not ask the right questions and find later that they haven't gotten what they wanted. So it would seem that some middle ground has to be found. Perhaps some information will be considered so obvious to the ordinary buyer that it need not be mentioned by the vendor, such as that Apple software won't work on an IBM machine. Other information will be considered irrelevant, for example, who worked on the software, what problems were encountered in development. The middle ground, it would seem, has to be tied to the notion of relevance to the buyer. That is, the vendor should supply the buyer with information that the vendor knows to be relevant to the buyer's decision. Oftentimes this means informing the buyer about the limitations of the software: what the software can do and what it can't do.

It is the same with coercion. Though it is highly unlikely to happen, it would be blatantly wrong for a software vendor to hold a gun to a customer's head and make the customer buy the software. There are more subtle ways that vendors can pressure customers, such as by offering them tempting "deals" that only hold for the next twelve hours and can't be voided after the purchase. It isn't easy to draw the line between coercive or manipulative sales techniques and those that recognize customers as freely choosing agents, but it is one that has to be drawn. Indeed, such lines have been drawn in law as well as in the courts.

CONTRACTUAL RELATIONSHIPS

At base, the producer- or vendor-buyer relationship is contractual in nature. One party (Party A) agrees to do certain things (usually to provide a product or service) and the other party (Party B) agrees to give money in return for the product or service. Often the relationship is established by means of a formal, written contract. When the contract is formal, the seller can be sued for breach of contract—for example, if a software system fails to meet the specifications outlined in the contract or in the time frame specified.

This, again, seems straightforward, but disagreements arise. In the early days of computing, buyers were often ignorant about computers and didn't know what to specify in the contract. These days buyers are more astute, or they hire lawyers and consultants to develop the specifications in the contract. Nevertheless, contractual issues arise having to do with what the seller is or is not obligated to do. An extremely complex body of case law has developed dealing with issues between manufacturers, vendors, and customers. This body of law employs concepts of implied warranties, express warranties and disclaimers, negligence, and strict liability.

Implied Warranties

You might think that people should be allowed to make whatever contract they like. That is, two parties ought to be allowed to agree to whatever conditions they find acceptable, assuming that each is honest with the other and neither is coerced. To a certain extent this is allowed by law, but there are limits. For one thing, there are laws which protect the customer by ensuring that he or she does not have to negotiate certain conditions of a purchase, they are always part of the purchase agreement (even when the agreement is not in writing). Implied warranties do just this. Under the category of implied warranty, two principles may be used as grounds for a legal suit: A product must have fitness for its intended purpose and it must be merchantable. Cases employing the principle of intended purpose often rest on evidence that the vendor knew what the buyer planned to use the system for and yet sold the buyer a system that was not suited for that purpose. In *Public Utilities Commission for City of Waterloo v. Burroughs Machines Ltd.*,[2] the court found that Burroughs had breached its implied warranty when it supplied hardware that was useless without the unsupplied software. The court held that the computer system was, therefore, unfit for the intended purpose. Burroughs was required to supply the software as part of the sale.

"Merchantability" involves fitness for the ordinary purposes for which the product is used. On this principle something sold as software must be capable

[2] See Larry W. Smith, "Survey of Current Legal Issues Arising from Contracts for Computer Goods and Services," *Computer/Law Journal*, 2611 (1979), p.479.

of doing what software ordinarily does. Breach of this warranty may be found when a system repeatedly fails or does not withstand normal shocks. The success of the merchantability claim often depends on additional factors such as a time period during which the purchaser is deemed to have accepted the system. But the courts have been fairly good in recognizing that buyers may spend some time and effort in trying to get a computer system working before they can conclude that the system is not "merchantable."

Implied warranties thus impose on software vendors a duty to sell software that is fit for its intended purpose and fit for ordinary purposes of software. Both of these legal principles seem to be connected with honesty in the sense that they require the vendor to provide the kind of product that the buyer implicitly expects. One might argue that the buyer is making assumptions that are never explicitly stated in the negotiation process, but the assumptions are quite reasonable given the context. For example, if you go to a software vendor in search of an accounting system that will work on an IBM machine, you explain this to the vendor, and the vendor suggests a product, it seems reasonable for you to expect that the package will allow you to put dollar amounts in and sum them in a variety of ways. And it seems reasonable for you to expect that these calculations will be made without errors, and without crashing your IBM-compatible machine.

Not only do these implied warranties seem fair to buyers but they serve the long-term best interests of software vendors. Because implied warranties lessen the risk that buyers have to take when buying computer software, they promote the buying of software. You would be more reluctant to buy software (or anything else for that matter) if you had no guarantee that what you were buying would come close to what the vendor said or what one might reasonably expect from a piece of software. In other words, without these implied warranties vendors would have a much harder time convincing customers to buy.

Many errors or malfunctions in software can be handled with the legal mechanism of implied warranty. Implied warranty, however, only ensures, in a sense, a minimum. When it comes to quality, the law is much less specific. Matters of quality are typically handled in a formal agreement.

Express Warranties and Disclaimers

Express warranties are elements of an agreement that are specified in writing. Generally these have to do with the quality of the software and what the manufacturer will do, if anything, to correct errors. An interesting and controversial element here is the use by software manufacturers of disclaimer clauses. Software manufacturers may alert the buyer to the limits of their guarantees with statements of the following kind: "There are no other warranties, express or implied, including but not limited to, the implied warranties of merchantability or fitness for a particular purpose." This means that the manufacturer makes no promises about the quality of the software and warns buyers that the manufacturer will not be liable for any faults beyond the implied warranties.

Manufacturers may also try to limit their liability by means of statements to this effect: "In no event will the manufacturer be liable for any lost profits or savings or other indirect, special, consequential or other similar damages arising out of any breach of this agreement or obligations under this agreement."

Courts generally recognize the validity of such clauses except when they find them to be "unconscionable." Literally, "unconscionable" means not guided or controlled by conscience; unscrupulous; excessive; unreasonable. This standard is not precise, it is not easy for a buyer to show that a disclaimer is excessive or unreasonable. In recognizing the legitimacy of disclaimers, the courts seem to be recognizing that buyers are rational, autonomous beings and, therefore, should be allowed to take risks if they want (as long as they are not deceived or forced). The appearance of the disclaimer statement in the contract serves as proof that the buyer was made aware of the risks.

As already mentioned, the use of disclaimer clauses is controversial. Many users see them as a mechanism that allows producers to avoid liability: All risk is transferred to the buyer. This would seem to tolerate, if not encourage, low standards for software. Why test and test before you put something on the market, when you can get it out there quickly with no consequence? On the other hand, the buyer is not being deceived or manipulated but is informed and agrees to take the risk. The buyer is thus making a free and informed choice, and it would seem wrong to interfere, except in extreme cases when the clauses are unconscionable. As well, we have to acknowledge that disclaimer clauses can have a beneficial effect insofar as they allow software producers to bring new software to the marketplace quickly. If software producers cannot disclaim any liability for quality, they will refrain from putting new, possibly useful or beneficial software into the marketplace until they are absolutely sure of every line of code. This makes the development cycle for software extremely slow and expensive. On the other hand, if software producers are allowed to develop software to the point at which they can stand by implied warranties but still can make disclaimers about other aspects of the software, they are more likely to get the software out quickly and it will be less expensive . One can argue that competition will be sufficient to keep the pressure on for improved quality.

Software: Product or Service?

American law treats the selling of products differently from the provision of services. When software first began to be sold, it was unclear which part of the law should be brought to bear. As we saw in Chapter 4 on property, software has challenged our traditional legal categories. Is software a set of mental operations implemented by a computer? Is it a set of electronic impulses? Is it a data set? Is it a process that a computer undergoes? A similar puzzle plagues liability law.

Those unfamiliar with the law might equate "product" with things that are tangible. Since software is in some sense not tangible, we could then say that it is not a product. The tapes and disks on which it is recorded are tangible, but the software itself is not. The problem is that the courts do not equate "product" with what is tangible, such things as leases and energy have been treated by the courts as products. Hence, we cannot rule out software as a product on grounds that it is not tangible.

We have to find some other way to decide whether software should be treated as a product or service, and we have to be careful not to assume that all software has to be treated one way or the other. One useful suggestion has been to use the distinction between "canned" software and customized software as the basis for distinguishing when software is a product and when it is a service.

Prince distinguished three different ways that software may be sold to a customer.[3] He makes an analogy with buying a suit. A customer may buy a suit that is ready to wear ("off the rack")—no alterations need to be made. Similarly, one may go to a computer store and buy a software package that is mass produced. This software is not supposed to be modified. Spreadsheets, games, graphics systems, and word processors are sold like this.

A second way that a customer may buy a suit is to have it made especially for him by a tailor. The customer goes to the tailor, tells the tailor what he wants, and the tailor makes the suit as specified. Analogously, a company may hire a person (or company) to build a computer system specifically for its use that will be designed to do what the customer specifies and will fit its special needs.

Finally, a customer may buy a suit "off the rack" and have it altered to fit her special measurements. In the same way, a company may buy a software system and arrange for it to be modified to fit the company's unique needs and circumstances.

Prince goes on to suggest that we might treat canned or packed software as a product and customized software as a service. The mixed case could then be treated as mixed. If there is a defect in the canned part, product law is brought to bear; if an error is made in the process of modification, we use the law dealing with services.

However, while this seems plausible, it is only intuitive at this point. We need some reason for drawing the distinction this way. Prince provides such an argument in examining the rationale for strict liability. Remember that strict liability is liability without fault. It is only used for products. If software producers were held strictly liable, then they could be sued for errors or malfunctions in software even when they had no reasonable way of knowing about these in advance, or preventing them. Prince argues that strict liability makes sense for canned software but does not make sense for customized software.

---

[3] Jim Prince, "Negligence: Liability for Defective Software," Oklahoma Law Review 33 (1980): 848–55.

He begins by asking what justifies us in imposing strict liability on those who sell products. [Strict liability applies to products under the Unified Commercial Code (UCC).] He identifies three factors that justify the use of strict liability, each having to do with the role or position of the manufacturer/vendor. First, to fall within the scope of strict liability, a thing has to be placed in the stream of commerce. This leads to a justification of strict liability on two counts: (1) Since the producer has placed the thing in the stream of commerce in order to earn profit, he or she should be the one that bears the risk of loss or injury and (2) since the producer has invited the public to use the product, implicit in the invitation is an assurance that the product is safe.

The second consideration is that the producer/vendor is in a better position than anyone else to anticipate and control the risks in the software, and thus imposing strict liability can have a positive effect. By holding producers/vendors strictly liable, we encourage them to be very careful about what they put into the stream of commerce.

Finally, the producer/vendor is in the best position to spread the cost of injury and risk of the product over all buyers by building them into the cost of the product. In effect, we make the producer/vendor pay for injury, knowing that he or she will recover this cost from the sale of the product. So instead of the burden being borne by those who are injured, it is spread to all who buy the product. When you pay for a product, you, in effect, pay for insurance. If you are harmed by the product, the producer/vendor will pay for it.

These three considerations show when and why strict liability makes sense. Strict liability imposes liability on the right person because it imposes it on the person who has made the product available in the first place, and this person is also in the best position to minimize risk and distribute costs. These considerations are consequentialist in character: We place liability where it will have a positive effect and discourage the release of dangerous, faulty products.

Now if we accept this justification for the use of strict liability, we can ask when, if ever, it makes sense to use it for software. None of these considerations seem to apply to customized software. Customized software is not placed by the vendor in the stream of commerce but rather is designed for a client at the client's request. Also, in this case, the producer is not necessarily in the best position to determine risk. The buyer may know more about the unique situation in which the software will be used than the systems designer. And, of course, if the software is just being sold to one customer, there is no issue of distributing the cost. Prince thus argues that it is inappropriate to use strict liability for customized software; hence, customized software should not be considered a product.

On the other hand, all three of these considerations do seem to apply to canned software. The producer places it in the stream of commerce, inviting use and hoping for profit. The producer is in the best position to anticipate dangers or errors. The producer is in the best position to distribute the cost of harm done by building it into the price of the software. Since it makes sense to use strict liability in the case of canned software, canned software ought to be treated as a product.

The mixed case (which is becoming more and more common) should be treated as mixed. If there is an error in the canned part, then this should be handled by laws that apply to products. If an error was made in the process of modifying the software, then this should be treated as negligence in providing a service.

Prince's argument seems quite sound and gives us a good deal of insight into strict liability law. Strict liability has been somewhat controversial in the law because it holds a person liable even when the person had no way of preventing whatever occurred. Our moral intuitions tell us that "ought implies can." We should not hold people responsible for failing to do what they were unable to do; yet that is exactly what strict liability seems to do. Of course, as always, things are more complicated.

The arguments generally given for strict liability are consequentialist in character. Strict liability has good effects. By threatening to make a person pay damages when a product is faulty, it encourages the person to take precautions before releasing the product. It encourages producers to be careful about what they put into the stream of commerce. So although strict liability is, in a sense, blind to what the manufacturer has done to make a product safe and reliable, it is imposed with an eye to pressuring manufacturers to make their products as safe and reliable as possible.

Also, strict liability does not seem unfair when it is used in civil law. That is, it would seem unfair to put people in jail for events or behavior they could not control, for example, to put a programmer in jail for failing to test a software package under every possible use. On the other hand, if programmers or systems designers are held civilly liable and are informed of this before they release a product, they can build the cost of this liability into the price of the software. They are not, then, personally harmed (punished) for failure to do something they had no way of knowing about.

If the preceding analysis is accepted, then canned or packaged software can be treated as a product and those who put it in the marketplace can be required by law to (1) be honest about their software, (2) live up to the implied warranties of fitness for intended purpose and merchantability, (3) not make unconscionable disclaimers, and (4) in certain circumstances be strictly liable. Customized software can be treated as provision of a service. The earlier discussion of honesty applies to the provision of a service as well. Other liability issues would be specified in a formal contract for services. Implied warranties would not apply. Most important, however, would be the issue of negligence, because, regardless of the contractual agreement, those who provide services have to provide competent services.

Negligence

Negligence is generally understood to be failure to do something that a reasonable and prudent person would do. It is based on common law, where it is assumed that people engaged in certain activities owe a duty of care. If a security guard is knocked unconscious by a burglar, we would not blame the guard for the robbery that takes place while he or she is unconscious. On the other hand, if the guard was drunk while on duty, making it easier for the burglar to break in and reach the guard so as to knock him or her unconscious, then we would say that the guard had been negligent in performance of his or her duties.

Negligence implies a standard of behavior that can reasonably be expected of any person engaged in a particular (often professional) activity. Programmers and systems designers are thought to have a duty of care in developing software. When they fail to do what can reasonably be expected of software developers, they can and should be considered negligent.

Of course, use of the concept of "negligence" to prosecute software developers poses a problem in determining what the prevailing standards are in the field. Generally, professional groups must develop their own standards because members will know better than anyone else what is reasonable to expect and what is blatantly a lack of competence. Typically, in court cases in which a professional is accused of negligence, members of the professional group will be called in to testify and establish standards in the field.

Testing is one area in which the issue of standards arises. A software developer may be accused of failing to test a piece of software adequately before releasing it to a client. The client would have to establish that the defendant had failed to do an amount or kind of testing that any reasonable, prudent software developer would do. Needless to say, it is sometimes difficult to identify prevailing standards for testing, especially in a field like software development wherein the technology continues to change rapidly. Moreover, testing procedures are likely to vary from one kind of software to another.

It is also important to note that standards are not entirely a technical matter but are as much a matter of ethics and social policy as they are of what is technically feasible. The analogy with other technologies should be obvious. When is an automobile safe enough? Automobile manufacturers can do any number of things to make automobiles safer, but additional measures of safety often increase the cost of the car, alter style, decrease fuel economy, and so on. Standards are set by balancing these factors against safety, by a mixture of marketplace feedback, government regulation, and competition. Technical feasibility is part of this, but remember that what becomes technically feasible is itself shaped by pressures from government (for example, fuel emission standards) and perceptions of what consumers want. Automobile companies invest in research that will help them meet targets set by government and appeal to customers.

Similarly, standards for the testing of computer software will balance a variety of factors. Testing levels, for example, will be a function of what is technically feasible now, what is reasonable to demand or expect, and what the social and economic effects will be of legally requiring that certain standards be met.

As with strict liability and implied and express warranties, therefore, negligence seems to be a morally acceptable legal mechanism. Whether it is just or unjust, of course, depends on the standards that are set. If these do not require software developers to do the impossible, if they ensure that software developers do not market blatantly unsafe or unreliable software, and if marketplace competition keeps the pressure on to develop better and better software and improve standards, then the use of negligence will help software development to flourish.

DIFFUSION OF RESPONSIBILITY

All of the preceding discussion focused on liability issues having to do with computer software as it is understood to be a relatively new entity in the marketplace. We now turn away from the buying and selling of software to the impact of computer technology on lines of accountability. All three of the scenarios at the beginning of this chapter depicted situations in which the lines of accountability became blurry or more complicated when computers were used. In scenario 7.1 creation and use of a computer program will aid in the design process but, at the same time, add a new branch of accountability. In scenario 7.2 the accountability of a pension plan manager is shaped in a new way by the introduction of an expert system. In scenario 7.3 we see individuals engaged in an activity that never quite existed before. That is, journalists talked to one another before and read each others' published work but never before through the medium of an electronic bulletin board. In this case, rules have to be established and/or implemented anew.

At the broadest level it seems that computers have a tendency to diffuse responsibility. In the early days of computing, there was some fear, expressed especially in science fiction (for example, in the film *2001*), that humans would lose control as computers took on more and more decision-making tasks. This fear was fed by organizations using their computers as the excuse for errors. For example, when customers complained about billing errors, companies would explain that their computer had made a mistake. This suggested that no person had done anything wrong and that the error was, somehow, beyond the company's control. Anyone who has experience with computers knows, however, that when "a computer makes an error," it is because the program being used is faulty, or because data was put into the computer incorrectly, or because the computer system was not being adequately monitored by a person.

Dismissing an error as the fault of a computer is a disturbing response, for it presumes that no humans are responsible for what the computer does. Indeed, if we treat computers as the locus of action and then presume that no humans are responsible for computers, then responsibility will be diffused and lost. But this will be a self-fulfilling prophecy, not a brute fact that we must accept. The thrust of the following analysis is to suggest that we should develop social conventions and expectations as well as laws and rules that assign responsibility for activities in which computers play a role, and we should do this with an eye to what will serve us best (rather than letting it happen as if it were following some natural course).

Admittedly, there are cases in which no human can fully understand what a computer system does. This is true when systems are designed in pieces— each piece may be designed by a different individual or team—and then the pieces are put together. It may happen as well when computer systems, in some sense or another, learn. For example, a person who designs a chess program that learns from each game that it plays may not be responsible (in some sense) for all the program's wins and losses, since the program comes to know more than its designer.

Such cases seem to defy our notions of responsibility. Nevertheless, a focus on these types of cases seems to lead us down the wrong path when they suggest that responsibility is an abstract, metaphysical notion following criteria independent of social choice. In fact, our notions of responsibility are much more a matter of social convention. Responsibility is assigned and designated. This will become clearer as we explore scenario 7.1. Scenario 7.1 raises a number of questions that are important to separate out. Suppose after checking out the programs produced by the programmers, the engineers use the programs to design a bridge. The bridge is built, and after only a few months, it collapses. A set of responsibility questions arise.

The first question is "Who is responsible?" It is important to note that this question is quite unclear. Using the distinctions made at the beginning of this chapter, it could be asking, Who is causally responsible? Or it could be asking, Who had role-responsibility to ensure the safety of the design? Or, Who, if anyone, was at fault? Or, Who is, by law, liable in this situation? I have posed these questions descriptively, but our "Who is responsible?" question might also be normative. We might ask, disregarding social or legal conventions, Who should be considered causally responsible? Who should be assigned role responsibility for safety? Who should bear the burden of liability in cases of this kind?

Several fruitful directions of analysis can be suggested here, directions of analysis that bring the complexity of the issues to light. First, it would make good sense in such a situation to try to trace back the chain of causality (causal responsibility). Indeed, one might argue that we cannot assign responsibility of any kind, and certainly not liability, until we figure out what happened and where, if anywhere, an error was made. Assuming the error was found to have been made in using the computer program, there is still a range of possibilities for who was "at fault." If the error was in the programming, the programmer's behavior will have to be scrutinized more carefully; if, on the other hand, the engineers gave the programmers inadequate information for design of the system, then the engineers will be likely candidates for being blameworthy and liable; if the engineers did not test the software after they got it from the programmers, then they, again, may be at fault; if, on the other hand, the county officials who hired the engineering firm to design the bridge did not give the engineering firm accurate information about the vehicles using the bridge, the range of weather conditions, and so on, then neither the engineers nor the programmers may have done anything wrong.

Notice that as I make these "if-then" statements, I am assuming a set of role-responsibilities: the engineers, I assume, have a duty to give the programmers accurate and adequate information from which to program the system; the programmers have a duty to write a program that works to the specifications given to them; clients (the county, in this case) must tell engineer-architects what conditions and uses to design for; architect-engineers must design bridges so that they don't collapse under expected, ordinary use; and so on. Any attempt to ferret out who was at fault will draw on presumptions about role-responsibilities and ultimately standards—standards of what competent programming is, what sound engineering practices are, what ordinary use is, and so on. In other words, while figuring out what happened and what went wrong is a starting place for our analysis, this starting place will itself be based on a complicated set of prior analyses—of role-responsibilities and standards.

Causal analysis is backward looking; that is, it looks at what happened. We might also want to consider this case in terms of setting some forward-looking precedents. We might want to ask where we should place "liability" so that it will do the most good. In assigning liability, we will in effect be alerting parties to their role-responsibilities. In other words, we want each party involved in the production of the bridge to be aware of what it is liable for. We can arrange liability so that it parallels causality, with each party legally liable for its work; or we can assign liability to the engineering firm so that it, in turn, must monitor and check the work of others. Or we can arrange liability in other ways. The point is that we should set up a system that has good consequences and is fair.

Returning to the question of the impact of computers on issues of responsibility, it seems that the introduction of a computer system in scenario 7.1 adds a layer of complexity. In addition to everything else involved in creation of a bridge, there is now the added issue of the software. Was it faulty? If it was faulty, how was the error brought in? How was the software used? and so on. Use of software adds another "set of hands," so to speak, to the many hands that were already involved in bridge building.

In a sense, this is not a unique characteristic of computers. Modern technologies generally are extremely complex and large scale—think of airplanes, skyscrapers, power plants, telephone systems, television networks, and so on. Creating such technologies typically involves dividing the task into pieces so that special expertise can be brought to bear on each piece. There seems no getting around the fact that large-scale endeavors involve many hands and many pieces. Computers are now an essential part of many of these technologies; hence, the "hands" of computer experts must be added to the lines of accountability.

LIABILITY IN BULLETIN BOARDS

Computer bulletin boards allow individuals with personal computers to communicate with one another over telephone lines on topics of special interest. Typically, an individual signs on to a bulletin board on a particular topic or chooses from a menu of possible interest areas and then posts messages or reads messages left by other subscribers. There are a variety of types of bulletin boards. Some are available through commercial computer services, such as CompuServe, which offer access to bulletin boards among an array of services; others are run by hobbyists who set them up on their home equipment; the government operates public boards, as well. It is difficult to estimate the number of electronic bulletin boards that now exist, but estimates range modestly up to 4500.[4]

Computer bulletin boards raise an interesting liability issue because they are a new form of communication. Jensen claims that computer bulletin boards have three unique characteristics: (1) The cost to set up an electronic bulletin board is much less than in other media, yet each bulletin board has a national reach; (2) electronic bulletin boards offer instant, multiple, interactive communication; and (3) in bulletin boards the "conversation" is written and anonymous.[5]

The situation described in scenario 7.3 suggests both the promise and the problem with electronic bulletin boards. On the one hand, they can be an enormously useful and entertaining resource, facilitating interactions among people, sharing of ideas, rapid communication, and so on. On the other hand, electronic bulletin boards can be used to instantly spread false, damaging, and criminal information across the world. The kinds of behavior that have become problematic in computer bulletin boards include defamation,[6] distribution of pornography, harassment, and posting of information that assists crime.

These forms of behavior are, of course, illegal off-line. They pose a special problem on-line because it is often impossible to determine who sent the message; we are, then, unable to use the criteria we ordinarily use in assigning responsibility. Consequently, some have suggested that we hold the bulletin board operator liable for the contents of the bulletin board. In the one criminal case that has been pursued, a user posted three stolen telephone access codes and encouraged subscribers to use them. The bulletin board operator

---

[4] Eric C. Jensen, "An Electronic Soapbox: Computer Bulletin Boards and the First Amendment," *Federal Communications Law Journal*, 39, no. 1 (1987), 220–1; Edward M. Di Cato, "Operator Liability Associated with Maintaining a Computer Bulletin Board," *Software Law Journal*, 4 (1990), 147.

[5] Jensen, "An Electronic Soapbox," pp. 223–4.

[6] Defamation is a form of libel. Libel, according to Charles, is the publication of a false, defamatory, and unprivileged statement to a third person by written or printed words or any other form of communication that has the potentially harmful qualities of written or printed words. See Robert Charles, "Computer Bulletin Boards and Defamation: Who Should Be Liable? Under What Standard?" *Journal of Law and Technology*, 2 (1987), 121–50.

was charged with violating a California penal code that punishes the publishing of credit card numbers. The operator denied any knowledge of the stolen numbers and eventually the charges were dropped.

While no statutes currently exist that directly regulate or license computer bulletin boards, a number of statutes are applicable to messages in electronic bulletin boards. For example, laws prohibiting child pornography and obscene, lewd, indecent phone calls may apply to messages in electronic bulletin boards. In addition, statutes addressing computer crime cover use of bulletin boards to commit crimes.

Holding bulletin board operators liable for the contents of their bulletin boards would not be wholly unfair. If it was conjoined with a licensing procedure so that operators would be informed of the law before they set up a bulletin board, it might simply be understood to be a form of strict liability. In effect, the law would say, if *you* (anyone) want to set up a bulletin board you may, but you will be liable for its contents. Those who go ahead must accept the risks.

However, whether we should in fact impose this sort of liability on bulletin board operators is another question. If we hold them liable for defamatory, harassing, or criminal messages, this will discourage individuals from setting up bulletin boards. (Some have already chosen to stop because of the potential liability issues.) Bulletin board operators would be forced to buy insurance to cover civil suits, and this would make bulletin boards much more expensive to set up. Certainly this practice would pressure operators to filter messages before they are posted. They would have to develop policies on what can and can't be included and then they would have to make sure incoming messages conform to these policies before they are posted for other subscribers.

The question of whether or not we should hold operators liable for the contents of bulletin boards poses a set of trade-offs. One of the benefits of this new medium is that it facilitates communication; some even say that it facilitates free speech in a way never possible before. Bulletin boards can be seen as small pockets of real democracy. Individuals talk freely to one another about the topics of the day without interference from anyone, which, some would argue, is much better than listening to mass media, which shapes (even distorts) information, appealing to the common denominator and promoting private interests. If we impose liability on bulletin board operators, we may well inhibit this free exchange. There is the real danger of a slippery slope here. As bulletin board operators filter out anything that looks defamatory, pornographic, or criminal, they start down a path that may lead to other forms of censorship. If this happens, then we lose the very thing the technology uniquely offers— unmediated communication between individuals anywhere in the world.

What will happen if we don't hold bulletin board operators liable? No one can see into the future—this new medium of communication is in its infancy and any number of things might happen. Consider some of the possibilities. Without any operator liability, it is possible that the potential of the medium will be undermined and ruined by irresponsible users who persistently input defamatory, harassing, or criminal messages. This in turn could lead to law enforcement agencies monitoring everything that goes on on-line, which, in turn, would significantly impede whatever privacy there may be in bulletin boards. Another possibility is that the quality of on-line discussion will deteriorate to such an extent that many individuals will opt out of using bulletin boards. We are already inundated with more information than we can handle—in newspapers, magazines, television, radio, discussions with friends, and so on. Electronic bulletin boards are yet another source of information, and if the quality of information is poor, many will simply choose other sources for information and discussion.

Another, perhaps more optimistic, possibility is that as a result of the problems already mentioned, a wide variety of kinds of bulletin boards will develop. Some will be unfiltered. When we sign on to one of these, there will be no guarantees about the quality of the information we well find. Other bulletin boards will be highly filtered; the operator will choose among submitted messages those which should be posted. Operators may select messages that are nondefamatory, nonharassing, noncriminal, and so on. Some operators will choose by content as well, intentionally shaping the dialogue to keep it on a certain level or within a certain domain. In between the unfiltered and highly filtered bulletin boards might be a variety of others with rules to suit diverse subscribers, purposes, and topics.

To see bulletin boards developing in this way is to see them developing along the lines of our newspaper and magazine system. We can buy newspapers filled with gossip and with very low credibility. Publishers of these are frequently sued for libel. At the same time, we can buy newspapers such as the *New York Times* and *Wall Street Journal,* whose publishers go to some lengths to check information before it is published. Readers know that the publishers select and shape the news. Or we can subscribe to professional journals on special topics, in which contributions from a narrow range of perspectives are filtered by a process of peer review. And so on.

Debate on the topic of operator liability has begun, at least in the law journals, and the arguments typically develop by making analogies between electronic bulletin boards and other forms of communication, such as common carriers, newspapers, traditional bulletin boards, and even social associations. Legal scholars look to how we have handled liability in these other forms of communication in the hopes of finding a principle or set of principles to use in this new case. In particular, the issue centers around whether First Amendment rights extend to electronic bulletin boards.

Although electronic bulletin boards are not exactly like any other form of communication, the analogies are provocative. Very briefly, when it comes to defamatory comments published in newspapers, publishers are protected under the First Amendment except when the defamatory statement was published with knowledge of its falsehood or with reckless disregard for its truth. In the case of common carriers, legislation specifically aims at not allowing the common carrier to interfere with communication. It is the users of the telephone rather than the telephone company who are treated as transmitters of a telephone message. Electronic bulletin boards might also be seen as a form of association. Individuals from across the country gather electronically just as a garden club, the Knights of Columbus, or a reading group might; such groups are entitled to constitutional protection.[7] Finally, the analogy with traditional bulletin boards is obvious. The courts have recognized that owners of traditional community bulletin boards "owe a duty of care to the public." This has meant that when a bulletin board owner has been informed about a defamatory message and he or she intentionally or negligently fails to remove it, the bulletin board owner is liable for republication.[8]

Bulletin boards are like and unlike each of these forms of communication, so that it is not easy to see which principles should apply to bulletin boards and when. There are important values at stake in what happens to electronic bulletin boards. We all have an interest in our First Amendment rights—we want free speech to flourish. Yet we also have an interest in protection from defamation, crime, and harassment. Balancing these will be difficult. We will shape bulletin board technology itself and balance these values as we shape legal liability for bulletin boards.

A FINAL NOTE

In Chapter 1 I suggested that computers are a mirror of our society and that the ethical issues they pose form a new species of generic problems. The discussion of liability for information in bulletin boards illustrates this point. While the physical form of communication is new, the problems are of a kind we have encountered before: false and damaging information, distribution of offensive materials, distribution of information assisting crime, and so on. Nevertheless, when activities are engaged in on-line, new rules, laws, and conventions are needed. We need to balance our old values in a new context. In this respect, electronic bulletin boards qualify as a "new species."

In general this chapter suggests that whenever we bring computers into an environment, we should anticipate issues of responsibility and liability. Many of the issues of liability will, no doubt, be settled in the courts through a process by which we find out, after the fact, what manufacturers, vendors, and users can be forced to pay. Some of this can be avoided by clarifying and assigning responsibilities and liabilities up front. The cost of neglecting these issues could well be a technology "out of control."

[7] Jensen, "An Electronic Soapbox," pp. 252–55.
[8] Charles, "Computer Bulletin Boards and Defamation," pp. 134–35.

STUDY QUESTIONS

1. Why do responsibility and liability issues arise around computers, computer software, and electronic information?
2. Distinguish four different meanings of the term "responsible."
3. How might legal liability be dependent on the different kinds of responsibility?
4. What does the categorical imperative require ofa those who sell software?
5. Explain the following terms:
   implied warranty
   merchantability
   express warranty
   disclaimer
   strict liability
   unconscionable
6. Explain Prince's argument for treating canned software as a product and the sale of customized software as provision of a service?
7. Can the use of strict liability ever be justified?
8. What is negligence? Why is it difficult to show that a software producer has been negligent?
9. How do computers diffuse responsibility?
10. How are electronic bulletin boards different than other forms of communication?
11. What are the potential benefits and problems with electronic bulletin boards?

CLASS EXERCISES/ESSAY QUESTIONS

1. Suppose you are on the staff of a state senator. The state senate is considering legislation to regulate electronic bulletin boards. The senator for whom you work for asks you to prepare a position statement on whether bulletin board operators should be held liable for the contents of their bulletin boards. Write up your analysis.
2. Develop a set of rules to be used by electronic bulletin board operators and users that might fend off regulation while maximizing the benefits of bulletin boards.
3. Consider scenario 7.1 or 7.2 or 7.3. Write an analysis that describes the problem depicted in the scenario and proposes a solution. Be sure to give reasons defending your proposal for a solution.

SUGGESTED FURTHER READINGS

CANGIALOSI, CHARLES. "The Electronic Underground: Computer Piracy and Electronic Bulletin Boards." *Rutgers Computer and Technology Law Journal,* 15 (1989), 265–301.
CHARLES, ROBERT. "Computer Bulletin Boards and Defamation: Who Should Be Liable? Under What Standard?" *Journal of Law and Technology,* 2 (1987), 121–50.

DI CATO, EDWARD M. "Operator Liability Associated with Maintaining a Computer Bulletin Board," *Software Law Journal*, 4 (1990), 147–59.

JENSEN, ERIC C. "An Electronic Soapbox: Computer Bulletin Boards and the First Amendment." *Federal Communications Law Journal*, 39, no. 3 (1987), 217–58.

NYCUM, SUSAN. "Liability for Malfunction of a Computer Program." *Journal of Computers, Technology and Law*, 7 (1979), 1–22.

SAMUELSON, PAMELA. "Liability for Defective Electronic Information" *Communications of the ACM*, 36, no. 1, 21–26.

CHAPTER 8

The Social Implications of Computers: Autonomy and Access

SCENARIO 8.1: POSITIVE FUTURISTIC VISION

It is the year 2020 and Professor Winder has just come into her office, a room in her house in San Francisco. Winder is a professor at an undergraduate college with administrative offices in New Jersey and students from across the world. As Professor Winder enters her office, she asks, "What's new?" and an automated voice tells her the messages that were left in her absence. Next, at her request, the voice tells her what she has scheduled for the day and lists any preparation she will have to do for meetings or deadlines in the future.

Professor Winder sits down and begins to work. She checks on her students first and finds a series of video communications from four of them. These communications consist of questions about last week's distribution and presentations they have prepared in response to an assignment. She replies to each. Then she prepares her distribution for this week. This takes some time as she pulls together text and video from her own files. This year she is covering new material so her files are not complete and she must call up various libraries throughout the world to find material to illustrate the points she wants to make. She downloads graphs and texts for the distribution to students.

SCENARIO 8.2: NEGATIVE FUTURISTIC VISION

In 1909 E.M. Forster wrote a powerful short story portraying the ultimate in our dependence on machines.[1] Patricia Warrick succinctly describes the world which Forster depicts as "an underground utopia where all needs and desires are fulfilled at the touch of a button. Each individual remains isolated in his cell, physically inactive, engaging only in intellectual activities. An elaborate global communications network using voice and picture permits remote communication with anyone in the world. No direct experience or communication is necessary or even desirable. Every event is tightly scheduled, controlled predictable, efficiently accomplished."[2]

The "Machine" that controls everything is beginning to break down and one of the unhappy characters explains to one who can not understand what is happening: "We created the Machine, to do our will, but we cannot make it do our will now. It has robbed us of the sense of space and of the sense of touch, it has blurred every human relation and narrowed down love to a carnal act, it has paralyzed our bodies and our wills, and now it compels us to worship it. The Machine develops—but not on our lines. The Machine proceeds—but not to our goal."[3]

INTRODUCTION

Many concerns have been expressed about the social impact of computers that go well beyond the topics discussed in the preceding chapters. At the heart of these concerns is a broad but unwieldy question about what is happening to the character and quality of our lives as a result of our widespread use of computers. This broad question encompasses many issues. Are computers making our lives better? Are they enhancing or eroding the values we hold most dear? Are they impeding or facilitating democracy? increasing safety or increasing risk? Are they making some of us better off at the expense of others? Do humans lose control as computers take over decision making?

Twenty or thirty years ago such questions might have been asked with an eye to deciding whether or not we should go forward with computer systems in such sectors as banking and government, or in such technologies as airplanes and power plants. That is rarely the issue today. Rather than asking whether we should go forward with computers, we now ask about the best ways to design, integrate, and use computer systems, and we look for better ways to deal with software ownership, privacy, liability, and so on.

[1] E.M. Forster, "The Machine Stops," in *Collected Tales of E.M. Forster* (New York. Alfred A. Knopf, 1947), pp. 144–97.

[2] Patricia S. Warrick, *The Cybernetic Imagination in Science Fiction* (Cambridge, Mass.: The MIT Press, 1980), pp. 44–45.

[3] E.M. Forster, "The Machine Stops," p. 176.

It would be impossible to discuss all the social effects of computers. And, indeed, some of the changes brought about by computers do not seem relevant for a text devoted to ethical issues. For example, the change from typewriters to word processors affects the work of secretaries and may affect the character of what gets written, but neither of these effects is ethical in character (at least not directly so). Similarly, when technologies such as automobiles, clocks, or airplanes switch over from mechanical to computerized parts, the character of those technologies is changed fundamentally, but this does not pose an ethical issue.[4]

Of course, in some sense ethics is concerned with what the good life is for human beings, and in this sense, all the social effects of computers are relevant to ethics. In particular, we have to be concerned about the cumulative effects of automating one sector after another of our society. The cumulative effects can easily slip through the cracks as we decide from the point of view inside each sector (the banking industry, the grocery store industry, the Internal Revenue Service, the transportation industry) that computerization looks beneficial, but then we end up with such an automated society that there is little room for human contact and individuality.

Social impact issues enter the domain of ethics in at least two other very direct ways. First, changes brought about by computers may affect precious values in our society. Chapter 5, on privacy, illustrates this point, but other values may be affected as well, such as democracy, equality, and autonomy. Second, social effects may enter the domain of ethics when the changes brought about by computers create a new territory that has to be organized and specified by rules, and the rules must be designed to create an environment that meets the requirements of morality, and to serve human well-being. We saw an example of this in Chapter 7 when we discussed liability for information in electronic bulletin boards. We saw, that is, how rules are evolving for this new environment and the rules need to be fair and to be shaped so as to protect civil liberties.

In this chapter, I explore a subset of the social effects of computing. The chapter is organized around values that are extremely important in our society—autonomy and access. These two values are crucial in a democratic society. In a sense, the starting place is with a Kantian conception of the value of human beings as ends in themselves, for this conception underpins the value of individual autonomy and the importance of democratic institutions. That is, this conception of human beings calls for a society in which individuals have opportunities to pursue their own plans for their lives and have a say in the governance of public institutions that directly and indirectly shape their lives. Just how computers are affecting individual autonomy is, then, the first concern of this chapter.

---

[4] In either of these cases, the change could have ethical consequences, if, for example, computerization of automobiles diminished their safety, or if word processing made writing less truthful; but, there is no reason to believe that all changes will have ethical implications.

The second concern is with access. It is counter to the value of individuals as ends in themselves that the autonomy of some be increased or improved at the expense of the autonomy of others. A just society is one in which freedoms and constraints, benefits and burdens are fairly distributed, and all individuals have access to opportunities to achieve their ends. This means, in particular, access to educational opportunities, and access to positions of authority and power. If the rules systematically skew things to the advantage of certain groups and to the disadvantage of others, then justice does not prevail.

Of course, although we aspire to the ideals of equal opportunity and just distribution, we do not always achieve them; hence, we must ask not just whether computers are *in principle* compatible with our ideals but whether they are *in fact* being used in ways that are moving us closer or further from our ideals, making our society more or less just.

As the issues of this chapter are discussed, it may be useful to return to the island analogy suggested in Chapter 1. Suppose you were one of the discoverers of the new island and it is now twenty years later. You, along with other members of the team that discovered the island, feel a strong sense of responsibility for its future. You all decide to get together and take stock of what has happened to the island. How is it developing? Is it becoming the place you had hoped it would become?

Something like this is much needed with regard to computers in our society. In a relatively short period of time—30 to 40 years—computer technology has been integrated into the fabric of the world. It touches the lives of every individual in one way or another. Information about you is entered into a database moments after you are born; you depend on computers when you drive a car, talk on the telephone, fly in an airplane, do your banking; many of you depend (or will depend) on computers in your work. Yet, we have had little public debate and little broad national or international planning for this technology.

We have let the market determine what applications are developed, the pace at which they are developed, who has access, and so on. To be sure, the market has been affected by privacy legislation and by property and liability law, which make it difficult to develop some of the potentials of the technology and easy to develop others. Nevertheless, these constraints on the market have come about in an ad hoc manner. A problem arises and we respond. For example, a problem arises with automated records of video rentals, we respond by passing legislation; a problem arises with computer hackers and we pass legislation. What we need, instead, is a vision of what we would like computer technology to do for us, and then a proactive plan for how to manage its development in that direction.

Now that we understand a good deal about its enormous power and potential, we would do well to have a public debate about the future development of computer technology. For example, in Chapter 5 I suggested that we think of personal information as part of the infrastructure of our society and that we manage it accordingly. We might do well to think generally about computer technology as infrastructure, and then manage its development, distribution, and integration to maximize positive effects, minimize negative effects, and gain efficiencies. This perspective might lead us to consider changes of the following kind: changing property laws to make more public domain software; investing in a national public network; establishing a personal information utility; ensuring that all citizens have access to terminals and certain databases in public libraries or post offices; and so on.

COMPUTERS AND SOCIAL CHANGE

Before we examine some of the social effects of widespread use of computers, we will find it useful to identify certain underlying assumptions that are often implicit in discussions of these effects. These underlying assumptions have to do with the role of computers in social change. Two examples illustrate. First, think about banking and ask whether it has changed fundamentally as a result of moving to a system in which funds can be transferred electronically. Some would say that banking has been radically and fundamentally altered in that the very meaning of "money" has changed. Money is no longer, at base, paper or coins; it is now electronic impulses. Others would argue that banking has not been transformed. The goals of the individuals involved and the character of the activities engaged in are essentially the same as before. Individuals aim to accumulate and exchange value and they move that value about to accomplish their plans. Whether that value is represented by coins and paper or by electronic impulses is insignificant. So, one underlying issue has to do with what counts as "real" or "significant" or "fundamental" change.

A second example has to do with the workplace. Is the workplace "revolutionized" when work changes so that workers now spend their time staring at computer screens and analyzing and interpreting symbols, whereas in the past they would use their bodies to move things about? Some would say there has been a fundamental change in that the knowledge needed to work has changed from being *embodied* to being *intellective*. A person has embodied knowledge when she knows with her body how materials and machines "feel" and "smell" and how they respond to her pulls or pushes. Instead of this, workers now interpret and manipulate symbols on a screen, using analytical skills and having little direct contact with the materials they are molding or the machines they are monitoring.[5] Others would argue that work has not really changed since businesses are still trying to make a profit by manufacturing and selling products or by providing services, employers are still telling employees what to do,

---

[5] The distinction between embodied and intellective knowledge is put forth by Shoshana Zuboff in *In the Age of the Smart Machine: The Future of Work and Power* (New York: Basic Books, 1988).

and employees are still trying to earn a living. Again the analysis tries to come to grips with what is significant change.

Below the surface of discussions of this kind is a set of interrelated issues about computers and social change, at least four of which can be separated out. (1) The first has to do with what is meant by "social revolution." What counts as "deep" or "fundamental" change, so that we would say it is revolutionary, and what counts as ordinary change, or superficial change? For many, social revolution means a change in political structure and in the distribution of power. Hence, when it comes to computers, the question is *not* just: Has the technology we use to produce things changed? Yes, we use computers instead of typewriters, robots instead of people. Rather, the question is: Has our social structure changed as a result of our use of computer technology? Has the employer-employee relationship changed? Has electronic banking altered the distribution of power? Remember here that computers are malleable so they can be fitted into an environment, rather than necessitating that the environment change to fit them.

(2) Related to the question of deep, fundamental change versus superficial or mere physical change is the second question: Do computers reproduce social patterns that already exist? If we look in particular at power relationships, we find some indication that computers, while changing the appearance or physical character of certain activities, reproduce old patterns of power and access (social hierarchies) and then entrench them even more deeply into the fabric of our society. This was suggested above in the work example. While we can argue that computers have changed the character of work, we can also argue that computers have given employers or managers more power to control workers. (Remember workplace monitoring devices, mentioned earlier). In this respect they may have solidified rather than changed the distribution of power in the workplace.

(3) A third issue has to do with whether it is computers or something else that cause social change. When we observe changes coming about in an institution, how do we sort out the role that computers have played? When it appears that computers are causing change, we have to remember again that they are malleable, and it may well be that other pressures and trends (existing long before computers) are determining the kind and direction of change, not computers per se. For example, one can argue that such things as competition (created by our market economy), pressure companies into using computers in the way they do. Companies are compelled to automate their operations and reduce the number of employees, and to gather as much personal data on consumers as possible, for if they don't, their competitors will, and they will be out of business. It is the competitive environment, then, not computers that brings about the change.

On the other hand, it is dangerous to suppose that computers are not an important factor in change. In Chapter 5 on privacy I noted that privacy is threatened not by computers per se but by the ways in which computers and information are used. At the same time I pointed out that we cannot dismiss computers as an insignificant factor in change since computers create possibilities to do things which could not be done without them.

(4) If this is the case, then computers may be a tool for change but may or may not be neutral with respect to the direction or character of the change. Hence, a fourth issue is whether computers are value neutral or value laden. Can we say that they can be used to bring about any kind of change, or do they have built-in biases that facilitate only certain kinds of changes or only change in a certain direction?

These are complex albeit extremely important issues. They are particularly difficult to resolve in the abstract. Only by coming to grips with particular examples can we even begin to sort them out.

AUTONOMY

As mentioned earlier, the Kantian notion of individuals as ends in themselves calls for a society in which the autonomy of individuals is recognized so that individuals have some degree of control over their own lives and some say in the public institutions that shape their lives. What, we should now ask, do computers have to do with this? Do computers enhance or erode autonomy? Do they enhance or erode democracy? Or, are they neutral with regard to these values?

Part of the answer has already been provided in preceding chapters. The discussion of privacy, for example, in Chapter 5 indicated how computers *can* be used in ways that significantly reduce the autonomy of individuals.When information about an individual is in the hands of organizations that will use the information to make decisions about the individual, and when the individual has no control over the information, then the individual loses autonomy in his or her dealings with these organizations. In Chapter 6 on hacker ethics, we saw how the autonomy of individuals might be enhanced through a network of computers that allowed individuals both to communicate with one another easily and to have access to vast quantities of information. At the same time, we saw how this potential of the technology might never be developed because of the activities of hackers or because of the activities of law enforcement agencies, or both.

These cases suggest that computers *can* be used to erode autonomy, but this does not mean that computers are inherently anti-autonomy. The effect that they have would seem to depend on how they are used. In order to get a grip on this matter let us take up the centralization-decentralization debate.

CENTRALIZATION-DECENTRALIZATION OF
DECISION MAKING

The notion of "centralized power" is tied to the notion of formal organizational hierarchies and decision making in these hierarchies. In any organization, whether it is a government, a government agency, a corporation, or a single workplace, there is usually a division of labor. Different units are assigned different tasks, and individuals within these units have designated domains of responsibility. The units are coordinated by means of an organizational structure designed to achieve the goals of the organization. Individuals at the top have the most overarching sphere of authority since they are responsible for the whole organization. Subunits have narrower spheres of responsibility; for example, in a corporation there may be units responsible for marketing, accounting, production, and training; and in a government, there may be divisions for budgeting, transportation, health and human services, commerce, and so on.

Generally, increased centralization of power is thought to occur when decision making authority is moved up the organizational hierarchy. Decentralization means just the opposite—decision-making moves down the hierarchy. In government, for example, when the locus of decision making moves from the individual to the local community, from the local community to the state, and from the state to the federal government, the individual has less and less control. The individual's input is more and more diluted. Similarly, in a company when the authority to make the decision on a particular matter moves from the salesperson, to the supervisor, or from the supervisor to a VP, or from a VP to the CEO, then decision making authority has been centralized. The authority of someone lower in the organizational hierarchy has been diminished.

In the late 1960s and early 1970s the first works on the social impacts of computers began to appear. While most expressed concern about privacy, several authors saw even the privacy threat as subsidiary to the threat of increased centralization of power. In a book that has now become a classic, *Computer Power and Human Reason* (1976), Joseph Weizenbaum suggested that many of our social and political institutions were becoming more centralized as a result of computers. Weizenbaum argued that many of our social institutions were under pressure to change after World War II because of the increased scale of operations. These institutions would have been forced to decentralize if computers had not come along when they did. For example, the stock exchange had grown to such an extent that the system was having difficulty handling the volume of activity taking place each day. There was pressure to move away from a system in which all activity was controlled by a single unit in one location. However, the computer came along just in time to allow the old system to continue; computers allowed the system to handle the increased (and increasing) level of activity.

Weizenbaum's speculation about the welfare system is also illustrative here. He writes:

> It may be that social services such as welfare could have been administered by humans exercising human judgment if the dispensing of such services were organized around decentralized, indigenous population groupings, such as neighborhoods and natural regions. But the computer was used to automate the administration of social services and to centralize it along established political lines. If the computer had not facilitated perpetuation and "improvement" of existing welfare distribution systems—hence of their philosophical rationales—perhaps someone might have thought of eliminating much of the need for welfare by, for example, introducing negative income tax.[6]

Weizenbaum's analysis is provocative. It suggests both that computers facilitate centralization of decision making, and that they prevent change rather than causing it. They prevent change by allowing us to continue to do things the way we had done them in the past, only on a larger scale.

Part of the concern about centralization of power can also be directly linked to the privacy issue. Many still fear that when government agencies have detailed records on individual citizens, they can use that information to control those citizens. To put this more abstractly, information is power, and more (information) power in the hands of government means less power for individuals. More power in the hands of those at the top means less power for those at the bottom.

Many of the concerns about centralization of power expressed in the 1970s were countered by computer enthusiasts who emphasized the potential of computers for democratizing our society. This potential became more and more apparent as microcomputers appeared, and as they became less and less expensive while they were becoming more and more powerful. Networking technology developed, as well, and its potential for linking individuals to one another became apparent.

The decentralists argued that computers, if used in the right way, can move information and decision making down an organizational hierarchy. An example often cited was that of having a computerized voting apparatus attached to televisions so that citizens might frequently vote on the issues of the day (after having watched the issue being debated).[7] Since then, a number of systems have been developed using computers together with closed circuit television to recreate town meetings and other forms of increased communications between citizens and political leaders.[8]

The question whether computers bring about more centralization or more decentralization of power is complicated because decision making may

---

[6] Joseph Weizenbaum, *Computer Power and Human Reason.* W.H. Freeman, 1976, pp. 30–31.

[7] Robert Paul Wolf mentions this in In Defense of Anarchism. HarperCollins, 1970.

[8] Christopher F. Arterton, *Teledemocracy: Can Technology Protect Democracy?* Sage Publications, 1987.

be centralized and decentralized in different ways. If local units of a national welfare system make the decisions about who qualifies for benefits, it appears that the decision is decentralized. However, if the decisions of the local unit must conform to detailed formal guidelines specified by a federal agency in Washington, D.C., then the decision making is decentralized only in a superficial way. The formal guidelines given from above effectively determine the local decision.

Suppose a large company with many outlets computerizes its inventory control system and as a result, individual stores lose control of their inventory. Each day cash register information (from each and every store) is sent to the main system which is maintained by a group of computer professionals located at the company's headquarters. The system keeps track of supplies at every store and makes decisions on when and what to send to each store. Decision-making power has been taken out of the hands of store managers.

It appears that we have here a simple case of centralization of decision-making, but there are ways in which the change might be viewed as decentralizing. For one thing, by having inventory decisions made automatically by a computer, a local store manager is freed to do other things. He or she is empowered in the sense of having more time to be active in the store, to better supervise employees, to have more contact with customers, and so on. Also, if the computer system was designed through a process that involved store managers, the system would incorporate the values and preferences of managers.

Yet another example is that of expert systems. An expert system, say, a medical diagnosis system, can incorporate the wealth of experience of hundreds of the best doctors in the world. Such a system could be made available to individual practitioners anywhere in the world. This might be seen as boosting the decision-making ability of individual doctors enormously. However, while it would increase their knowledge, it would not necessarily increase their autonomy. If the automated medical diagnosis system gained so much credibility that it defined standards in a field of practice, then doctors would have to follow the computerized diagnosis for fear that if they did not, they might be sued for malpractice. In other words, if an expert system gains too strong a foothold in a field, its effect would be to centralize decision making rather than to increase the autonomy of individual practitioners.

It would seem that those who fear centralization of power from computers are thinking of computers in the hands of those who already have power, that is, government, managers, employers; those who see computers as the great democratizers are thinking of computers in the hands of individuals. Whether or not computers cause centralization or decentralization of power is an extremely complex matter. Moreover, it is one thing to claim that *computers by their very nature cause centralization of power* (or decentralization of power), and it is quite another to claim that *people tend to use computers in ways that bring about centralization* (or decentralization).

One possibility here is that computers, by their nature, are neutral with regard to centralization-decentralization, but because it is generally the already powerful that get computers first (or get the best computers and software first), computers tend to be used to favor those already in power. Those already in power—those at the top—will typically (though not always) use computers to obtain more control; hence, there will be more centralization.

Most recently George and King (1991) have argued that it is no longer useful to frame the debate in terms of centralization and decentralization. Initially they identify four alternative positions: (1) computers cause centralization; (2) computers cause decentralization; (3) computerization and centralization are unrelated; and (4) computerization reflects centralization. After emphasizing the powerful role of management decisions in structuring the use of computers George and King argue for what appears to be a version of (4).

> At the broadest level, features of the environment such as availability of technology and expertise, social and legal structures, and community opinion shape both what is possible and what is desirable regarding both decisions authority structures and use of computing technology. Moving to the organizational level, each organization's history further shapes the opportunities and constraints surrounding organizational structure and use of technology. Finally within this web of opportunities and constraints, management can exercise significant influence on the specific choices of decision authority structure and the uses of computing technology to reinforce those choices. The causal relationships in this milieu are not uniformly clear or consistent. Instead, what emerges is a strong and observable tendency toward use of computing technology to reinforce the decision authority status quo.[9]

This is important to keep in mind. At the same time, we should not, as suggested earlier, neglect potential cumulative effects. If significant decision making authority is taken away from individuals in the workplace, and then taken away from them when it comes to public decision making (for example, as computer decision procedures are used to determine public policy), and then taken away from them in the marketplace (as companies interpret cash register receipts and thereby select what is advertised to an individual), and so on, we will end up with a society which might give "lip service" to individual autonomy, but in fact has little.

ACCESS

Computers as a Resource

The centralization-decentralization debate focuses on how computers structure a decision-making environment, but computers are powerful tools for many other purposes. They can be used in education, business, medicine, government, manufacturing, communicating, monitoring, and so on. The bot-

---

[9] Joey F. George and John L. King, "Examining the Computing and Centralization Debate," *Communications of the ACM* 34, 7 (July 1991), 70.

tom line is that computers are a resource, a resource for achieving an organization's or individual's ends. From this arises the question of who has (and should have) access to this powerful resource. How should this resource be distributed in our society? in the world?

We live in a world in which we must compete for many of the things that we most need and want. We must compete for educational opportunities, for jobs, for customers or clients, for protection of our interests, for wealth, and so on. It hardly needs saying that in a competitive environment, those who have access to powerful tools (resources for achieving their ends) are better off than those who do not. One of the concerns that has been expressed about the social effects of computers is that they have widened (and will continue to widen) the gap between the haves and the have-nots, in our society and in the whole world.

This point can be illustrated in a number of different contexts. College students who bring personal computers to college may have an advantage over those who cannot afford to buy a personal computer; start-up companies with few resources are at a disadvantage in competing with large companies that can afford to automate their production activities, and purchase and use large databases of potential customers for their marketing activities; industrialized countries like the United States can overpower Third World rivals with very sophisticated computerized surveillance technologies and weapons; and so on.

In one sense, this is nothing new—the same could be said about many resources. It is usually the wealthy and powerful who first get access to new medical technologies; children in wealthy neighborhoods have access to the newest and best textbooks; large, established companies benefit from efficiencies of scale in production; industrialized countries use their wealth and knowledge to secure their interests. In this respect, the impact of computers is nothing new or unique, computers are simply the latest powerful resource to be used.

Some may counter this claim by pointing out that computers are different, because they are not a "scarce" resource. As mentioned earlier, they have become cheaper and cheaper as they have become more and more powerful. In a short period of time, they have become relatively inexpensive and, hence, are abundant and available to many. Computers have become easier to use, as well, so that you do not need advanced training to take advantage of many applications.

Still, whether or not computers are expensive or cheap, hard or easy to use, scarce or abundant are all relative matters. Computers certainly are not equally distributed among citizens of this country or among countries of the world. Distribution of computers does not follow some natural order arising from their character but is determined by social, economic, and political factors. In the United States, computers are distributed through our market economy.

In Chapter 4 we discussed how property rights in the U.S. are designed to encourage invention: companies design hardware and software, and our patent, copyright, and trade secrecy laws protect these companies so that they can put their products into the stream of commerce. If the hardware or software is something that consumers want or need (and if there is no better, cheaper product that does the same job), then there is a good chance that the product will sell.

There is, however, one catch. Consumers who want or need the technology must have the money to pay for it. This is no small point. In a capitalist economy: Things are not produced unless there is someone to pay for them. For example, software and hardware have enormous potential to help the disabled, but since the disabled are not all rich, this potential will not be realized, at least not through the market alone. Computer applications for the disabled arise when insurance companies and government policies assure that the new technology will be paid for. Government can spur this development in a number of ways, such as by subsidizing research in the field, or by providing funds (through Medicare) to the disabled for purchase of technology that makes their lives better.

Nevertheless, the point is that while computers and computer software have the potential for innumerable (possibly infinite) applications, only a subset of these applications is likely to be developed, and it is cultural, political, and economic factors that will largely determine which directions and which applications are developed. Hence, while it is possible in principle for software to be developed to help the have-nots, such software is *less* likely to be developed because the have-nots cannot pay.

To illustrate, imagine a software system that would help the newly unemployed identify what benefits they qualify for and then would assist an individual in navigating his or her way through various state and federal bureaucracies. It could identify offices to be contacted, procedures for application, timeframes, where and how to appeal negative decisions, and so on. The system would help ensure that unemployed citizens would receive the full benefits to which they are entitled. To be sure, such a system might be expensive to develop, but it would not be technically difficult to create. The question is, why isn't it being developed? The answer, I believe, is that those who would use such software could not afford to buy it. In other words, there is no market for such a system.

In a sense, this points to a flaw in capitalism, but that is not the important point for our purposes. Rather, the thing to remember is that many of the potentials of computer technology may never be realized. It is social context that shapes the development of the technology and determines which applications are developed.

Computers for Information

We are led to the same conclusion when we focus on computers as a means of access to information. That "information is power" has now become a cliché in our society. It is a statement that can be debunked in certain contexts, but in a competitive environment there is a good deal of truth to it. Think of businesses competing for customers or politicians competing for votes. The more information they have about potential customers or about voters, the better they are able to reach them. Think also about libraries and educational institutions brought into every citizen's home, and about a public network through which individuals could tap into information and discussion on whatever topic they chose. These uses of the technology could create a better informed and better educated citizenry than ever before.

In this respect, the technology has the potential to enhance democracy. Will this potential be realized? Perhaps. But it will not happen by some natural course of technological development. It will take an enormous public and political effort (and investment) to put such a system into place. Computer technology has the potential to enhance democracy and to equalize access to information, to help the disabled and the have-nots, but these potentials will only be realized by conscious action in the form of public policy and personal and professional choice.

ARE COMPUTERS VALUE LADEN?

The issues of autonomy and of access touch on another question about computers, and that is whether they are value neutral or value laden. If computers favor centralization, that is a value; if they favor those already in power, that is a value.

There are several different ways in which computers are uncontroversially value laden. Systems designers often intentionally design systems to favor some or promote particular values. For example, an inventory control system might route new inventory to stores with the lowest inventory, favoring those stores. A computer system used in college admission might list applicants in order of highest SAT scores or highest grade point average, so that the admissions office can respond to the "best" students first. These systems are value laden, though they are laden with the values that the designers and users choose to build in. Favoring stores with the lowest inventory and students with the highest SAT scores is thought by the users of the system to be appropriate.

Of course, concerns about the value ladenness of computer systems generally do not have to do with these sorts of values, but with values that are considered "biases." (I use "bias" here to refer to values that are thought to be inappropriate or unfair.) Bias may be built in intentionally or unintentionally. For example, the admissions system that lists male applicants with a certain grade point average before female students with the same grade point average might be "biased." Likewise, an inventory system that routes inventory to stores in white neighborhoods before stores in black neighborhoods is biased, and it is difficult to imagine this being done unintentionally.

Often, when the issue of value ladenness arises, the question is whether computer systems by their very nature favor certain values. The one argument that might be made to show that computers have an inherent bias is the claim that computers skew things toward the quantitative. This was a fear expressed in the early days of computing. Those who expressed this concern usually had in mind simulation and statistical analysis systems. They worried that such analyses would always lack something because computers only take as input that which can be put into quantifiable form.

For example, suppose a politician uses a survey of her constituency to decide how to vote on an issue. A questionnaire is distributed and the responses to each question are coded as numbers 1-5. In other words, five possible responses are identified and a person filling out the questionnaire can mark any of the five possible responses to each question. The politician might receive the results of the survey in the form of a summary that tells her how many people indicated 1, 2, 3, 4, or 5 in response to each question. More likely, she would receive an average score for each question.

The process of summarizing the data in this form filters and may even distort the information. Some would say a good deal is lost when answers to a questionnaire are coded in this fashion. Indeed, if a politician looks only at this summary data, never talks to her constituency, and doesn't even read comments that have been written in on the questionnaire, she would not get a good picture of what people are thinking.

One may object here that the poor quality of the data has less to do with computers and more to do with the use of questionnaires. Moreover, it can be argued that there is a good deal to be gained from such studies. Without the aid of a computer, the politician would not have access to the thoughts of nearly as many people. She would not have time to read individual responses to a questionnaire filled out by thousands of people. The process of quantifying and summarizing provides a *quantity* of information that a person could not deal with otherwise. The quality of the data may well be sacrificed in the process, but there is also something to be said for hearing more people. Quality seems to be traded off against quantity.

The argument that computers favor the quantitative has not been made in recent years, and one cannot help but wonder whether the quantitative has simply won out, so that it is now considered the most valuable in any process. Have you heard the saying, "If you can't measure it, it does not exist"?

At the same time that this issue has become more invisible, computers are being used more and more in decision making. Computer systems are now an important part of the decision making process in many public and private sectors. Think, for example, of the complex computer models used in investing, planning for national health care, controlling air traffic, reducing the national debt. Computer systems used in these activities may incorporate thousands of factors (modelling the interactions of these factors) so as to predict what will happen if there is a change in the real world, a change in interest rates, or a change in the weather, depending on the context. Typically such systems have difficulty taking into account important human values such as the value of human life, aesthetic value, the importance of leisure time, national pride. When such systems do incorporate such values, they do so by assigning a dollar value to them. For example, in the computer models used to plan for our national forests, use of land for recreational purposes is assigned a dollar value so that this use can be compared to using the land for lumbering. And, we have all heard about computer models that evaluate the risks of certain undertakings by putting a dollar value on the occurence of certain diseases so that the costs (in terms of human health) can be balanced against the benefits of the undertaking—for example, building a hazardous waste disposal facility in a neighborhood, or producing a product that depletes the ozone.

As mentioned earlier, studies of this kind can be very valuable. The problem is that those who use these studies should understand their limitations when they are used in decision making.

Perhaps, the most important thing to remember in the debate about the value ladenness of computers and computer systems is that to a large extent it does not matter whether the values are inherent in the computer or put into systems when they are designed and used. Values are embedded in computer systems and we ought to be well aware of this when we use them. Those who design systems ought, in particular, to be sensitive to the values they are building in.

COMPUTER PROFESSIONALS

In the end, whether or not computer technology promotes or erodes autonomy, whether or not access is equal or biased all depend on how the technology is developed, designed, and used. In this regard there is no doubt that computer professionals have an important role to play. As computers become more and more a part of our society and as we become more and more dependent upon computer systems, we become more and more dependent on *computer professionals*. Within organizations computer professionals exercise power in how and for whom they design systems. As computing becomes an integral part of an organization, organizations become more dependent on the computer professionals who maintain the computers. As our society becomes more dependent on computers, we all come to rely on computer professionals to ensure the smooth functioning of our social institutions.

In Chapter 3 I argued that we need computer professionals to act for the good of humanity. Hence, we cannot leave this chapter without returning to the theme of Chapter 3 on the social responsibilities of computer professionals. Because of their special expertise and their positions, we need computer professionals to see themselves as having a special duty to exercise their power with special care.

It would be ideal if we could say that computer professionals are in the best position to anticipate the effects of computers on power and access. Then we could argue that computer professionals have a duty to bring these effects to the attention of their clients, employers and the public. However, the matter is not so simple. Computer professionals do, of course, work most closely with computers, but they are not always trained to see and understand the social effects of their work. Moreover, some of the effects are not immediate or apparent and thus it is hard to argue that computer professionals bear the entire burden of anticipating and controlling the social effects of computers.

Still, the more computer professionals can do, the better. There seems little doubt that our society will be better served if computer professionals are sensitive to the social effects of computers. In addition, we will be served by computer professionals acting as a group on matters of public interest. Some may see this as a threat to business, but it seems rather to be a matter of the profession taking a leadership role in the future development of the technology.

STUDY QUESTIONS

1. How does a Kantian conception of the value of human beings lead to a focus on autonomy and access?
2. What questions or issues often underlie analyses of computers and social change?
3. What is centralization of power? What is decentralization of power? Give examples of how computers might cause each.
4. Why do computers affect the relationship between haves and have-nots? Explain.
5. Why aren't computer systems likely to be developed for the have-nots unless some deliberate social efforts are made?
6. Explain how computer systems may be value laden versus their being biased?

ESSAY QUESTIONS/EXERCISES

1. Imagine that you were part of a team that developed the first computers. You are having a reunion to take stock of your creation and develop guidelines to shape future development. Each member has been asked to write a statement presenting his or her ideas. Write yours.
2. Are computers causing a social revolution? Be sure to consider both sides of the issue. That is, whether you say "yes" or "no" or "both," consider what someone on the other side would say and respond.
3. Do computers reinforce social patterns of power and access? Again consider arguments on both sides and explain what you think.

SUGGESTED FURTHER READINGS

DUNLOP, CHARLES, and ROB KLING. *Computerization and Controversy Value Conflicts and Social Choices.* Orlando, Fla.: Academic Press, 1991.

FORESTER, TOM (ed.). *Computers in the Human Context: Information Technology, Productivity, and People.* Cambridge, Mass.: MIT Press, 1989.

GEORGE, JOEY F. and JOHN L. KING. "Examining the Computing and Centralization Debate," *Communications of the ACM,* July 1991 34, 7, 62–72.

WEIZENBAUM, JOSEPH. *Computer Power and Human Reason.* New York: W. H. Freeman, 1976.

ZUBOFF, SHOSHANA. *In the Age of the Small Machine: The Future of Work and Power.* New York: Basic Books, 1988.

Appendix: Codes of Professional Ethics

ACM CODE OF ETHICS AND PROFESSIONAL CONDUCT*

Preamble. Commitment to ethical professional conduct is expected of every member (voting members, associate members, and student members) of the Association for Computing Machinery (ACM).

This Code, consisting of 24 imperatives formulated as statements of personal responsibility, identifies the elements of such a commitment. It contains many, but not all, issues professionals are likely to face. Section 1 outlines fundamental ethical considerations, while Section 2 addresses additional, more specific considerations of professional conduct. Statements in Section 3 pertain more specifically to individuals who have a leadership role, whether in the workplace or in a volunteer capacity such as with organizations like ACM. Principles involving compliance with the Code are given in Section 4.

The Code shall be supplemented by a set of Guidelines, which provide explanation to assist members in dealing with the various issues contained in the Code. It is expected that the Guidelines will be changed more frequently than the Code.

The Code and its supplemented Guidelines are intended to serve as a basis for ethical decision making in the conduct of professional work. Secondarily,

* Adopted by ACM Council. October 16, 1992.

they may serve as a basis for judging the merit of a formal complaint pertaining to violation of professional ethical standards.

It should be noted that although computing is not mentioned in the imperatives of section 1.0, the Code is concerned with how these fundamental imperatives apply to one's conduct as a computing professional. These imperatives are expressed in a general form to emphasize that ethical principles which apply to computer ethics are derived from more general ethical principles.

It is understood that some words and phrases in a code of ethics are subject to varying interpretations, and that any ethical principle may conflict with other ethical principles in specific situations. Questions related to ethical conflicts can best be answered by thoughtful consideration of fundamental principles, rather than reliance on detailed regulations.

1. General Moral Imperatives.   As an ACM member I will . . .

1.1   Contribute to society and human well-being.
1.2   Avoid harm to others.
1.3   Be honest and trustworthy.
1.4   Be fair and take action not to discriminate.
1.5   Honor property rights including copyrights and patents.
1.6   Give proper credit for intellectual property.
1.7   Respect the privacy of others.
1.8   Honor confidentiality.

2. More Specific Professional Responsibilities.   As an ACM computing professional I will . . .

2.1   Strive to achieve the highest quality, effectiveness and dignity in both the process and products of professional work.
2.2   Acquire and maintain professional competence.
2.3   Know and respect existing laws pertaining to professional work.
2.4   Accept and provide appropriate professional review.
2.5   Give comprehensive and thorough evaluations of computer systems and their impacts, including analysis of possible risks.
2.6   Honor contracts, agreements, and assigned responsibilities.
2.7   Improve public understanding of computing and its consequences.
2.8   Access computing and communication resources only when authorized to do so.

3. Organizational Leadership Imperatives.   As an ACM member and an organizational leader, I will . . .

3.1   Articulate social responsibilities of members of an organizational unit and encourage full acceptance of those responsibilities.
3.2   Manage personnel and resources to design and build information systems that enhance the quality of working life.

3.3   Acknowledge and support proper and authorized uses of an organization's computing and communication resources.

3.4   Ensure that users and those who will be affected by a system have their needs clearly articulated during the assessment and design of requirements; later the system must be validated to meet requirements.

3.5   Articulate and support policies that protect the dignity of users and others affected by a computing system.

3.6   Create opportunities for members of the organization to learn the principles and limitations of computer systems.

4. Compliance with the Code.   As an ACM member, I will . . .

4.1   Uphold and promote the principles of this Code.

4.2   Treat violations of this code as inconsistent with membership in the ACM.

GUIDELINES

1. General Moral Imperatives.   As an ACM member I will . . .

1.1   Contribute to society and human well-being.
This principle concerning the quality of life of all people affirms an obligation to protect fundamental human rights and to respect the diversity of all cultures. An essential aim of computing professionals is to minimize negative consequences of computing systems, including threats to health and safety. When designing or implementing systems, computing professionals must attempt to ensure that the products of their efforts will be used in socially responsible ways, will meet social needs, and will avoid harmful effects to health and welfare.

In addition to a safe social environment, human well-being includes a safe natural environment. Therefore, computing professionals who design and develop systems must be alert to, and make others aware of, any potential damage to the local or global environment.

1.2   Avoid harm to others.
"Harm" means injury or negative consequences, such as undesirable loss of information, loss of property, property damage, or unwanted environmental impacts. This principle prohibits use of computing technology in ways that result in harm to any of the following: users, the general public, employees, employers. Harmful actions include intentional destruction or modification of files and programs leading to serious loss of resources or unnecessary expenditure of human resources such as the time and effort required to purge systems of "computer viruses."

Well-intended actions, including those that accomplish assigned duties, may lead to harm unexpectedly. In such an event the responsible person or persons are obligated to undo or mitigate the negative consequences as much as possible. One way to avoid unintentional harm is to carefully consider potential impacts on all those affected by decisions made during design and implementation.

To minimize the possibility of indirectly harming others, computing professionals must minimize malfunctions by following generally accepted standards for system design and testing. Furthermore, it is often necessary to assess the social consequences of systems to project the likelihood of any serious harm to others. If system features are misrepresented to users, coworkers, or supervisors, the individual computing professional is responsible for any resulting injury.

In the work environment the computing professional has the additional obligation to report any signs of system dangers that might result in serious personal or social damage. If one's superiors do not act to curtail or mitigate such dangers, it may be necessary to "blow the whistle" to help correct the problem or reduce the risk. However, capricious or misguided reporting of violations can, itself, be harmful. Before reporting violations, all relevant aspects of the incident must be thoroughly assessed. In particular, the assessment of risk and responsibility must be credible. It is suggested that advice be sought from other computing professionals. See principle 2.5 regarding thorough evaluations.

1.3 Be honest and trustworthy.

Honesty is an essential component of trust. Without trust an organization cannot function effectively. The honest computing professional will not make deliberately false or deceptive claims about a system or system design, but will instead provide full disclosure of all pertinent system limitations and problems.

A computer professional has a duty to be honest about his or her own qualifications, and about any circumstances that might lead to conflicts of interest.

Membership in volunteer organizations such as ACM may at times place individuals in situations where their statements or actions could be interpreted as carrying the "weight" of a larger group of professionals. An ACM member will exercise care to not misrepresent ACM or positions and policies of ACM or any ACM units.

1.4 Be fair and take action not to discriminate.

The values of equality, tolerance, respect for others, and the principles of equal justice govern this imperative. Discrimination on the basis of race, sex, religion, age, disability, national origin, or other such factors is an explicit violation of ACM policy and will not be tolerated.

Inequities between different groups of people may result from the use or misuse of information and technology. In a fair society, all individuals would have equal opportunity to participate in, or benefit from, the use of computer resources regardless of race, sex, religion, age, disability, national origin or other such similar factors. However, these ideals do not justify unauthorized use of computer resources nor do they provide an adequate basis for violation of any other ethical imperatives of this code.

1.5   Honor property rights including copyrights and patents.
Violation of copyrights, patents, trade secrets and the terms of license agreements is prohibited by law in most circumstances. Even when software is not so protected, such violations are contrary to professional behavior. Copies of software should be made only with proper authorization. Unauthorized duplication of materials must not be condoned.

1.6   Give proper credit for intellectual property.
Computing professionals are obligated to protect the integrity of intellectual property. Specifically, one must not take credit for others' ideas or work, even in cases where the work has not been explicitly protected by copyright, patent, etc.

1.7   Respect the privacy of others.
Computing and communication technology enables the collection and exchange of personal information on a scale unprecedented in the history of civilization. Thus there is increased potential for violating the privacy of individuals and groups. It is the responsibility of professionals to maintain the privacy and integrity of data describing individuals. This includes taking precautions to ensure the accuracy of data, as well as protecting it from unauthorized access or accidental disclosure to inappropriate individuals. Furthermore, procedures must be established to allow individuals to review their records and correct inaccuracies.

   This imperative implies that only the necessary amount of personal information be collected in a system, that retention and disposal periods for that information be clearly defined and enforced, and that personal information gathered for a specific purpose not be used for other purposes without consent of the individual(s). These principles apply to electronic communications, including electronic mail, and prohibit procedures that capture or monitor electronic user data, including messages, without the permission of users or bona fide authorization related to system operation and maintenance. User data observed during the normal duties of system operation and maintenance must be treated with strictest confidentiality, except in cases where it is evidence for the violation of law, organizational regulations, or this Code. In these cases, the nature or contents of that information must be disclosed only to proper authorities. (See 1.9)

1.8   Honor confidentiality.
The principle of honesty extends to issues of confidentiality of information whenever one has made an explicit promise to honor confidentiality or, implicitly, when private information not directly related to the performance of one's duties becomes available. The ethical concern is to respect all obligations of confidentiality to employers, clients, and users unless discharged from such obligations by requirements of the law or other principles of this Code.

　　2. More Specific Professional Responsibilities. As an ACM computing professional I will . . .

2.1 Strive to achieve the highest quality, effectiveness and dignity in both the process and products of professional work.
Excellence is perhaps the most important obligation of a professional. The computing professional must strive to achieve quality and to be cognizant of the serious negative consequences that may result from poor quality in a system.

2.2 Acquire and maintain professional competence.
Excellence depends on individuals who take responsibility for acquiring and maintaining professional competence. A professional must participate in setting standards for appropriate levels of competence, and strive to achieve those standards. Upgrading technical knowledge and competence can be achieved in several ways: doing independent study; attending seminars, conferences, or courses; and being involved in professional organizations.

2.3 Know and respect existing laws pertaining to professional work.
ACM members must obey existing local, state, province, national, and international laws unless there is a compelling ethical basis not to do so. Policies and procedures of the organizations in which one participates must also be obeyed. But compliance must be balanced with the recognition that sometimes existing laws and rules may be immoral or inappropriate and, therefore, must be challenged. Violation of a law or regulation may be ethical when that law or rule has inadequate moral basis or when it conflicts with another law judged to be more important. If one decides to violate a law or rule because it is viewed as unethical, or for any other reason, one must fully accept responsibility for one's actions and for the consequences.

2.4 Accept and provide appropriate professional review.
Quality professional work, especially in the computing profession, depends on professional reviewing and critiquing. Whenever appropriate, individual members should seek and utilize peer review as well as provide critical review of the work of others.

2.5 Give comprehensive and thorough evaluations of computer systems and their impacts, including analysis of possible risks.
Computer professionals must strive to be perceptive, thorough, and objective when evaluating, recommending, and presenting system descriptions and alternatives. Computer professionals are in a position of special trust, and therefore have a special responsibility to provide objective, credible evaluations to employers, clients, users, and the public. When providing evaluations the professional must also identify any relevant conflicts of interest, as stated in imperative 1.3.

　　As noted in the discussion of principle 1.2 on avoiding harm, any signs of danger from systems must be reported to those who have opportunity and/or responsibility to resolve them. See the guidelines for imperative 1.2 for more details concerning harm, including the reporting of professional violations.

2.6 Honor contracts, agreements, and assigned responsibilities.
Honoring one's commitments is a matter of integrity and honesty. For the computer professional this includes ensuring that system elements perform as intended. Also, when one contracts for work with another party, one has an obligation to keep that party properly informed about progress toward completing that work.

A computing professional has a responsibility to request a change in any assignment that he or she feels cannot be completed as defined. Only after serious consideration and with full disclosure of risks and concerns to the employer or client, should one accept the assignment. The major underlying principle here is the obligation to accept personal accountability for professional work. On some occasions other ethical principles may take greater priority.

A judgment that a specific assignment should not be performed may not be accepted. Having clearly identified one's concerns and reasons for that judgment, but failing to procure a change in that assignment, one may yet be obligated, by contract or by law, to proceed as directed. The computing professional's ethical judgment should be the final guide in deciding whether or not to proceed. Regardless of the decision, one must accept the responsibility for the consequences.

However, performing assignments "against one's own judgment" does not relieve the professional of responsibility for any negative consequences.

2.7 Improve public understanding of computing and its consequences.
Computing professionals have a responsibility to share technical knowledge with the public by encouraging understanding of computing, including the impacts of computer systems and their limitations. This imperative implies an obligation to counter any false views related to computing.

2.8 Access computing and communication resources only when authorized to do so.
Theft or destruction of tangible and electronic property is prohibited by imperative 1.2 - "Avoid harm to others." Trespassing and unauthorized use of a computer or communication system is addressed by this imperative. Trespassing includes accessing communication networks and computer systems, or accounts and/or files associated with those systems, without explicit authorization to do so. Individuals and organizations have the right to restrict access to their systems so long as they do not violate the discrimination principle (see 1.4). No one should enter or use another's computer system, software, or data files without permission. One must always have appropriate approval before using system resources, including .rm57 communication ports, file space, other system peripherals, and computer time.

3. Organizational Leadership Imperatives. As an ACM member and an organizational leader, I will . . .

BACKGROUND NOTE: This section draws extensively from the draft IFIP Code of Ethics, especially its sections on organizational ethics and international concerns. The ethical obligations of organizations tend to be neglected in most codes of professional conduct, perhaps because these codes are written from the perspective of the individual member. This dilemma is addressed by stating these imperatives from the perspective of the organizational leader. In this context "leader" is viewed as any organizational member who has leadership or educational responsibilities. These imperatives generally may apply to organizations as well as their leaders. In this context "organizations" are corporations, government agencies, and other "employers," as well as volunteer professional organizations.

3.1   Articulate social responsibilities of members of an organizational unit and encourage full acceptance of those responsibilities.
Because organizations of all kinds have impacts on the public, they must accept responsibilities to society. Organizational procedures and attitudes oriented toward quality and the welfare of society will reduce harm to members of the public, thereby serving public interest and fulfilling social responsibility. Therefore, organizational leaders must encourage full participation in meeting social responsibilities as well as quality performance.

3.2   Manage personnel and resources to design and build information systems that enhance the quality of working life.
Organizational leaders are responsible for ensuring that computer systems enhance, not degrade, the quality of working life. When implementing a computer system, organizations must consider the personal and professional development, physical safety, and human dignity of all workers. Appropriate human-computer ergonomic standards should be considered in system design and in the workplace.

3.3   Acknowledge and support proper and authorized uses of an organization's computing and communication resources.
Because computer systems can become tools to harm as well as to benefit an organization, the leadership has the responsibility to clearly define appropriate and inappropriate uses of organizational computing resources. While the number and scope of such rules should be minimal, they should be fully enforced when established.

3.4   Ensure that users and those who will be affected by a system have their needs clearly articulated during the assessment and design of requirements; later the system must be validated to meet requirements.
Current system users, potential users and other persons whose lives may be affected by a system must have their needs assessed and incorporated in the statement of requirements. System validation should ensure compliance with those requirements.

3.5 Articulate and support policies that protect the dignity of users and others affected by a computing system.

Designing or implementing systems that deliberately or inadvertently demean individuals or groups is ethically unacceptable. Computer professionals who are in decision making positions should verify that systems are designed and implemented to protect personal privacy and enhance personal dignity.

3.6 Create opportunities for members of the organization to learn the principles and limitations of computer systems.

This complements the imperative on public understanding (2.7). Educational opportunities are essential to facilitate optimal participation of all organizational members. Opportunities must be available to all members to help them improve their knowledge and skills in computing, including courses that familiarize them with the consequences and limitations of particular types of systems. In particular, professionals must be made aware of the dangers of building systems around oversimplified models, the improbability of anticipating and designing for every possible operating condition, and other issues related to the complexity of this profession.

4. Compliance with the Code. As an ACM member I will . . .

4.1 Uphold and promote the principles of this Code.

The future of the computing profession depends on both technical and ethical excellence. Not only is it important for ACM computing professionals to adhere to the principles expressed in this Code, each member should encourage and support adherence by other members.

4.2 Treat violations of this code as inconsistent with membership in the ACM.

Adherence of professionals to a code of ethics is largely a voluntary matter. However, if a member does not follow this code by engaging in gross misconduct, membership in ACM may be terminated.

This Code and the supplemental Guidelines were developed by the Task Force for the Revision of the ACM Code of Ethics and Professional Conduct: Ronald E. Anderson, Chair, Gerald Engel, Donald Gotterbarn, Grace C. Hertlein, Alex Hoffman, Bruce Jawer, Deborah G. Johnson, Doris K. Lidtke, Joyce Currie Little, Dianne Martin, Donn B. Parker, Judith A. Perrolle, and Richard S. Rosenberg. The Task Force was organized by ACM/SIGCAS and funding was provided by the ACM SIG Discretionary Fund. This Code and the supplemental Guidelines were adopted by the ACM Council on October 16, 1992.

ACM CODE OF PROFESSIONAL CONDUCT*

PREAMBLE

Recognition of professional status by the public depends not only on skill and dedication but also on adherence to a recognized code of Professional Conduct. The following Code sets forth the general principles (Canons), professional ideals (Ethical Considerations), and mandatory rules (Disciplinary Rules) applicable to each ACM Member.

The verbs "shall" (imperative) and "should" (encouragement) are used purposefully in the Code. The Canons and Ethical Considerations are not, however, binding rules. Each Disciplinary Rule is binding on each individual Member of ACM. Failure to observe the Disciplinary Rules subjects the Member to admonition, suspension or expulsion from the Association as provided by the Procedures for the Enforcement of the ACM Code of Professional Conduct, which are specified in the ACM Policy and Procedures Guidelines. The term "member(s)" is used in the Code. The Disciplinary Rules of the Code apply, however, only to the classes of membership specified in Article 3, Section 4, of the Constitution of the ACM.

CANON 1

An ACM member shall act at all times with integrity.

Ethical Considerations

EC1.1. An ACM member shall properly qualify himself when expressing an opinion outside his areas of competence. A member is encouraged to express his opinion on subjects within his area of competence.

EC1.2. An ACM member shall preface any partisan statements about information processing by indicating clearly on whose behalf they are made.

EC1.3. An ACM member shall act faithfully on behalf of his employers or clients.

Disciplinary Rules

DR1.1.1. An ACM member shall not intentionally misrepresent his qualifications or credentials to present or prospective employers or clients.

DR1.1.2. An ACM member shall not make deliberately false or deceptive statements as to the present or expected state of affairs in any aspect of the capability, delivery, or use of information processing systems.

DR1.2.1. An ACM member shall not intentionally conceal or misrepresent on whose behalf any partisan statements are made.

DR1.3.1. An ACM member acting or employed as a consultant shall, prior to accepting information from a prospective client, inform the client of all factors of which the member is aware which may affect the proper performance of the task.

DR1.3.2. An ACM member shall disclose any interest of which he is aware which does or may conflict with his duty to a present or prospective employer or client.

* Adopted by the ACM Council in 1973.

DR1.3.3. An ACM member shall not use any confidential information from any employer or client, past or present, without prior permission.

CANON 2

An ACM member should strive to increase his competence and the competence and prestige of the profession.

Ethical Considerations

EC2.1. An ACM member is encouraged to extend public knowledge, understanding, and appreciation of information processing, and to oppose any false or deceptive statements relating to information processing of which he is aware.

EC2.2. An ACM member shall not use his professional credentials to misrepresent his competence.

EC2.3. An ACM member shall undertake only those professional assignments and commitments for which he is qualified.

EC2.4. An ACM member shall strive to design and develop systems that adequately perform the intended functions and that satisfy his employer's or client's operational needs.

EC2.5. An ACM member should maintain and increase his competence through a program of continuing education encompassing the techniques, technical standards, and practices in his fields of professional activity.

EC2.6. An ACM member should provide opportunity and encouragement for professional development and advancement of both professionals and those aspiring to become professionals.

Disciplinary Rules

DR2.2.1. An ACM member shall not use his professional credentials to misrepresent his competence.

DR2.3.1. An ACM member shall not undertake professional assignments without adequate preparation in the circumstances.

DR2.3.2. An ACM member shall not undertake professional assignments for which he knows or should know he is not competent or cannot become adequately competent without acquiring the assistance of a professional who is competent to perform the assignment.

DR2.4.1. An ACM member shall not represent that a product of his work will perform its function adequately and will meet the receiver's operational needs when he knows or should know that the product is deficient.

CANON 3

An ACM member shall accept responsibility for his work.

Ethical Considerations

EC3.1. An ACM member shall accept only those assignments for which there is reasonable expectancy of meeting requirements or specifications, and shall perform his assignments in a professional manner.

Disciplinary Rules

DR3.1.1. An ACM member shall not neglect any professional assignment which has been accepted.

DR3.1.2. An ACM member shall keep his employer or client properly informed on the progress of his assignments.

DR3.1.3. An ACM member shall not attempt to exonerate himself from, or to limit his liability to clients for his personal malpractice.

DR3.1.4. An ACM member shall indicate to his employer or client the consequences to be expected if his professional judgment is overruled.

CANON 4
An ACM member shall act with professional responsibility.

Ethical Considerations
EC4.1. An ACM member shall not use his membership in ACM improperly for professional advantage or to misrepresent the authority of his statements.

EC4.2. An ACM member shall conduct professional activities on a high plane.

EC4.3. An ACM member is encouraged to uphold and improve the professional standards of the Association through participation in their formulation, establishment, and enforcement.

Disciplinary Rules
DR4.1.1. An ACM member shall not speak on behalf of the Association or any of its subgroups without proper authority.

DR4.1.2. An ACM member shall not knowingly misrepresent the policies and views of the Association or any of its subgroups.

DR4.1.3. An ACM member shall preface partisan statements about information processing by indicating clearly on whose behalf they are made.

DR4.2.1. An ACM member shall not maliciously injure the professional reputation of any other person.

DR4.2.2. An ACM member shall not use the services of or his membership in the Association to gain unfair advantage.

DR4.2.3. An ACM member shall take care that credit for work is given to whom credit is properly due.

CANON 5
An ACM member should use his special knowledge and skills for the advancement of human welfare.

Ethical Considerations
EC5.1. An ACM member should consider the health, privacy, and general welfare of the public in the performance of his work.

EC5.2. An ACM member, whenever dealing with data concerning individuals, shall always consider the principle of the individual's privacy and seek the following:

—To minimize the data collected.
—To limit authorized access to the data.
—To provide proper security for the data.
—To determine the required retention period of the data.
—To ensure proper disposal of the data.

Disciplinary Rules

DR5.2.1. An ACM member shall express his professional opinion to his employers or clients regarding any adverse consequences to the public which might result from work proposed to him.

IEEE CODE OF ETHICS*

We, the members of the IEEE, in recognition of the importance of our technologies in affecting the quality of life throughout the world, and in accepting a personal obligation to our profession, its members and the communities we serve, do hereby commit ourselves to the highest ethical and professional conduct and agree:

1 to accept responsibility in making engineering decisions consistent with the safety, health and welfare of the public, and to disclose promptly factors that might endanger the public or the environment;
2 to avoid real or perceived conflicts of interest whenever possible, and to disclose them to affected parties when they do exist;
3 to be honest and realistic in stating claims or estimates based on available data;
4 to reject bribery in all its forms;
5 to improve the understanding of technology, its appropriate application, and potential consequences;
6 to maintain and improve our technical competence and to undertake technological tasks for others only if qualified by training or experience, or after full disclosure of pertinent limitations;
7 to seek, accept, and offer honest criticism of technical work, to acknowledge and correct errors, and to credit properly the contributions of others;
8 to treat fairly all persons regardless of such factors as race, religion, gender, disability, age, or national origin;
9 to avoid injuring others, their property, reputation, or employment by false or malicious action;
10 to assist colleagues and co-workers in their professional development and to support them in following this code of ethics.

* Approved by the IEEE Board of Directors, August 1990.

Index